HOPE AND PLANNING

JÜRGEN MOLTMANN

Hope and Planning

1817

Harper & Row, Publishers
New York, Evanston, San Francisco, London

Translated by Margaret Clarkson
from selections from the German
Perspektiven der Theologie: Gesammelte Aufsätze
(Chr. Kaiser Verlag, München, and Matthias-Grünewald Verlag,
Mainz, 1968)

CONTENTS

PREFACE

The articles collected here were written between 1960 and 1968. They are the preparatory work for and the sequel to *Theology of Hope*, which was published in German in 1964 (and in English in 1967). To a great extent the subject matter was determined by meetings, university symposia, *Festschriften* for teachers and friends, and the discussions of other theological approaches. The articles were published in learned journals, both theological and cultural. Nevertheless, all these occasional elements are random only at a superficial level. In the end, the articles carry on the contemporary discussion that theology needs if it is not to become abstract. Certainly theology has its own subject matter. But it can only understand and develop this subject matter when it enters into current problems and, in this way, shares the difficulties as well as the opportunities of its contemporaries. This led me to give the German edition the title *Theological Perspectives*.

A perspective permits something to be seen. It brings a matter into the present circle of history. It presents an opinion and opens up a view. It is based on the present and points out the special aspects of a concern. At the same time, a perspective is closely related to practice. It reaches out into the possibilities of the future, searches for goals and develops directives for action. Perspectives of vision and perspectives of practice are, as the words themselves indicate, aware of the difference between the idea and the matter itself, between theory and practice. Perspectives ought not to confuse the appearance with the matter itself. They are open for critical elaboration by other perspectives. They cannot illusionarily confuse the present vision of the future with the oncoming future itself. Perspectives always have a heuristic and experimental character. They have something to do with the reality of fantasy.

Theological perspectives attempt to discover relevant aspects of the matter of Christian faith in the changing conditions of time. It is not only the rapid changes of history that force theology to make a permanent revision of its concepts, so that dogmatic systems become obsolete more quickly than the authors of these systems would like to admit. When the concern of Christian faith involves the final changing of the world as it has appeared in and through Christ within history, then this concern is, in essentials, the driving force for permanent change, criticism, renewal and the transformation of theology.

Theological perspectives, on the other hand, seek to discover theological dimensions within present reality and to bring this present into public discussion. Theology cannot raise itself to the status of the supreme, all-embracing science. Nor, if it is to do justice to its concern, may it withdraw into its own private sphere. It can, however, in productive tolerance and active provocation, join in the present discussion of the fate and the needs of the world in order to represent that truth which is always greater than itself. This modest awareness of its own relativity has nothing to do with resignation. It receives its strength from that hope for the victory of truth over the fragments and perspectives in which it is represented here.

These articles fall into two groups. The first comprises articles on the perspectives of theology and theologians. They deal with the concept of God and the understanding of the Word in which God proclaims his presence. The second comprises studies on the theological perspectives for Christians in their vocations in the world. They deal with scientific and ethical questions. They strive to cross over the borders within the areas of social ethics, sociology, science of history, planning, revolution and utopia. The division between the two groups cannot be strictly maintained. In each, it ought to be clear that theology is not only a reflection on the proclamation of the minister but also a reflection on the tasks and experiences of Christianity in the world.

JÜRGEN MOLTMANN

ABBREVIATIONS

CW	*Die christliche Welt*, Leipzig
EvTh	*Evangelische Theologie*, Munich
MPTh	*Monatsschrift für Pastoraltheologie*, Göttingen
PhB	Philosophische Bibliothek, Hamburg
*RGG*³	*Die Religion in Geschichte und Gegenwart*³, Tübingen, 1957ff.
WA	Martin Luther, *Werke*, Kritische Gesamtausgabe, Weimar, 1883ff.
ZEE	*Zeitschrift für evangelischer Ethik*, Gütersloh
ZTK	*Zeitschrift für Theologie und Kirche*, Tübingen

PART ONE

THEOLOGICAL PERSPECTIVES

I

THE REVELATION OF GOD AND THE QUESTION OF TRUTH

The Christian faith speaks of God on the basis of historical revelation. 'The biblical theologian proves that a God exists because he has spoken in the Bible', affirms Kant somewhat dryly, in order to progress from the rational theologian to the pure faith of religion as quickly as possible.[1] The real problem seems to be whether or not Christian talk of God, based on the historical witness of the Bible, has a universal significance. In what universally binding sense does the Christian proclamation of God address itself to all men? The naked positivity of the Bible and the affirmation of the church's proclamation of revelation are not enough. They make Christian talk of God seem arbitrary. For that reason, one must question the divinity of this God and the general conditions for the understanding of revelation as a revelation of God. The hermeneutical situation must be sought in which this talk of God appears meaningful and necessary. For Christian talk of God claims not only to speak of a God on the contingent foundation of the Bible, but also, on the basis of this foundation, to proclaim the *one* God. The Christian talk of God not only claims to speak of the God of Israel and of the God of the Christians, but it also proclaims this God as the God and Lord of all men. Thus, the Christian talk of God leads necessarily to the question of the universal divinity of this God.

However, the question is not just who or what shows this biblically based Christian talk of God to be meaningful. In more radical terms, the question is: is it in fact God from whom and in whose name the biblical witnesses and, after them, the

Christian proclamation speaks and is spoken of? Who conceals the diversity which Christian proclamation displays to men in the name of God? Who guarantees the truth of the proclamation and the truthfulness of the proclaimer? What gives foundation to the faith that is based on it? By what reality do the words validate their truth or what reality validates the truth of these words?

If Christian theology is reflection on proclamation, then in the name of truth it is always concerned with such inquiries into the Christian talk of God. This can lead to the point where theological reflection on the particular, historical proclamation tries to offer verification which basically tries to be immediately obvious to all men. However, on the other hand, this can also mean that theological reflection seeks to formulate the specific question of faith concerning the divinity and universal rule of this God, a God from whom faith has only the historical witness of the Bible; a question which it asks in solidarity with and as a representative of the whole longing creation.

In the course of its history, Christian theology has developed three great schemes of verification to deal with the historical perplexities of the problem of truth,[2] to make what is Christian believable and to show that, against a generally binding background and within a unified horizon, Christian talk of God is meaningful and necessary. The constant problem is that of the presuppositions of revelation in historical witness in order to show that it is *God's* revelation. This always involves a search for the general conditions for an understanding of the special revelation and the discovery of a far-reaching solidarity in which revelation unites the believers with all of suffering creation. Christian theology presupposes a reality in the disclosure of which revelation can be shown to be meaningful, necessary and useful. It presupposes a 'natural' element against which it is able to point to its own supernatural character. It presupposes a fragmentary element against which it can show its completeness. It presupposes something that is called into question against which it can show itself to be the answer. It assumes an element of need in order to point out its own necessity. Even if one says that it presupposes exclusively itself, in the very act of doing this the problem of the 'presupposition' of revelation presents itself.[3]

By means of such presuppositions, a general canon of interpretation for the 'contingent' biblical truths of history is sought from a reality which has already dawned on every man in knowledge or experience. With such a canon of interpretation, the historical witnesses are then read like a palimpsest. For the concrete texts of God, a generally approachable text is substituted through which the Bible is to become more readable and more understandable.[4] The text is brought into a hermeneutical situation in which man's talk of God is shown to be necessary and, as such, is meant to bring illumination. Interpretation then becomes a bridge between the witnesses of a specific history and a sphere of generally accessible possibilities which recur through the ages.[5] For only the general within the particular seems to be what is reasonable.

I *The scheme of verification in cosmology and universal history*

Christian talk of God as the *one* God, who reveals his divinity in and to Jesus of Nazareth, can be made generally meaningful when it is implied that this is precisely the God for whom all finite beings ask in their discontinuity, groundlessness and disunion. 'Being refuses to be poorly managed', said Aristotle. 'Wholeness is not found in the rule of many; only one is the ruler.'[6] Thus all being longs for unity, wholeness and order and, with its longing, points towards a divine world monarchy. All being is aware of God in the question of its yearning and longing for his monarchy in which alone it can find its wholeness and its totality, i.e., its basis and continuance *extra se* in a foundation established on itself. Not only man, but all finite creatures with him ask in this way, for they are threatened with transitoriness, death and chaos, and are delivered over to futility. This is the divinity about which they ask with their whole finite being. If the presupposition and implication is that it is the question of the same God, about whom, on the one hand, all being asks, and of whom, on the other hand, the biblical historical witnesses speak, then Christian monotheism can be shown to be the truth of all problematic reality. The Logos for which all that exists questiòningly longs, so that it establishes foundation and continuance, meaning and totality, has appeared in the full person of Jesus.

Christian talk of God, then, represents the revelation of God in Christ as the completion of that which is fragmentary, as the putting right of that which is upside down, as the foundation in eternal being of that existence which is subjected to the transitory and as the gathering together of what is scattered. In Christ, the restlessly propelling force of reality is brought into order and into eternal truth. Christ is the fulfilment of the metaphysical longing of the universe. His cross is erected in the cosmos in order to secure that which is unsteady. The incarnation of the Logos is the true *diacosmesis*.

If the reality presupposed is understood not only in cosmological but also in universal-historical terms, then the act of God in Christ can correspondingly be represented as the final turning point of the world and can be presented as perfection. The universal-historical scheme of verification for the Christ-event is related to the cosmological scheme and represents a further development of it. Against a universal-historical background, the Logos which appeared in Christ proves itself to be not only the cosmological Logos but also the prolepsis of the end of all things; it becomes the unifying principle of all historical forces.[7]

Finally, then, on the basis of both schemes of verification, a political scheme can also be developed. The Logos which appeared in Christ forms the archetypal unity of a universal kingdom of peace. The church composed of Jews and Gentiles brings together that truth which has been scattered throughout the nations and becomes the exemplary fulfilment of the universal search for the unity of mankind. 'Everything that is good and beautiful belongs to us', said Justin.[8] In this way, the church of Christ brings true peace into human society and calls its corresponding political endeavours into life. *Pax christiana* and *pax romana*, Christ and Augustus, are connected in parallel by providence.[9] This cosmological, world-historical and political scheme of verification verifies the particular Christian talk about God in that reality of the world that is called in question in its unity, its satisfaction, and in its foundation and justification. Presupposition and consequence, horizon and mid-point, universality and specific history are found here in a reciprocally illuminating relationship. Only the Logos which appeared in Christ really clarifies the needs which are present and that which is being questioned. Questioning reality points out the completeness of Christ's Logos. In no way is this presupposed pre-understanding merely a cosmological theory of objectifying thought which arises from a failure to take existence seriously. In this way, God is expressed in relation to man by his being expressed in relation to the whole of questioning and unstable reality. This, then, is not a concept of God in which God is either above or outside the world. Rather, the concept of God developed within this scheme is a concept of relationship. It is presupposed that the experience of chaos in the world calls God's divinity into question, and therefore God's revelation of his divinity in Christ is developed against this continuing question. Every statement about God is at the same time a statement about the world as a whole, and *vice versa*. Thus an ellipse of theological thought and talk is presupposed. This ellipse includes God and reality as a whole, and in this way reveals that reality which is specifically human. It envelops biblical history in such a way that the universal reality of God and of the world becomes visible in and directly through this history.

II   The anthropological schemes of verification

Alongside this cosmological and universal-historical scheme of verification (shaped by gnosticism, the classical philosophy of life and Augustine),[10] another scheme of verification has grown up which is closely related to current talk of God. When man can no longer understand himself in terms of the world and its relationships, but rather must understand the world and its

relationships in terms of those designs which he himself develops
for the purpose of reforming the world, it seems that the reality
of the world which surrounds him is no longer to be understood
as the hermeneutical context for the verification of God's
revelation in Christ. That context is, rather, man himself who
discloses the world. As, in the cosmological scheme, Christian
talk of God was related to man in the context of reality as a
whole, so now it is related to reality as a whole to the extent to
which this reality is experienced, manipulated and controlled
by man. Although the subject – *hypokeimenon* – is changed, the
method remains the same. The hermeneutical locus is changed
in which Christian talk of God becomes meaningful and necessary. The presupposition is changed. The whole of reality in
terms of its most comprehensive horizon is no longer understood as cosmos or history but rather in terms of man who, as
subject, makes himself into its mid-point. The method, however,
of showing Christian revelation to be the fulfilment of the longing of that which is finite remains as the completion of what is
striven for and as the answer to the questionability that is presupposed.

To the degree to which man, by means of scientific explanation and technical structuring, removes the religious character
from the world, the world loses the protective character of its
surroundings, the home and that direction-giving order into
which he can integrate himself. The world can no longer provide answers to the questions 'Who is man?' and 'Why does he
exist?'[11] In this way, man himself becomes a question; he
becomes more radical, but also more than ever alone. He now
no longer sees the questionability in all things, but rather only
in those problems which concern his own existence. He is no
longer aware of this questionability in theoretical reason, but
rather only in his conscience. In the 'experience of passivity',
especially in birth and death, he is confronted with the irrefutable recognition that he is not his own creator.[12] That is,
existence finds in itself neither foundation nor continuance
against the transitory; it represents nothing but a question, an
unrest, a longing. This questionability as a now exclusively

human phenomenon becomes the subject's relation to revelation:

> The phenomenon as such (viz., that human existence is occupied by the question about itself) is the relation of the matter to the manifestation.[13]

> . . . apart from the resolve to be a human being, a person who accepts responsibility for his own Being, not a single word of Scripture is intelligible as a word with an existential relevance.[14]

How does this phenomenon – and not the various types of explanation – look? It is described as that experience of the self which cannot be lost,[15] as that question which brings man to his authenticity and his integrity, as his irrefutable historicity,[16] and the momentary quality of his very reality. It is the primary experience in which man becomes aware of his finality.[17] It is the condition of the anxiety of an ecstatic existence or, put more simply, its anxiety of existence, its anxiety of conscience.

Now if, as here, it is presupposed that this questionability of existence is to be called the question of God and the 'God' who is asked about in this questionability; if, further, it is presupposed that, in the Christian talk of revelation, this same God is concerned, then – as above – God's revelation in Jesus can be interpreted as the fulfilment of man's questionability. Its truth is evident in that it brings questioning man to himself; in the instant of the kerygma, it makes a decided wholeness possible in justification, it grants him a foundation and continuance *extra se*. At this point, however, the anxiety of the human condition becomes the hermeneutical context in which God is recognized as the one 'who turns towards the anxious'.[18] The phenomenon of his own questionability becomes the controlling instance of the 'touchstone' (Lessing) for the recognition of God in revelation. God and Jesus become understandable within the 'system of coordinates' of the 'may' and the 'ought' in accord with conscience.[19]

> If his existence were not motivated (whether consciously or unawares) by the inquiry about God in the sense of the Augustinian . . . *cor inquietum* . . . , then neither would he know God as God in any manifestation of him.[20]

Here, too, there is a criterion for the universal truth of Christian talk of God. It is man's coming to himself in historical integrity that is presupposed and is called into question. This is no objective proof of the existence of God in theoretical reason. But it is certainly a proof of God through existence in the conscience. Whether or not human talk of God corresponds to God is confirmed by one's own conscience in that which is effected by this word in homologic existence. Where in conscience a man experiences a difference to himself, he also experiences God in the event of an identity of conscience.

Christian talk of God becomes meaningful in this scheme of verification against the background of anthropological questionability. Presupposition and consequence are again so dialectically related that, on the one hand, only revelation really points out what is being called into question and, on the other hand, the presupposed questioning makes revelation meaningful. Here, too, the concept of God is a concept of relationship and, therefore, it participates in all the characteristics of relation. If man withdraws from himself, then God is also withdrawn. If man is not objectifiable, then God is not objectifiable either. If man is historical, then God is an 'event'. If God is found only in relation, then, seen in terms of that relation, he also receives 'transformations'.

Here the theological ellipse covers both important points: God and existence. Christian talk of God is represented in it as fulfilment. The true is the whole, but the whole is disclosed from its centre, the potentiality of human existence for totality, and not by its furthest circumference, the world. The truth of God's revelation becomes evident, therefore, in that existence which is brought to truth and historical integrity. The presupposed pre-understanding is 'naturally' no cosmological theory, but rather man's need to understand himself. The word 'God' is not veiled by the unity of reality in the whole, but rather by the collective unity of resolute existence in the 'hard currency' of truthfulness. Here, too, the Bible is read as a palimpsest – man's eternal question about himself and about God is found under every historically accidental sentence. A historical source such as the Bible is interpreted as a pure 'historic' phenomenon when it is set against the background of the 'historicity' of human existence, a historicity which is characterized by death, through which it is also presupposed 'that in it a possibility of human existence has been grasped and expressed'.[21] Interpretation, therefore, translates the concrete and contingent texts into universal and recurring possibilities of existence.

III   The onto-theological scheme of verification

We have concerned ourselves up to now with Christian talk of God within the framework of the cosmological proof of God and the proof of God in existence. We now come to the possibility of Christian talk of God within the framework of the ontological proof of God – the proof of God from 'God'. The ontological proof of God is the most recent among the proofs of the existence of God. It could only appear in the Christian world in which subjectivity comprehends itself and, therefore, must overcome its contrast to objectivity.[22]

What God in Jesus has to say to man will not be able to preserve its function as a norm either in the world as a whole or in the human potentiality for totality.[23] 'Reality as a whole', now or then, in terms of cosmology or universal history, will not prove the divinity of God, nor can the ontic abyss of human need become the measure of God's divinity. Both presuppositions are certainly adequate to point out the universally binding character of what is Christian; but they are also apt to transcend the particular Christian element in what is universally accepted and, by doing so, to destroy its history. Now if Christian talk of God cannot be verified either in the whole of reality or in the whole man, on what can it be verified?

The conclusion suggested is that the proof must be a self-proof and not something other and foreign. It must presuppose only itself. In that case revelation is not a source of light which illuminates a reality which is questionable but which is always dawning, whether in knowledge or in experience. Above all, it is the self-revelation of God in which God himself makes himself

evident through himself. His revelation must then be taken as
that proof of God which originates from himself, and therefore
the proof can no longer be presupposed in the *praeambula ad
articulos fidei*. The hermeneutical locus of proclamation is not
universal history or the historicity of existence and its personal
character, but rather the church. The light in which God's
revelation becomes understandable is not the light of 'natural
theology' but rather the light of the Holy Spirit. This is not a
'positivism of revelation', as some have misunderstood it to be,
but rather the *argumentum ontologicum* according to which being
and knowledge coincide in God himself.

Putting aside the two schemes of verification retained earlier,
Christian talk of God on the basis of the 'little pieces of information' concerning Jesus of Nazareth[24] acquired from the time of
the Roman empire takes on the protective covering of a third,
namely the arguments of the ontological proof of God. The
question which is also the basic question of the other two – *an
Deus sit?* – is answered by the statement *Deum esse est per se, i.e. per
verbum suum, notum.* The advantage of this way of thinking lies in
the fact that what is Christian does not, as in the other schemes,
have a norm in terms of external referents, but rather can begin
with itself and its own concerns. Its weakness lies in the fact that
the ontological proof of God from 'God' cannot actually exist
alone for itself, but must always be explained in relation to the
world and to existence. Taken by itself, it is as incapable of
being attacked as it is of attacking. Its problem is how to begin
to show that something begins with itself.[25]

If I see the situation correctly, a quite independent onto-
theological thought has developed in Karl Barth in his discussion of the anthropological attempts by Brunner and Gogarten
to found and explain Christian talk of God (1927–31).[26] In the
Christliche Dogmatik im Entwurf (1927), the new image of the
'closed circle of the *Deus dixit*' replaces the Schleiermacherian
ellipse of God and the self in the theology of consciousness.[27]
God's word is not founded in any other thing. In his word and
his revelation, God is the sovereign subject and, for this reason,
he enters into no correlation and into no circle of human con-

sciousness. Therefore, he is not a point of relation to be inquired for in advance from an *a priori* of world and existence, which is already known in the form of the question. The sovereignty of God which is inaccessible to the world and existence validates itself in the act of revelation. By confronting the 'I' of man as indissoluble subject and therefore also as his God and Lord, God reveals himself here to be the 'Thou'. In this way, revelation remains 'an act which has happened, a decision which has been made', and never becomes the manipulable object of man. Yet revelation does not appear in place of a concrete objectivity as an abstract reality which keeps encountering me. Rather, God, beyond the alternatives of objectivity and subjectivity, is revealed through himself. His word alone proves his reality. It comes into contact with man by itself, i.e. in the power of the Holy Spirit. God's sovereignty, therefore, must be theologically preserved in the processes of knowledge and understanding. This, however, is only possible by means of a trinitarian pneumatology, which, according to that God who reveals himself out of the reality of his revelation, creates the possibility of understanding. Since he 'gives' himself to be understood, he also creates the conditions in which it is possible to confess and acknowledge him, to hear and obey him, to understand him and correspond to him.

In his book on Anselm,[28] Barth, in order to formulate this sovereign self-revelation of God, interpreted the ontological proof of God anew, freeing it from the last remnants of an anthropological foundation and explanation of Christian doctrine. Anselm declared that 'God' cannot be thought of as 'that than which nothing greater can be conceived' without his existence. Hegel said that the Absolute Spirit thinks itself in its concept. Barth says that God reveals himself in his name. The Word of God presents that reality which it proclaims – God's divinity and lordship. One can, therefore, talk of God only in a truthful and justified way on the basis of his self-revelation in his words. Knowledge of God is only possible, therefore, through the self-revelation of God and through recognition by him. To think of God means to rethink his thoughts of himself and what is thought of by him. The question of the divinity of God, therefore, cannot correctly be presented on the foundation of the experiences of world or existence, but rather must be presented as a further inquiry about his being based on the hearing of his revealed name. One must not think of God in order to illuminate the unity of the world or the reason for one's own existence. When, however, one thinks of God on the basis of his self-word, one is compelled to think of his existence.[29]

Theology here presupposes that event in which God expresses himself. Theology cannot critically ask whether it is true, but only explain the extent to which it is true and necessary as it is said. God must be the ground of everything that is and that is thought. This ground, however, cannot be there only for the sake of providing a foundation, but rather must be determinable through itself and in itself. The *Church Dogmatics* shows the thought of the self-revelation of God in a trinitarian exposition, first as God's subjectivity and sovereignty, then as an inference from 'God' to God. The doctrine of the Trinity becomes the canon of interpretation for the proclamation of the lordship of Christ – the doctrine of the Trinity is that which witnesses; that which is witnessed to is the lordship of Christ.[30] The applications of this theological thinking, which are important for our discussion, appear in all Barth's writings: (1) God's divinity can be validated neither objectively in the world and history nor subjectively in man's self or his existence, for God proves his divinity himself. Revelation is that proof of God which comes from God himself; therefore, all other proofs of God would compete with the uniqueness of his self-revelation. His word makes itself believable and, therefore, needs no universal background. It establishes itself in the power of self-verification. In place of Herrmann's knowledge of God as the 'defenceless expression of religious experiencing', the self-word of God is now found in the same defenceless state – unprovable and undeniable, unfoundable and undestroyable in that ground which is founded in itself, in God himself, and occurring within the closed circle of the *Deus dixit*. (2) Now this onto-theological thinking would hang like a circle in the air[31] if it presupposed the process and the superiority of God's self-disclosure in contrast to the human knowledge of God only for its own sake and not for the sake of a definite event. Like the doctrine of the Trinity, onto-theological thinking can only be the canon of interpretation for a fixed reality, and therefore one to be pre-supposed – that is, for the person and history of Jesus Christ. If the uniqueness and the finality of this person and history is explained in onto-theological and trinitarian terms as God's self-revelation, then in this way the unique finality of man's reconciliation by God with God is presupposed. The Christ-event can only be understood as God's self-revelation if God really grants the godless fellowship with himself here. Therefore, the idea of the reality of reconciliation in Christ, perfected and concluded in itself, must be added to the basic thought of the self-revelation of God in Christ. The one attests to and founds the other. Therefore, the 'closed circle of the *Deus dixit*' is no circle *supra nos*, nor is it an exclusive circle; it is, rather, an open circle *pro nobis* and an inclusive circle which, in and through Christ, already encloses man and the world and, in the exten-sion of the kerygma, discloses this inclusive ground of all creation.[32]

IV   Eschatological revelation

The schemes of verification presented here all presuppose that the validation of what is Christian must be found in the fact that word and reality, word and existence, word and name are congruent, and that truth is experienced in correspondence, conformity and agreement. The question is whether Christian truth must not burst apart the immediate correspondences of this concept of truth. Christian revelation does not introduce something which was already there independent of it, some-thing which was always beginning or is eternal. Rather, it makes present that which does not yet exist. It presents the future, and calls that which does not exist into existence. If the event of revelation is found in the resurrection of the crucified one, then truth must also be understood eschatologically and dialectic-ally. If that which is Christian does not correspond to reality that can be known or experienced, then the observed contradiction between the word of God and reality can become not only an argument against what is Christian but even an argument against reality. To follow Hegel somewhat carelessly: this contradiction can be just as bad for the word of God as for the facts. It seems more important, therefore, first to raise the contradiction in which the cross of Jesus suggests that God and reality are analogies which do not yet exist.

Atheists and Christians find themselves in solidarity in the contradiction that is disclosed. For unbelief, this contradiction becomes the occasion to put God in the wrong. For faith, it becomes the occasion to put reality, as it presents itself, in the wrong. For faith, it means that faith can only think of both God and reality in the resurrection of the crucified one by explaining reality as the transitory reality of sin and death and, *contra experientiam*, hopes, waits and searches for the victory of the crucified one. This, however, means that the question about the proof of the divinity of God's Jesus is not only the question of unbelief but also the question of faith; it is not only the question of doubt but also the question of hope.[33] 'Pauline eschatology, like that of the Apocalypse and of the whole of primitive Christianity, centres upon the question whether God is indeed God and when he will fully assert himself as such.'[34] If, according to the psalm quotation in Rom. 3.10f., universal unrighteousness consists in the fact that no one asks about God, then justification by faith is still alive because it steadfastly stands by the question about God and intercedes in the sighs of the Spirit for the freedom of the whole creation in God's lordship (Rom. 8.26). The question about God and the demonstration of his universal divinity arises from that concrete history in which God himself announces his glory in promises and initiates his glorification in the resurrection of the crucified one. In this contradiction, in which his future and his glory intercede for the misery of present creation, are founded the controversial quality of faith and the controversy with which faith confronts suffering reality. Correspondence to God is only possible through the contradiction; conformity with his word is possible only in confession to the cross; anticipation of the future of his truth is possible only within the experience of history, that is, in solidarity with the suffering of the eager expectation of creation.

A

According to the witnesses of whom the 'biblical theologian' speaks, the revelation of God constitutively bears the character of promise.[35]

The usual oriental way of talking about the manifestation and the self-presentation of the deity were bound up very early in Israelite thought with the understanding of the divine talk of promise. In the tradition, the divine talk of promise appears more and more as the authentic content of the scenes of revelation. Interest moves from the tangible theophanies to the word of the proclamation of God's activity, a word which is to be heard and followed. The history of divine activity is, therefore, remembered and anticipated within that horizon which is opened up by God's promises. If God's revelation, however, is recognized in this way in promise, revelation does not reveal present history, and does not illuminate a historicity that is always beginning, but rather opens up history by the promise of something new and by hope aroused. In this way, however, God's revelation provokes a more or less sharp contradiction to that which is present, that which was or that which has always existed. Perceived as promise, revelation must be understood as the historical disclosure of that which does not yet exist, but which comes into view. Its truth is not concealed by a reality that can be recognized or through revelation that can be experienced, but rather by the anticipation of the future. The *kabod* of Yahweh was already announced in his *dabar*. The verification scheme of promise is not just 'promise and fulfilment', but rather 'promise and glorification', for it is clear that God's promises are not simply prophecy about a coming, alien reality. The promising God himself creates what he promises; the appearing promise itself opens up the history of his creative activity and, to that extent, cannot be separated as word from that reality which it announces. Rather, promise itself is reality coming from the reality of the glorification of God. Finally, therefore, the name of God stands over the promises of his future as they appear, as well as over the glorification in the future as it takes place. The name of God makes clear *who* God is. The history of promise and glorification makes clear *what* his divinity is. The promise appears in his name, and history, which is opened up and announced by it, serves the glorification of his name. The name and word of God do not coincide here. The name of God also announces the eschatological goal of the *debarim Yahweh*. Therefore the words of God are found in his name, and history, in which they appear, serves the glorification of his name. If these words, however, are promises, then an internal difference exists between the word and the name of God. Through hope, this difference is experienced as history.

B

That the revelation of God in promise does not 'disclose' history or existence, but rather 'opens up' history and existence within a new horizon, becomes even clearer in the fact that revelation is always connected with calling, commission and sending into historical service in the promised future.

The so-called visions of revelation are primarily visions of calling. The calling and mission to the promised future follows where God's revelation opens up new historical horizons. One 'corresponds' to the God of promise by breaking away from the old and setting out into the new, by change and transformation. Hope, which mobilizes to a new obedience, is therefore always bound up with a criticism of the present. The corresponding consciousness of history is thus, first and foremost, a consciousness of sending and, only then and because of this knowledge, about the historicity of the world and man's own historicity. History, therefore, is first and foremost a relationship to the promised future of God, and only then is it the relationship of man to the world and to himself. His future is 'the Spirit' of the age and the corresponding experience of this age. Revelation in promise and sending does not, then, effect a new self-understanding and a new world-view, but rather an openness to that future of God which is conditioned by hope.

C

The question about the divinity of God is asked on the basis of the expectation of his promise and calling, and it has the form of a question which holds all of history in suspense, a question about the coming of God's glory to all men.

The question of God is not asked *out of* the universal questionability of all transitory things. It is not asked out of the phenomenon of the questionability of human existence. It is asked out of the appearance of his promise and calling, and is the question of the divinity of *this* God. It is, however, a question with which all things and the existence of all men are confronted because of their future in the coming of his glorification. The question of God does not generally come from the world and from human existence, but rather from the concrete, contingent and special history of Israel and of Jesus Christ. This question, however, directs itself *to* the world and *to* the existence of every man in the anticipation of God's demonstration in them and in the hope for their transformation. God is known in the persistent and universal question of the coming of his divinity. This persistent question calls everything that is into question and does not allow it to remain as it is. One does not ask about God on the basis of the world, but rather about the 'world on the basis of God'. One does not ask about God on the basis of human existence, but rather about 'human existence on the basis of God'. This is never the world or the man as they are, but rather as they could and will be.

D

The New Testament speaks of God's revelation in the light of the Easter appearances of the crucified one, for it recognizes the coming of God's glory in them.

If the Easter appearances of Christ are the 'springboard' for Christian talk of revelation, then in the face of the cross of the risen one they can only be expressed eschatologically. Whatever it was that happened there and was understood as his glory can find no other analogy in the world of the cross of Christ, of sin

and of death, than the gospel's categories of promise and contradiction. Jesus reveals God, and God reveals Jesus. What,
however, appears as life from death, justice from judgment,
wealth from the poverty of the crucified one, can only be understood as the appearance and promise of the divinity and glory of
God in contrast to the visual appearance and the experienceable
God-forsaken state of the world. This must also be understood as the coming of the kingdom to the poor, the coming of
life to the dying, the coming of justice to those without legal
rights. Resurrection as the apocalypse of the eschaton in the
crucified one reveals Jesus as the one who, in fact, he is – the
risen and exalted one is identical with the crucified and
humiliated one. But it reveals him in such a way that his future,
his victory and his lordship are to be confidently hoped for.
Resurrection, therefore, not only reveals the significance of his
person and his cross, but opens up to all the world the coming
lordship of the crucified one. Resurrection as revelation is thus
not only the illumination of the real but also the opening up of
the new. The great theme of God's revelation is not to be understood 'without the perspective of the resurrection of the dead'.[36]

The revelation of Christ as the Lord in his lordship is a
revelation which is not concluded in itself because it points
beyond its own appearance. It is concluded *ad personam* – he is
the Lord, the first to rise from the dead, the leader of life, the
firstborn among many brothers. It is, however, unconcluded
ad opera, as the *taxis* sequence in I Cor. 15 points out in Paul's
eschatological christology. Because it is an event which, as it
were, is an unconcluded event and is still temporary in its
universal claim of salvation, the revelation of God in the resurrection of Christ is a promise up to and including its structure
as event.[37] It exhibits a new reality which does not yet exist,
and throws existing reality into non-being (I Cor. 1.26–9). As a
result, it finds in history only an analogy – the confession of
hope, the missionary process in which the gospel involves the
nations and the obedient acceptance of the cross of the present
in the 'power of the resurrection'.

E

What was treated as 'natural theology' in the general presuppositions and conditions of understanding for Christian talk of revelation is, in truth, pneumatology. What in a trinitarian pneumatology was treated as being a possibility of understanding opened up by the reality of revelation is, in truth, of eschatological universality.

The *locus classicus* of 'natural theology' (Rom. 1.19ff.) can only be understood in relationship to Paul's apocalyptic. In parallel phrases, Paul describes the revelation of the wrath of God now manifest over the whole God-forsaken state of man and the revelation of his saving justice which now appears in the gospel.[38] Misery, sin, transitoriness and death and even the Greek concept of conscience thus receive an un-Greek-like, eschatological function. In the appearance of the gospel, the whole world moves into the light of the eschaton. With the revelation of God's justice, at the same time the misery of the world is revealed. The question of God is asked from the point of view of faith, but what becomes questionable in this question is the world in its God-forsakenness and transitoriness. Therefore faith, as Romans 8.18ff. indicates, comes into a unique solidarity with the whole eagerly awaiting and suffering creation. Faith's question about God and its cry for freedom are the question and outcry of the whole of creation in the present suffering.[39] Its hope for glory and freedom directs itself towards the future of the whole of suffering creation and intercedes on behalf of it. The language of 'natural theology', the revealing of the questionability of all finite beings who are delivered over to that which is transitory, is therefore the language of the Holy Spirit. What unites all creation is that misery which is revealed in the afflictions which are still to come at the end of time and the future of the kingdom, the justice and life from God which is promised to the poor because it was revealed in the crucified one. What is treated in 'natural theology' as being the universal presupposition for the particular revelation of salvation, in reality means the solidarity of the children of God at the end of time with the whole creation in the present suffering. Christian proclamation does not acquire its universalism in all the world from a commonalty that is present and always beginning, but rather from that common future which determines all creation and to which, as one can say in this regard, all creation is destined.

On the other hand, the effect and the sending of the Spirit are also understood apocalyptically. In Acts 2.17, Luke follows Joel 3: 'And in the last days it shall be, God declares, that I will pour out my Spirit upon all flesh. . .' The eschatological determination of time is bound up here with a universal determination of place. Paul understands the activity of the Spirit eschatologically when he speaks of the 'guarantee of the Spirit', of the pledge of the future in the spirit of hope. The Spirit is the spirit of the resurrection of the dead which comes to believers from the resurrection of Christ as the power of life. In this spirit, the coming of the promised and opened future of God is completed. While one can say that a charismatic community takes shape in the body of Christ, one cannot say that it is still spatially limited to the sphere of innerness or the church. It must be understood within time and history, because the future of the judgment and the kingdom of all of God's creation reveals both the misery and the hope of the body of Christ. The sighing of the Spirit for the revelation of God's glory and the freedom of creation creates a solidarity between the longing of all creation and the longing of the troubled people of God. Therefore, this sighing for God and for freedom resounds through the community of the crucified one as well as through the whole of suffering creation. Consequently, in the eschatological understanding of the gospel there is a coincidence between what is expressed in 'natural theology' and what is expressed in pneumatology.[40]

V

If we understand the revelation of God in the way presented in these theses, we must now return to the three schemes of verification.

1. The 'closed circle of the *Deus dixit*' must open. It is not broken open from the outside, but rather opens outwards. The Word of God is, and yet is not, the self-proof of God. There is a difference between the appearance of the Word of God and the glorification of God, a difference which allows questioning, on the basis of the word, about the coming glorification of God. The Word of God already offers what it promises, namely God himself, reconciliation and community with him. And it offers him in such a way as to promise himself, his glorification. The Word heard in the gospel of the one who awakes the dead and creates out of nothing lets us wait confidently for the event of this word (I Cor. 15.54). God himself announces himself in his revealed name, but in it he also announces his universal lordship. In relation to this lordship, one must say that God is present in the *lumen verbi et fidei*. This light, however, points towards the future of God in which the *maiestas divina per sese revelabitur*. [41] Therefore, on hearing the Word of God the question is not silenced. Rather, it is this that calls into life. It appears in the prayer for the coming of the kingdom of God in the *parousia* of Christ. The word of the gospel and the liberating word of justification are spoken within the horizon of the resurrection of Jesus and are an eschatological word of the word with which God is glorified in all that is transitory, forsaken and suffering.

The 'closed circle' of the ontological proof of God is given a new shape by the 'biblical theologian' who wants to prove that there is a God because he has spoken in the Bible. It becomes – to keep the metaphor – a parable open to the eschaton. All lines point towards this universal eschaton which is coming towards us and in which, seen from this future of God, all light rays coincide at one point – the knowledge of God's glory in the face of Jesus Christ.

2. The ellipse which gathers all theological statements into the correlation of God and existence, or self and conscience, opens itself up in a similar way. Theological statements which, on the basis of promise, relate to the universal glorification of God, must also prove themselves in the interpretation of human

being. They will not point out God's divinity in man's existential anxiety, but they must outline the appearance of that existence which is brought into view by the future of God. Man, who is encountered by God's revelation in promise, is identified and finds himself; at the same time, however, he is differentiated and goes searching for his true life which is concealed in Christ (Col. 3.3). He finds himself, but only in hope, for he is not yet excluded from death, he is not yet risen. He is not yet in an eschatological existence of immediateness to God, but rather in an existence that is determined by the Logos, that is, an eschatological existence which mediates community with God to him within the community of Christ. The word of life that he has gives him hope for the salvation of his body and allows him to struggle for physical obedience. He, who is justified in his guilt, hungers and thirsts for righteousness. For the one who loves, the suffering of creation becomes intolerable. In this way, the one who believes becomes the one who hopes. He comes into harmony with himself – *in spe* but not *in re*. It is the believer who becomes a puzzle for himself, an open question, a *homo absconditus*. *Cor inquietum*, conscience and the open questionability of life are more the consequences of Christian faith than the presuppositions of faith. The promised identity, the freedom, which is brought into view by Christ, therefore leads man to the emptying of himself. He finds himself by abandoning himself. He finds life from death where in love he is delivered over to the pain of the negative. In this way, that truth comes towards him which points towards the resurrection of the dead. To be able to think, at the same time, of both God and existence in the name of the crucified and risen Christ, does not result in an ellipse which allows the unconditional to be recognized in the conditional; the other-worldly in the this worldly, the eternal in the temporal,[42] in a 'paradoxical identity',[43] but rather assumes a real dialectic[44] which, by virtue of the contradictions coming together in it, puts the *agon* of history from itself and is oriented towards an eschatological transcendence. Reconciliation is oriented towards overcoming when it does not become the confirmation of given conditions. The overcoming of enmity occurs in the reconciliation of the enemy, if it is not to become the terror of annihilation.

3. The ellipse which gathers together all statements regarding God and reality as a whole opens itself in a similar way. If, in the event of promise, man's existence appears as determined for the future of God by hope and sending, this does not occur without a new understanding of reality into which hope reaches, love empties itself and work gives everything a new shape. One can only speak of historical existence together with a historical world,[45] and one can only speak of the radical openness of existence for the future with a world which is full of everything that is possible (to God). Without eschatological ontology, eschatological existence is inexpressible. Without a new understanding of the world, no self-understanding of faith can be formulated. But to think both of the God of the resurrection and the reality of the world is not possible in the direct way attempted in the cosmological proof of God, for this would presuppose an ordered world and a divine plan of history which is identical with the course of history. In the face of the reality of suffering and the God-forsaken state of this world and history, both are illusionary. To think at the same time of God and the reality of the world or world history is possible neither in indirect nor in paradoxical co-existence, but rather only within a real dialectical process which by virtue of its driving antagonism evokes the historical process for the future of truth. In the face of the cross of Christ and as expressed in his resurrection, the judgment of God on reality can only be, 'See, I make everything new.' It is not yet, 'See, everything is very good.'

4. *Conclusion.* The revelation of God in the word of Christ from the cross, which opens up the future, is the promise of glorification in all men. The schemes of verification mentioned above, from the world, from existence and from the revealed name of God, are plans which anticipate the glorification of God within the present reality of his Word, his world and his image. They are plans based on promise and hope and, therefore, remain open for that new existence which God, according to his Word, will realize.

As long as real conditions have not yet reached this point, the eschatological question about the divinity of God and the freedom of suffering creation is greater than all possible answers. All answers by which the world might be shown to be God's world and man to be in God's image can be understood as necessary but provisional doxologies which press in on this future in the insufficient material of the present, a future in which God will become all in all. Christian faith appears in the persistent question about God, in the continuing prayer concerning the glorification of his name, the future of the kingdom and the doing of God's will 'in heaven as on earth'. This question cannot yet be answered by the illumination of the present and the reality that is always dawning. Rather, it finds its answer first in that transformation of all things which projects its appearance in Christ and the Spirit.

God is not yet present in such a way that everything is silenced in us. He is, however, present in Word and Spirit in such a way that everything in us and with us questions, searches, hopes and also begins to suffer from the misery in the world. Christian faith is alive in the steadfastness of hope, not the jubilation of those who are saved. In solidarity with the whole of this eagerly awaiting creation, Christian faith announces the truth.

NOTES

This article was first published in: *Parrhesia. Karl Barth zum 80. Geburtstag am 10. Mai 1966*, ed. Eberhard Busch, Jürgen Fangmeyer and Max Geiger, 1966, 147–72.

1. I. Kant, *Der Streit der Fakultäten* (PhB 252), 1959, 15; Akademie-Ausgabe VII, 23.
2. Cf. also H. U. von Balthasar, *Glaubhaft ist nur Liebe*, 1963, who describes on 8ff. 'the cosmological reduction' and on 19ff. 'the anthropological reduction'.
3. H. U. von Balthasar has shown that in Barth's theology the 'presupposition of revelation' is to be understood actively: *Karl Barth. Darstellung und Deutung seiner Theologie*, 1957, 129: 'Consequently, we shall see that the key problem of Karl Barth's theology in its final form is compressed into the *concept of presupposition* in the sense that the specific and original assumption

of God, *in the very act of its assumption, presupposes something about itself.*' Cf. also
E. Jüngel, 'Die Möglichkeit theologischer Anthropologie auf dem Grund
der Analogie', in *EvTh* 22, 1962, 544f.

4. I have borrowed this formulation from H. U. von Balthasar, *Glaubhaft
ist nur Liebe*, 1963, 32, and would point out that, like Melanchthon, one
could understand the law of Moses as a new version of the general law of
nature, in order by this broad understanding of the law to show the universality of the gospel. Even if, like Bultmann, one understands Old Testament
history as a conflict 'which belongs to human existence as such – the conflict
of being created for God and called to God, and yet of being imprisoned in
secular history' (*Essays Philosophical and Theological*, trans. J. C. G. Greig,
1955, 207), and universalizes it in this paradigmatic way, one accepts it as
a palimpsest. Cf. also H. G. Geyer, 'Zur Frage der Notwendigkeit des
Alten Testaments', *EvTh* 25, 1965, 218.

5. W. Kamlah, *Christentum und Geschichtlichkeit*, 1951, 345ff.; H.
Gollwitzer, *The Existence of God as Confessed by Faith*, trans. J. W. Leitch,
1965, 81ff.

6. *Metaphysics*, I, 1076, ed. W. Jaeger, Oxford 1957, 262.

7. This is the theological intention of W. Pannenberg. See *Revelation as
History*, trans. David Granskou, 1968, 141f.: 'The one and only God can be
revealed in his deity, but only indirectly out of a totality of all events. This
was also the lead thought regarding the true form of the divine in Greek
philosophy. It is only that this philosophy did not understand the totality of
reality as a history always open to the new contingency, but rather took it
to be a world with unchangeable structures of order. . . . The biblical
experience of reality as history is more inclusive, since the contingency of the
real event is included in this conception. . . . In such a situation, the God
who is revealed out of the totality of history in this indirect way would also
be the dominant answer to the philosophical question about God.

'Now the history of the whole is only visible when one stands at the
end. . . . It is only the eschatological character of the Christ event that
establishes that . . . from now on the non-Jew can acknowledge the God of
Israel as the one true God, the one whom Greek philosophy sought. . . .'

8. Justin, *Apology* II, 13.4.

9. Cf. E. Peterson, *Der Monotheismus als politisches Problem*, 1935; H.
Berkhof, *Kirche und Kaiser*, 1947.

10. Cf. B. Groethuysen, *Philosophische Anthropologie*, 1928, 78ff.

11. This reminds one of Nietzsche's poem:

> The world – a gate
> to a thousand deserts, silent and cold!
> He who has lost
> what you have lost
> has nowhere to stay.

After the metaphysical concept of God within the horizon of cosmology lost
its power, it did not help to establish talk about God within the horizon of
the ethical. The disintegration of morals followed the disintegration of
cosmology. 'Now we have destroyed morality, we have again become quite

incomprehensible to ourselves', declared Nietzsche, *Will to Power*, no. 594. See also R. Musil, *Der Mann ohne Eigenschaften*, 1952, 150: 'The disintegration of the anthropocentric attitude which has for so long understood man to be the mid-point of the universe (an attitude which has now been receding for centuries), has probably finally reached the ego itself; for to most people the idea that the most important thing in experiencing is that one should experience this experiencing and the most important thing in doing is that one should do this doing seems naïve.

12. G. Ebeling, *Word and Faith*, trans. J. W. Leitch, 1963, 350f.

13. R. Bultmann, *Essays*, 257f.

14. R. Bultmann, *Kerygma and Myth*, ed. H. W. Bartsch, trans. R. H. Fuller, 1957, 194.

15. R. Bultmann, *Essays*, 136.

16. R. Bultmann, *Faith and Understanding* I, 1969, 323.

17. R. Bultmann, 'The Idea of God and Modern Man', *Journal for Theology and the Church* 2, 1965, 89 n.27, against H. G. Gadamer's question: 'Must we not say that human existence finds itself moved by the question of god only by God, that is, in the light of faith?' (*Wahrheit und Methode*, 1960, 313): 'I am of the opinion that the pre-understanding is given precisely in that experience which Gadamer designates as the "authentic experience", namely, the experience in which "man becomes conscious of his finiteness" (339f.). This experience is certainly not always realized, but it surely persists as an ever present possibility.'

18. G. Ebeling, *Theology and Proclamation*, trans. J. Riches, 1966, 80: 'It is essential that we should follow the urgent dictates of conscience as a guide for the proper interpretation of theology.'

19. H. Braun, 'The Problem of a New Testament Theology', *Journal for Theology and the Church* 1, 1965, 182: 'God is understood not as a holy given, but in the system of the coordinates "I may" and "I ought".'

20. R. Bultmann, *Essays*, 257.

21. R. Bultmann, *Faith and Understanding* I, 150.

22. D. Henrich, *Der ontologische Gottesbeweis. Sein Problem und seine Geschichte in der Neuzeit*, 1960, 201.

23. H. U. von Balthasar, *op. cit.*, 5.

24. K. Barth, 'The Christian Understanding of Revelation', *Against the Stream*, trans. E. M. Delacour and S. Godman, ed. R. Gregor Smith, 1954, 211.

25. Thus Hegel, according to a quotation by D. Henrich, *op. cit.*, 206.

26. It is not intended to tie Karl Barth's theology down to a simple ontological mode of thinking. No method grasps its theological object in such a way that it is already understood with the method. Karl Barth's theology, in its complexity, makes this unforgettably clear. We discuss in what follows only that aspect of Barth's theology which contributes to the discussion of the above-mentioned schemes of verification. In the comparison, however, his onto-theological thinking with its prevenience and the predominance of the ontic over the noetic become particularly clear. Cf. also M. Josuttis, *Die Gegenständlichkeit der Offenbarung. Karl Barths Anselmbuch und die Denkform seiner Theologie* (Bonn dissertation), 1962, and

E. Jüngel, *Gottes Sein ist im Werden: Verantwortliche Rede vom Sein Gottes bei Karl Barth. Eine Paraphrase*, 1965.

27. *Die Christliche Dogmatik im Entwurf*, 1927, 319.

28. *Anselm: Fides Quaerens Intellectum*, trans. Ian Robertson, 1960.

29. H. G. Geyer, 'Theologie des Nihilismus', *EvTh* 23, 1963, 104.

30. *Church Dogmatics* I/1, trans. G. T. Thomson, 1936, 349ff., 'The Root of the Doctrine of the Trinity'; 431ff., 'The Meaning of the Doctrine of the Trinity'. For the significance of the doctrine of the Trinity for hermeneutics see F. Schmid, *Verkündigung und Dogmatik in der Theologie Karl Barths: Hermeneutik und Ontologie in einer Theologie des Wortes Gottes*, 1964, 145ff.

31. The image of the closed circle keeps recurring in the *Church Dogmatics* (cf. e.g. I/1, 351, 436; II/1, trans. T. H. L. Parker *et al.*, 1957, 246ff.). IV/3, trans. G. W. Bromiley, 1961, 85f., states: 'our line of argument is informed by the true spirit and import of the "ontological proof" of Anselm of Canterbury. The point of our whole exposition is positively: *Credo ut intelligam*, and polemically: "The fool hath said in his heart, There is no God." As we have put it, the declaration of the prophecy of the life of Jesus Christ is valid as and because it is a declaration concerning the life of Jesus Christ. But is not this begging the question? Are we not arguing in a circle? Exactly! We have learned from the content of our presupposition and assertion, and only from its content, that because it is true it is legitimate and obligatory, and in what sense this is the case. *Honi soit qui mal y pense*. Only fools can say in their hearts that this is a *circulus vitiosus*, as though there could not also be, and in this case necessarily is, a *circulus virtuosus* as well.

32. See *Church Dogmatics*, IV/2, trans. G. W. Bromiley, 1958, 274ff. The confession of the Kyrios has an inclusive significance. The divine decision on sinful man made in Christ presupposes an 'ontic connection' between Christ and all men. He becomes the 'legal ground' of the universal kerygma. He does not make the kerygma irrelevant or even superfluous, but founds it. The ontological statement of the confession of the Kyrios thus has a dynamic, missionary character.

33. H. J. Iwand has recently called attention to this question – *an Deus sit?* – which faith and unbelief have in common (*Glauben und Wissen. Nachgelassene Werke* I, 1962, 112f.). He thus yields to the sort of questioning with which Thomas Aquinas' doctrine of God begins (S.Th.I, Q.2), and rejects the defence of this question by the thesis '*Deus esse est articulus fidei*' as being a retreat into the subjectivity of faith.

34. E. Käsemann, *Essays on New Testament Themes*, trans. W. J. Montague, 1964, 182.

35. For the following short theses see my *Theology of Hope*, trans. J. W. Leitch, 1967.

36. H. J. Iwand, 'Meditation zu 1 Kor. 15.54–8', in G. Eichholz (ed.), *Herr, tue meine Lippen auf* IV, ³1961, 260.

37. Cf. E. Jüngel, *Paulus und Jesus*, ²1964, 272: 'In Paul, the present is disclosed in terms of the past *for* the future as the time of hope.' H. G. Geyer, 'Geschichte als theologisches Problem', *EvTh* 22, 1962, 103f.: 'The proclamation of the revelation of God which occurred in the history of Jesus Christ is the promise of this event in the sense of the proclamation of Jesus

Christ himself as the universal promise contained in the future of all things, which, as a result, concerns all things and therefore in this concern graciously waits for all things. If it is true that the history of Jesus Christ is an event stemming from the mode of promise, then this implies the impossibility of trying to understand it as a fact of the past. . . . This coming fulfilment (sc. his coming parousia which includes our resurrection) is the only possible and conceivable verification of the witness of the resurrection. . . .'

38. G. Bornkamm, 'The Revelation of God's Wrath (Rom. 1–3)', *Early Christian Experience*, trans. P. L. Hammer, 1969, 47ff.

39. E. Käsemann, 'Der gottesdienstliche Schrei nach der Freiheit', *Haenchen Festschrift*, 1964, 142ff.

40. Cf. also P. Stuhlmacher's pertinent remark in *Gerechtigkeit Gottes bei Paulus*, 1965, 72: 'With the help of the apocalyptic world-view of his time, Paul understands that man and the world have a common destiny, that this destiny must be understood as the temporal context of suffering, i.e. as history, and that God, in the power of his word, is and remains the Lord of this event.'

41. With this distinction, Luther (WA 18,785) also expressed the *absconditas Dei* in this life as, so to speak, the eschatological reservation and the eschatological projection of God.

42. R. Bultmann, 'The Idea of God and Modern Man' (see n. 17), 94: 'Only the idea of God which can find, which can seek and find, the *unconditional* in the conditional, the beyond in the here, the transcendent in the present at hand, as possibility of encounter, is possible for modern man.'

43. For this concept see G. Hasenhüttl, *Der Glaubensvollzug: Eine Begegnung mit R. Bultmann aus katholischem Glaubensverständnis*, 1963. It has been criticized by G. Bornkamm, *Theologische Rundschau* NF 29, 1963, 111ff., esp. 138, because 'the dimension of history has no place' in the concept of paradoxical identity.

44. The return of the Kierkegaard-oriented concept of paradox to the more comprehensive dialectic of Hegel and Marx has been brilliantly called for by D. Sölle, 'Paradoxe Identität', *MpTh* 53, 1964, 366ff. The paradox preserves its world-encompassing power in the 'history of the world', the dialectic, on the other hand, its world-illuminating power' (p. 372). 'The man who is not satisfied by a paradox searches the horizon of his life for possibilities which can be planned and anticipated because for him God is not the paradoxical "other" but rather the one who is dialectically "changing all things".' This is the intention of *Theology of Hope*.

45. W. Pannenberg points out this necessity in 'Hermeneutic and Universal History', *Basic Questions in Theology*, trans. G. H. Kehm, 1970, 54ff.

2

GOD AND RESURRECTION

Resurrection Faith in the Forum of the Question of Theodicy[1]

I   The question of God and the question of the resurrection

Today, the most intense conflicts in theology are being carried on in regard to the question of God and the resurrection faith.

The conflict over the content of reality and the practical meaning of the Christian resurrection faith is at the centre of discussion within theology. 'If Christ has not been raised, then our preaching is in vain and your faith is in vain': this is the way in which one group repeats the judgment of the apostle Paul (I Cor. 15.14) in order to force doubting belief to come to a resolute confession.

Others, however, ask: how can we believe today in a super-natural event such as the resurrection of the dead when we no longer know, feel or fear the almightiness of a God, without being dishonest to our intelligence and alienated from the suffering of our contemporaries? If Christian faith exhausts itself in self-confirmation by the mere repetition of biblical formulae, it becomes sterile. Christian theology is thus caught between the danger of external irrelevance and an internal loss of meaning. It is impossible for it to reduce itself to a biblical language game within its own areas of influence. It is equally impossible for it to canonize the present conditions in thought and life as conditions for theology. In doing so, it would have nothing new to say to its contemporaries and nothing to say to conditions which would change them.

The question of the resurrection today is a conflict *in* theology; the question of God, however, is a conflict *with* theology.

The two questions are much more closely related than in earlier times. Earlier protests were made in the name of religion against belief in the crucified one and, for the sake of the gods, Christians were called 'atheists'. Today, atheism shrugs its shoulders at Christians as the last people who believe in God. Earlier, the existence of God was accepted even without a Christ, a mediator and saviour. Christians did not doubt the existence of God either. Under the influence of Christian cultural history, however, conditions have been reversed, so that now belief in God is itself at stake in belief in Jesus. 'God' increasingly becomes the concern of faith itself and is no longer its universally demonstrable presupposition.

But how, and in what situations, are the questions of God and the resurrection related?

The God-question is only superficially the theoretical question about the possibility of conceiving the existence of God. Actual misery lies behind this question. 'Suffering precedes thinking', remarked Ludwig Feuerbach.[2] From this, Herbert Marcuse drew the conclusion: 'No realization of reason is in the offing until that suffering has been eliminated'.[3] Thinking brings an awareness of the painful suffering caused by the difference and dissonance of life. Man only gives his attention to that in which he is interested, and he is interested where he experiences reality in pain as another and strange reality. The passion of his thinking is kindled by suffering. In what sort of pain is this passionate thinking about God brought to life?

Is it not that character of the world which produces suffering (the world's crisis of identity)?

Is it not also the uncertainty of man's own existence in this world (man's crisis of identity)?

Is it not the despair resulting from the inability of thought and faith to change the world concretely and to offer this intolerable reality more than illusions and compensations (the identity crisis of human activity in the world)?

'Why do I suffer? That is the rock of atheism', said Georg Büchner. And it is precisely in this experience of anguish that we find a great solidarity between Christians and atheists. In it, faith suffers from the God who has withdrawn his presence. In it, unbelief hungers for a present meaning. Behind the various forms of atheism stemming from the Enlightenment and post-Enlightenment periods, we find that suffering which is expressed in the question of theodicy, which can neither be dismissed nor redeemed.[4] It is the experience of the separation of God and the world, of justice and reality, of essence and existence. Since the Enlightenment's dream of harmony faded away in the Lisbon earthquake (1755) and in the historical crises of the French Revolution, Job has appeared on the scene of the modern spirit. Job's philosophical, theological and poetic friends discuss the penetrating question of meaningless suffering: is God the 'sun of righteousness' – is God the dark power of nothingness?[5] Those who offer one positive theodicy after another to the person who is arguing with God for the sake of God have been succeeded through the atheists who, following the example of Job's matter-of-fact wife, say to him, 'Do you still hold fast your integrity? Curse God and die' (Job 2.9). If only this were the simplest solution to the question of theodicy – that no God exists, in other words, negative theodicy! If only there were no God, then everything would be all right and the excitement would be to no purpose. If the old question is *si deus justus, unde malum*?, then with this absolute presupposition the radical questioning of suffering would be taken up in conscious agony. One can come to terms with meaningless suffering when one no longer asks about meaning or asks only about meaning within certain boundaries. If man becomes accustomed to over-stated questions about the meaning of world events and a particular determination of his life, then he will contentedly allow himself to adjust and no longer question anything critically.[6]

The unavoidable character of the question of theodicy is found precisely in the fact that neither theism nor atheism solves it. Even if the answers have disappeared, the questions and the agony have not been taken care of (E. Bloch).[7] Today they have only been intensified. Lisbon was a natural catastrophe. What is Auschwitz? The question persists long after the event. The traditional faith in God cannot provide a common denominator for the atrocities of history with God or with history. Here nothing seems to fit. Nihilism is impossible, because it would withdraw the foundation from the elementary protest against the event, against God and man. Even the revolt must be directed against someone, said Camus (*The Rebel*, 1953, 30). What is developing here? A piety of unbelief against the Enlightenment solution to the question of theodicy? A protest theology of 'no longer not being able to believe'?[8] Is there a theological experience in which God is against God and, for God's sake, is judged with God? The old phrase *'nemo contra deum nisi deus ipse'* forces man back into his situation. Positively stated, however, it can also mean that God is hidden and unrecognizably present in those who quarrel with God, destroy all images of God, and are never satisfied.

We have now seen the question of theodicy at various levels. The depth of the criticism is directed towards the strength of the affirmation. We recognize it in the ancient world in the form of universal cosmology: if there is a God who is the orderer and the ruler of the universe, why then is there evil?[9] Why is creation so subject to futility, so that fear and longing permeate everything that exists (Rom. 8.20)? In Israel, we recognize it in the form of election and God's covenant with his people: 'Why must the just suffer while the godless prosper?' 'Why has Israel been given over to the Gentiles as a reproach? Why has the people whom you loved been given over to godless tribes?' (II Esdras [IV Ezra] 4.23). Already in Israel's national laments, in the Psalms, in the Suffering Servant passages of Deutero-Isaiah, in Job and in apocalyptic, the question of suffering and pain caused by forsakenness is much stronger because the preceding affirmation of God is much stronger.

We recognize it in still another form in the words of those who proclaim the gospel of the coming kingdom of the poor and personify it in themselves. It is the cry of Jesus from the cross: 'My God, why hast thou forsaken me?'[10] The mystery of the open question and lament with which Jesus dies is not solved by his repetition of the words of Psalm 22. These rather, for example in Mark, only intensify the paradox. The paradox is found in the fact that, in spite of his being, for the witnesses to the event, the Son of God, he was not heard (cf. Heb. 5.7 with Harnack's correction). Not without reason, the biblical history of tradition increasingly silenced this offensive cry and replaced it with the words of surrender (compare Luke 23.46 with Ps. 31.6: 'Into thy hands I commit my spirit').

To sum up, we find an increase in the presupposition of the question of theodicy on the way from universal-cosmological presence to particular historical presence, to personal presence in the suffering righteous one and the presence of God in the one who incorporates his nearness. At the same time, on the other hand, we find an infinite intensification of suffering in the world, in history, in personal destiny and in helplessness – to the agony of God. Conversely, however, cosmic, historical and personal suffering come into the horizon of solidarity with Christ's suffering.

Christian theology which is to think of God for the sake of Christ becomes relevant when it accepts this solidarity with present suffering, brings an awareness of this suffering in agony and expresses it in the cry for God and for freedom. Suffering also precedes the thinking of Christian theology – the open questions precede the answers of Christian theology. It is not possible to express God before the world without first and at the same time expressing the world before God. The one who believes does not live in a redeemed enclave in the midst of an unredeemed world, but rather becomes the spokesman for unredeemed creation.[11] Where freedom is close at hand, the chains begin to chafe. Where life begins to live, death begins to die. Where God's nearness is announced, the condition of God-forsakenness becomes torture. Precisely because faith intends to lead man out of this world, it leads him ever deeper into solidarity with groaning creation. The one cannot be realized without the other.

'No realization of reason is to be expected as long as suffering is not overcome.' For Christian theology, Jesus' cry from the cross is the most extreme horizon of the question of God. All its answers must always return to this fundamental question, for no

conclusion can be reached through historical answers. With the
question of the crucified one – as with all questions – the horizon
of the future is opened up in which there appears what is called
'God', for it is the question of the one who dies in God. Thus in a
Christian context, the words 'God' and 'resurrection' characterize that event of the future which is asked about in the cry
and the agonies of the crucified one on earth. What keeps arriv-
ing in new and surprising reality, whatever 'God' and 'resurrection' and 'Spirit' and 'faith' and 'hope' deserve to be called,
enters into the specific horizon of the questioning and lamenting
openness of the crucified one and can only be shown to be
'Christian' within this horizon. Here questioning reason,
through the suffering of the world, becomes theological reason,
i.e. becomes the passionate question of the understanding of that
vision of which the gospel of John says, 'Then you will no longer
ask me'. Christian reason asks with the dying Jesus about God
and can only be satisfied with a vision which means the transformation of the viewer in the vision and the transformation of
the new creation of the whole of reality in the presence of God.
Therefore, this reason is not oriented towards explanations but
towards changes, not towards agreement, but rather towards
fulfilment in the new. In 1924, Karl Barth wrote, 'Without any
doubt at all the words "resurrection of the dead" are, for him
(sc. Paul), nothing else than a paraphrase of the word "God".'[12]
Conversely, one can say that in that case 'God' is historically
paraphrased by that event in the crucified one which is characterized as 'resurrection'. 'God' appears within the horizon of
the crucified one, not as 'the totally other', but as the one who
changes things; he appears not only in the infinite qualitative
difference but also in the surprising newness of the qualitative
change. The as yet hidden arrival of the coming God and the
redemption of creation through the crucified one is precisely
what is expressed by the Easter faith.

After these introductory remarks on the question of theodicy
and the resurrection faith, we now turn to the question of
how the God who is called into question and announced in
this way within the cross of present reality can relevantly be

expressed in the language of knowledge, faith, practice and hope.

II   The resurrection faith: from the historical criticism of the Easter faith to the critical theory of the present in the light of the cross[13]

At first glance, for the modern consciousness everything seems to be historical. The truth must be contained in the facts (Vico). In the first approach, we shall accept the historical question and reject those prejudices according to which either the resurrection of Jesus can be historically supported because it must be historically supported, or cannot be historically supported because it ought not to be historically supported. We shall ask: (1) What the Christian Easter faith says and does not say historically; (2) Where this historical criticism leads the Christian faith in its ground of reality.

(i) The witness and the witnesses which we cross-examine speak of two experiences of Jesus which, at first glance, seem to be contradictory. They describe how he was forsaken by the God whose nearness he had announced and how, unable to do anything about it, he died on the cross. They attest it by abandoning him themselves and, in the collapse of their faith, by fleeing from him as he is forsaken by God. They then announce that the one who was forsaken by God has appeared to them in the glory of God's righteousness and attest it by returning to Jerusalem, the place of his crucifixion, in anticipation of his future in the coming glory of God. Not one of them claims to have seen what happened to Jesus himself between the time of his experience on the cross and the Easter visions. In order to recount what had happened, they explain the Easter visions in eschatological language and proclaim 'God's resurrection of Jesus from the dead'. The expression itself is an interpretation and a conclusion from experience and appearance to an event which was not experienced and not observed. It is not occasioned by their universal apocalyptic disposition, but rather, concretely, by the aporia of their experience of God's nearness to Jesus and their experience of his God-forsakenness. The

expression is not, however, arbitrarily chosen, but rather conceals an inner necessity; for (1) it expresses the fact that the one
who was killed now 'lives', that the executed one is now lifted
up to God's right hand, and that the future belongs to the one
who has been slain; (2) it excludes every thought of a revival of
the dead into the old life leading to death, and speaks of a new
life which qualitatively changes this 'life leading to death'. The
'raising of Jesus' is a hope for justice and means (3) retrospect-
ively the justification of the present proclamation of the coming
kingdom of God through Jesus and, together with this, the
constitution of the eschatological person of Jesus as the revelation of the coming God in his living and dying; (4) prospectively,
the anticipation of the coming transformation of the world
through the presence of God in the crucified Jesus and (5) the
present summons to faith which transcends the world and to
love which permeates the world. The expression itself can be
replaced and interpreted – as can already be seen in primitive
Christianity – by other expressions such as 'resurrection',
'exaltation', etc., but these five points can hardly be abandoned.

(ii) Can the real content of this event, characterized and
understood in this way, be communicated historically? The
Christian Easter faith in fact describes a historical person, Jesus
of Nazareth, a definite time, after his crucifixion under Pontius
Pilate and before those appearances which brought the disciples
to new faith, and finally a definite place, Jerusalem. What,
however, has happened to this historical person in this time at
this place eludes historical questioning, for there is no witness
to the event itself and there are no analogies in the same
category from which analogous conclusions can be drawn.
History can transmit the fact that there was an Easter faith; it
can say who was affected by it, what it looked like, what it did
and did not proclaim, but the event itself eludes the drawing of
both positive and negative conclusions. On the one hand, Jesus,
the crucified one, is historically comprehensible; on the other
hand, so is the Easter faith of the disciples. The basis of this
Easter faith in God and Jesus, however, transcends historical
opinion. Apart from faith, it is not evident in itself as a 'saving

fact'; nor, however, is it understandable as a fantastic projection of faith.

(iii) Where does historical criticism lead Christian faith? First of all, to the recognition that even the Easter witnesses do not assert that the crucified one has already appeared in an event that is available to everyone and in an experience that can be repeated at all times. He has only appeared to particular persons (I Cor. 15.3–6) who, on the strength of that, strive to fill the whole world with the gospel. Their faith was extended between particular experiences and universal expectations founded on these experiences. For them, Easter was no finished event of the past recognizable by anyone who made the attempt to observe it in a methodically correct way. It was, rather, an event of the future which forms the basis of universal world-transforming hope within the 'ambiguous and historical' and is, therefore, necessarily bound up with the risk involved in such a faith.

When historical criticism in this way throws faith back on faith and robs it of its universally accepted supporting proofs in the realm of sight and experience, it leads faith away from illusions of history and utopias of the future back to the cross of Christ. The advantage and disadvantage of history for faith is not found by giving faith a firm foundation within the conflicts of history but rather by bringing faith into the conflict of the cross. Here critical history is confronted by the iconoclastic power of Christian hope, and the prohibition of images is fulfilled in the destruction of images of religious fetishism on the one hand and of religious dreams of the future on the other. Christian faith does not prejudice God and the future but rather, as faith in God's lordship, it is openness for the surprising new element in this future. Historical criticism brings Christian remembrance out of the glorificatory gilding of the isolated facts of Easter and back to the real cross of the resurrection.

Paul did not proclaim the Damascus experience, but rather the crucified one as the future of the world. In other words, Easter is a light of the *novum* into which one cannot look directly without being blinded or deluded. It does, however, allow the one who is illuminated by this light to be seen – and that is Jesus, the crucified one, alone. Easter is the invisible ground of faith, but the crucified one is the visible object and the continuing encounter of faith. If, in historical criticism, we find a retrospective destruction of images, then this happens – if it is not prejudiced by humanism – in the sense of the second commandment, for the sake of God's divinity and *against* it. If it leads the men involved back to the conflict of the cross, then it does not serve the abstract hiddenness of God in the beyond, but the concrete hiddenness of God in the agony of Christ. The risen one then become visible in the cross, the exalted one in the forsaken one, the just one in the condemned one. Here is the decision between the acceptance of the cross as exasperation at God and the acceptance of the cross as justice for the godless; between the cross as aporia for the religious and the righteous and the cross as justification of those who murmur, hunger and are without justice.

(iv) If Christian faith takes up historical-critical iconoclasm, then at the same time it must also go further and move from historical criticism of the power of the past over the present to a critical theory of the cross of the present. Once historical criticism itself stood in the service of revolutionary enlightenment and the liberation from mythos of lordship in society, state and church. The 'dialectic' of this enlightenment has, however, changed the function of history in such a way that positivism soon moved into history. From the criticism of the power of the past over the present, a science has developed which has history as its object.[14] The historicization of the past leads to a neutralization of the present by history. It was no coincidence that in the quest for the historical Jesus, the designation 'Jesus of Nazareth', which connected his history with his origin, replaced the title Christ, which connected his history with his future. It was no coincidence that the cross of Jesus was reduced to the private person of Jesus and the significance of his agony for the agony of the whole world was negated. The history in which the present must take responsibility for the past before a future which is not yet decided, degenerates into the registration of facts when it does not incorporate the necessary abstracting character of history into the fundamental questions of history. Is what has happened true because it has happened? I suffer, therefore I am, and I ask about justice and truth. Historically, man and his society are caught in the conflict between being and non-being.[15] The historical criticism of the power of the past serves to liberate the open possibilities and tasks of history. Therefore historical criticism can be taken up into a new critical theory of history.

To begin with, we called this fundamental question of history the question of righteousness, and we considered it within the various forms of the question of theodicy. If we incorporate history within the larger context of the question of history which is open to the future, it does not mean that we need a theodicy from history writing in the pattern of Hegel, nor does it mean that analytical history should again be involved with speculation on world history. It does mean, however, that this recounting of history pushes the past into the agony of the present and thus produces a critical awareness of the historical solidarity of unredeemed being.[16]

III The ground, way and goal of the resurrection faith

In our second consideration of the problem, we shall ask about the ground, way and goal of the resurrection faith within the open horizon of the question of theodicy. Hegel was to restore

. . . to philosophy the idea of absolute freedom, thus bringing out absolute suffering or the speculative Good Friday which was otherwise historical . . . in the full truth and severity of its godlessness, from which severity alone . . . the highest totality can and must rise again in all its seriousness and from its deepest foundation, at the same time in an all-embracing fashion and in the most cheerful freedom of its form.[17]

Conversely, in relation to this restored 'speculative Good Friday', 'the abyss of nothingness into which all existence sinks', the feeling 'God is dead', Christian theology is forced again to bring the 'historical Good Friday' of Jesus into view and to

interpret its significance. It cannot undertake this speculatively
in view of world history, but rather only in a concrete dialectic
with concrete negatives. We shall make the attempt here in a
series of open circles, which refer to each other with internal
logic, beginning with the dialectic of christology.

1. God in the crucified and risen Christ

The suffering and dying of the crucified one in God is not
understood if it is not seen in the light of Easter. At the historical level, the 'life of Jesus' (W. Herrmann) certainly
precedes 'the end of his life' (M. Kähler). At the level of
matters to be understood, however, the future precedes the past,
the end the beginning.[18] Only with Easter does the cross of
Jesus become a puzzle. Why did the Messiah have to suffer such
a thing? The Easter appearances of Jesus did not solve the
puzzle of his forsakenness on the cross, but rather made his
forsakenness the puzzle of his being forsaken *by God*. Where and
who is 'God' at the end of Jesus' life, at the end of his beginning
and at the new beginning of his end?

The first simple answer, in the missionary sermons of Acts,
ran: 'You have crucified him on the cross; God, however, has
raised him up.' According to this, God's act and revelation are
found wholly in the resurrection of Jesus from that death which
men had prepared for him. God is recognized as the one who
calls those who do not exist into being, who raises the dead and
who shows himself to be the power of freedom in all humiliated
and transitory being. In that case, Jesus' resurrection is the
answer to the cry of the forsaken and the glorious beginning of
the resolution of the question of theodicy in the world. The cross
of Jesus has lasting meaning only as the conquered, dark past
which is on its way towards a glorious future.

The second, more profound answer, however, is: Does God
from his divinity give a prior indication in the resurrection of
the crucified one of where he was and who he was in the crucifixion itself? Did God permit this only because he restrained
himself? Did he hide himself when it occurred? If the Easter
faith makes a puzzle of the cross of the forsaken one, then

obviously the cross must first explain this Easter faith. By abandoning him, the God who accepted him sacrifices him. The suffering and dying of the crucified one in God then acquires the significance of his sacrifice in the world, and in Jesus' sacrifice is found the sacrifice of God himself. In Jesus' suffering God suffers; in his death, God himself tastes of damnation and death. 'God wills to lose in order that man may gain' (Barth).[19] In this way, the old image of God, the image of fatherly or cold authority against which the question of theodicy rebels, is transformed in the cross. 'God is other.' In the crucified one he withdraws from power and lordship and humiliates himself to the point of this death. Why and for whom does God's Christ suffer? Georg Büchner is wrong: *this* is the rock of the Christian faith.[20] Here the abstract superior power becomes the concrete suffering of God; the abstract immortality of God becomes the 'death of God' in Christ. As happened in a hidden way in Job and in the Suffering Servant of Isaiah, God no longer stands before the forum of the human question of theodicy, but is himself incorporated into it, is at stake in it in a game in which the loser wins. The cross of the risen one, then, reveals who and where God is. Only under the presupposition 'God in the face of the crucified one', i.e. God no longer as the heavenly opponent but rather as the earthly and humane God in the crucified one, does the cross of Christ acquire its full judicial significance and future meaning within the question of theodicy. God is no longer the defendant in the human question of theodicy; rather, the answer is found in this question itself. The cross of Christ then becomes the 'Christian theodicy' – a self-justification of God in which judgment and damnation are taken up by God himself, so that man may live.

This apparently paradoxical dialectic of the presence of God in the one who was crucified and surrendered is no closed paradox, but rather an open dialectic. We meet the openness of this dialectic towards the future where we define the God who demonstrates his power to the witnesses through the resurrection by the God who, for all men, is involved in the cross of Christ. In the resurrection of the crucified one can be seen a preview in the night of the forsaken one of the kingdom in which God is God and finds his identity in that creation in which man receives freedom; and justice and peace rule the earth. In the resurrection of Christ, a real anticipation of God's comprehensive future becomes tangible, for he is transformed 'ahead of us' into the kingdom of freedom in which we live even in this 'body of death', in this 'kingdom of necessity'. This is expressed in the first, proleptic titles of Christ such as 'firstborn of those who have fallen asleep', 'first to rise from the dead', 'leader of life'. Such a real anticipation of a future which qualitatively changes things does not just help those who live 'in darkness and the shadow of death'. It serves as a prefiguration of freedom, but not as a concrete liberation. Why then does the kingdom of freedom not arrive all at once? What justifies its delay?[21] The problem of theodicy then returns to Christianity in the form of the 'delayed parousia'. Only the cross of the risen one makes resurrection, freedom and new life in the cross of reality meaningful. The proleptic character of the resurrection of the one before the others is reflected and becomes concrete in the solidarity, the vicarious character of his crucifixion for others. The prolepsis of the new future in his resurrection turns towards earth and towards that which is earthly in the pro-existence of the crucified one. In this sense, the resurrection of Christ reveals the significance of the future of his cross and, conversely, his cross reveals the significance of the presence of his future. Freedom is born from his suffering; life from his death; the exaltation of the man of God from the self-humiliation of God. Resurrection faith is faith in the crucified one; and hope which overcomes the world, which can hope against hope, is born in the community of the crucified one. Therefore the 'members of God's kingdom' meet in the world as the 'community of the cross'. The theology of the exodus from the gods of the fatherland and of the *status quo* is a theology of the disgrace of Christ before the gate (Heb. 13.13f.). Conversely, *theologia crucis* is a *theologia viatorum*. In the world of the cross, which still awaits the resurrection, the resurrection of Christ becomes relevant through the proclamation of the saving event of his cross.

2. The dialectic of belief in unbelief

In the first dialectical circle of christology, we found that resurrection and crucifixion mutually interpret each other. But for what reason has Christ died and risen? How does the God on earth who is present in him affect the world? The recognition of God in the cross of Christ cannot be generalized into a speculative expression of history, but must be practised in the concrete dialectic of belief in unbelief. The Christ-event is not realized in Christian theories and eschatological speculations, but rather in the word from the cross, i.e. in the proclaimed gospel and that belief which acquires from this gospel the power to overcome unbelief. In the 'word from the cross', those christological anticipatory and vicarious structures are repeated.[22] The word which pronounces the sinner just and calls the godless into the community of Christ proclaims that the crucified Jesus is the justice of God and that the power of salvation is revealed in his suffering; the freedom of life in his death.

The word represents the Christ-event in each person that it reaches. But the fact that it does this already as word and that through this word the freedom of the crucified one becomes active is an anticipation of the future of perfect freedom. In and as the word that justifies and calls, Christ is present to all men in the mode of the anticipation of his universal presence. The word that mediates his action is the anticipation of his future that is contained in this word. In representing the God even in the cross of Christ it anticipates the future of a qualitative transformation of the world. As the 'word from the cross' it is already 'the power of the resurrection', as Paul said. By pointing back to the cross of Christ, the word points out beyond itself into the parousia of the kingdom of freedom. Correspondingly, faith, which is created through the word, is wholly directed towards that Christ-event. But because a future event is realized in it, as faith it is hope.[23]

If the believer is accepted in his unbelief and his dispute with God and with life through the mediated knowledge of God in the crucified one, he acquires the freedom to accept himself as he is, and it is just this freedom that lifts him above himself and his faith. In this way faith, which is indebted to the word of Christ, is freedom within the conditions of compulsory obligations. The believer acquires certainty in the midst of the ambiguity of history, reconciliation in hostility and peace in the midst of conflict. This is the first effect of that Christ-event; what has happened on the cross finds its first future and arrives at its first goal in the event of word and faith. So 'who was put to death for our trespasses and raised for our justification' (Rom. 4.25) is the correct interpretation. The word that justifies and calls in a world in which it would be better if one were silent, and the resurrection of belief in the midst of unbelief: these are the first goals of the history of Christ.[24] There is no access to the knowledge of God in the cross of the risen one other than concrete participation in the power of the Spirit which is present in word and faith.

3. The dialectic of love in alienation

Now this belief finds itself not only in its own unbelief, but also in a world which does not correspond to God in the cross, but rather contradicts that event. It is contested belief, in itself and in the world. The justification of faith does not yet mean the salvation of the world. Precisely when man is free on the basis of faith, the chains of his own body and the torture of the whole of unredeemed creation begin to chafe. In this way, we leave the dialectical circle of word and faith on the basis of the greater misery of the world and of the overflowing promise of the Christ-event and move logically into the next dialectical circle of the obedience of faith in the body of death and of love in a world of dead, petrified conditions.

An analogy to faith, to the word and to Christ can again be found formally within the structure of concrete obedience. It is the discipleship of Christ and therefore leads, through the acceptance of the cross, to the acceptance of the form of the crucified one. It is an analogy to the word of justification in the act of the just. In such analogies, however, physical obedience is an anticipation of the resurrection of the dead and the salvation of the body from the compulsive forces of the law and anxiety, and also from the repression which both cause. As a real analogy to Christ, the obedience of faith is the anticipation of the qualitative transformation of this reality.[25] In the struggle between justice and injustice, love and lovelessness, in the world, the interpretation of the Christ-event extends from the circle of word and faith into the circle of the lordship of Christ and the earthly obedience of those who belong to him. Why did Christ die and rise? To be the Lord, and for those who belong to him to spread his humanity in obedience. If, however, in this way they anticipate his liberating future in the midst of the enslaved creation, then not only do they attest a totally other and distant kingdom of heaven in the hopeless kingdom of earth, but they also take up the struggle for the liberation of God's creation from godless and inhuman powers.

What meaning does this new condition of the body have in modern society? For this analysis, we take up the categories of 'being and having' introduced by Moses Hess in social criticism and by Helmut Plessner and others in anthropology.[26] The originally Cartesian category of 'having' is expanded without limit in scientific technical civilization. Man understands his body as his property, but no longer identifies himself with his physical existence. His physical and social life is something that he has, something that represents him but that he is not. An environment develops in which all things are interchangeable and all human relationships are replaceable. In love, we identify ourselves with our physical, social and political existence. Both the body and external existence vibrate with the movement of self-surrender, of engagement and of mission. This, however, makes us vulnerable and capable of being disappointed. Therefore the mechanism of self-protection suggests that man should continue to live but should hold back his soul and his interests. The categories of making and having which make possible an increasing differentiation of man from the reality of his life have replaced the identification of the self with physical existence. This leads man to experience everything coldly and without feeling, to enter into human relationships without love and to follow social callings as if they were roles in a play. How can I identify myself with physical life when I have still physically to await death and the decay of happiness – and I experience it daily in loss and in disappointments? Conversely, how can I live at all without identifying myself with this transitory, guilty and mortal existence? It is evident that the suffering which arises from the sacrifice of love is the very place where Christian faith has produced hope in the resurrection. Love in which a man surrenders himself and identifies himself with this vulnerable earthly life and hope in the resurrection belong together. They mutually interpret each other. 'For whoever would save his life will lose it; and whoever loses his life for my sake and the gospel's will save it' (Mark 8.35). The resurrection hope prepares the way for a life of total sacrifice. This is the 'profound this-worldliness of Christianity' of which Bonhoeffer said that it always has the knowledge of death and resurrection present in it'.[27]

Conversely, then, that creative and self-sacrificing love is the reflection of the resurrection within the conditions of this life. Love which takes the cross of self-sacrifice upon itself is therefore an anticipation of the resurrection of the dead. In the acceptance of the body through love and in unreserved identification with the social and political body, there is an anticipation of the liberation and salvation of this body of death. In this way the body is already free from the constraints of fear, as it is free from law and from the constraints of the law. The body comes into the effective sphere of freedom. This has wide-reaching psychological consequences and provides a starting point for discussion with psychoanalysis.[28] It also has socio-political consequences for the overcoming of the superior forces of that category of having, the world of things and substitutes, for the benefit of a society of authentic human existence. Life in the spirit of the resurrection brings about the 'reviving of dead conditions' (Hegel) and the humanization of inhuman conditions. In this interpretative circle of life in the body of death and of love within these petrified conditions of life, the resurrection of Christ gains the significance of the revolt of life against death and of the revolt of the new humanity against the superior force of oppressive conditions.

The force of mind is only as great as its expression; its depth only as deep as its power to expand and lose itself when speaking and giving out its substance.[29]

4. The dialectic of hope in death

Love is supposed to be stronger than death, yet love experiences death as a power which is inhuman and contrary to God. Therefore the dialectic of love in alienation still once more points out beyond itself. Certainly it is itself already the power of the transformation of life, but only under the conditions of agony and death. It does not conquer death. It does not overcome all violence now. It does not save creation. It is, however, the analogy to that qualitative transformation of existence and therefore lives from the hope of the kingdom. We now come to the final and broadest horizon of the interpretation of the God-event in the crucified Christ. It is the eschatological horizon in which God is confronted with the misery of all creation, which cries to heaven. There is no other access to the observation of this eschatological horizon than through the concrete historical dialectic of belief in unbelief and love in alienation, but it becomes necessary out of this concrete history because the future, which is opened up in Christ, extends further and wants to incorporate all fields of the negative within the dialectic of the new creation. 'If I must give up a man, or give up hope for an area or an earth, then Jesus is not risen for me. You are not the light of the world if I must give up hope anywhere', said Christoph Blumhardt in his Easter sermon of 1899.[30]

In the conflict between belief and unbelief, hope arises from patience and experience, and finally overcomes. In the agony of love, which attempts to hold fast to the dead, hope is awakened in the victory of the living over the hell of death. The more faith is in harmony with the groaning of the whole creation, and the more love is in solidarity with all forsaken beings, the more comprehensive the horizon of hope in God and his coming presence in a new creation becomes. This vision of an end of the history of torture, by the earthly indwelling of God in a new creation without suffering, death and lamentation, is in no way the negation of the cross of Christ in the midst of this history, but rather the perfection of his lordship. Christian hope for the world is not directed towards an abstract other-worldly pantheism in which all that Christ has done to overcome the world disappears, but rather towards the fact that 'God will be all in all'. Eschatology is no final theodicy according to the motto: if the end is good, everything is good. Rather, the eschatological interpretation of the Christ event means: '. . . Christ died and lived again that he might be Lord both of the dead and of the living' (Rom. 14.9). In the language of I Corinthians 15, the Son will hand over the kingdom to the Father and, in this way, God will become all in all. The sonship of the Son is not put aside as the role of a forerunner and representative of God on earth, but rather the sacrifice of Christ on the cross is completed in the handing over of his lordship in the lordship of God the Father. Through the 'Son of man', God will be 'all in all'. Therefore, finally, in the metaphorical language of the Apocalypse, the city of God has as its sun 'the lamb that was slain'. This all indicates that the presence of God in a new creation is life with the Father and the Son in the kingdom of the Spirit; it does not threaten a new slavery, but brings the kingdom of freedom, a likeness to God created by the cross. If the crucified Christ is the ground of this freedom, then he is also the focal point of that hope which encompasses the world and overcomes death. Christian hope anticipates the transformation of the world from no one else, but even from 'a greater God'. It anticipates it in that God who appeared concretely in the crucifixion and resurrection of Christ, and in no heavenly authority which is abstracted from this. In him who overcame in God, or in him in whom God decided for man, lies the hope for both the question and the answer of theodicy.

IV Who is God?

We began from the question of theodicy, in the area in which religious and irreligious, theists and atheists carry on their debate. Between them we found Job in his heap of ashes arguing with God and justified by God. Between them, we found Christ in his God-forsakenness on the cross accepted by God. In Job, we found God arguing with God. In the crucified one, we found God forsaking God and God overcoming for men the agony of God in himself. So we must consider the question: what do we mean by the word 'God'? The image of the authority in heaven, which one can accuse, justify, deny or affirm, is past. The judging God is found in the man who argues with God. The glory of the totally other world of God as a transforming power in this world is present in the Christ who was forsaken by God and sacrificed by him. In this way, we abandon the centuries-old, weak Christianization of the God concept and are on the way towards a fuller understanding of God in the crucified Christ. Who is 'God' in the Christ event? He is the power of the transformation of the world in vicarious suffering. Who is 'God' in the corresponding event of belief in unbelief? He is the word of the justification of the godless. Who is 'God' in the event of love in alienation? He is the power of freedom in self-surrender. Who is 'God' in the event of hope in the face of death? He is the power of a qualitatively new future. Finally, who is 'God' in the new creation? He is the eternal presence of the victory of the crucified Christ.

According to a saying of Luther's, one does not become a theologian simply by reading and studying, but rather by conflict, temptation, being condemned, dying and living. 'To recognize God means to suffer God', says ancient theological experience. Today, however, it is no longer the inner struggles involving justification before God but also the external social and political struggles involving justice in the world. The question of theodicy leads us into these struggles. Only the future of the coming God leads us out of them. For both these struggles, however, in which one can become a 'theologian' in the most profound sense of the word, the advice which Hermann Friedrich Kohlbrügge gave his student Wichelhaus is valid: 'I certainly understand what you mean when you write that you have become a *theologus* through many struggles. Even so, do not let your shirt know that you think you are a theologian.'[31]

NOTES

This article was an inaugural lecture, given on 19 June, 1968 at the University of Tübingen.

1. Today it is again recognized that Christian theology has its broadest and most controversial relationship to the world within the horizon of the question of theodicy. Cf. John Hick, *Evil and the God of Love*, 1966; H. Küng, *God and Suffering*, 1969. We find it again in the still largely inarticulate discussion on 'after Auschwitz'.

2. L. Feuerbach, 'Vorläufige Thesen zur Reform der Philosophie', in: M. G. Lange (ed.), *Kleine philosophische Schriften* (PhB 227), 63. 'Only that which suffers deserves to exist. Only that being which is fullest of suffering is a divine being. A being without suffering is a being without being. A being without suffering is nothing but a being without senses, without matter' (67). Cf. also F. J. J. Buytendijk, *Über den Schmerz* (1948). If we accept these reflections on suffering in connection with the suffering of Christ, we shall also arrive at a new understanding of the physical relevance of the resurrection hope and the new corporeality.

3. H. Marcuse, *Reason and Revolution*, [2]1955, 270.

4. Cf. G. Rohrmoser, 'Zum Atheismusproblem im Denken vom Pascal bis Nietzsche', *Internationale Dialogzeitschrift* 1, 1968, 130ff., 142. The experience behind Nietzsche's remark about the death of God involves 'the question of theodicy which was abandoned after the move away from German idealism and then arose with a new urgency'. Following Kant, Protestant theology was fond of personalizing the question of theodicy posed by nature and world history in terms of the subjective attitude of man. Cf. R. Bultmann, *Primitive Christianity in its Contemporary Setting*, trans. R. H. Fuller, 1960, 219: 'This radical openness for the future in absolute surrender to the grace of God is prepared to accept all encounters as tokens of his grace. Incidentally, this provides the answer to the problem of suffering.' This individualizing of relationships with God deals adequately with subjective anguish, but does not deal either with objective suffering or with the suffering of others, the suffering of love. There is a limitation of existentialist interpretation, as has been seen very clearly by G. Bornkamm, 'Die Frage nach Gottes Gerechtigkeit', *Das Ende des Gesetzes*, 1952, 209ff. Cf. also E. Käsemann, *Jesus Means Freedom*, trans. Frank Clarke, 1969, 132f.: 'Its drawback (sc. that of the existentialist interpretation) is that, although it

enables one to see the historicity of man, it does not give an adequate view of world history. It will not do for us to reduce world history, as a matter of course, to the historicity of human existence.' E. Peterson, 'Zeuge der Wahrheit', *Theologische Traktate*, 1951, 187f., refers to the fact that according to the Revelation of John there is something in the 'suffering of Christ' that permeates the whole cosmos. 'All of creation participates in this suffering (Rom. 8.19). . . Suffering in this cosmos is universal, because it is a suffering with the suffering of Christ who has entered this cosmos and yet has burst it open by his resurrection from the dead and ascension into heaven.'

5. Cf., for example, A. Döblin, *Berlin Alexanderplatz*, 1955.

6. W. W. Bartley, *Flucht ins Engagement*, 1964. The feeling of meaninglessness and of an empty life which is coming to an end is based only on the fact that man is accustomed from the time of his early youth to 'exaggerated measures' according to which an absolute reasonableness and total meaningfulness is demanded of all that is encountered. If this requirement is removed, everyone will be satisfied with the course of his life and the condition of his society. According to A. Gehlen, *Urmensch und Spätkultur* (1956), 69, the institutionalization of man's historical world in fact results in the 'suspension of the question of meaning'. Anyone who still asks the question has either lost his way or is looking for other institutions. Still, paradoxically, even for Gehlen the life which is adapted and institutionalized (289) 'is called into question from its unfathomable depths'.

7. E. Bloch, 'Studien zum Buch Hiob', *Auf gespaltenem Pfad: Susman Festschrift*, 1964; cf. also M. Susman, *Das Buch Hiob und das Schicksal des jüdischen Volkes*, ²1948.

8. Here I take up questions arising from the discussion of the Jewish philosophy of religion in America. Cf. R. L. Rubinstein, *After Auschwitz*, 1966; E. B. Borowitz, 'Hope Jewish and Hope Secular', *The Future as the Presence of Shared Hope*, 1968.

9. Cf. H. Blumenberg, *Die Legitimität der Neuzeit*, 1966, 79: 'The problem which antiquity left behind unsolved was the question of the origin of evil in the world.'

10. For the understanding and history of the interpretation of this passage see W. Schrage, 'Das Verständnis des Todes Jesu Christi im Neuen Testament', in: F. Viering (ed.), *Das Kreuz Jesu Christi als Grund des Heils*, 1967, 67. For the use of Ps. 22 as a horizon of interpretation see H. Gese, 'Psalm 22 und das Neue Testament', *ZTK* 65, 1968, 1–22, here 17: 'death intensified to the deepest experience of suffering together with that activity of God which delivers from death leads to the breaking in of the eschatological kingdom of God. He who has proclaimed this kingdom in his life brings it about in his death.'

11. Cf. U. Hedinger, *Hoffnung zwischen Kreuz und Reich*, 1968, 135.

12. Karl Barth, *The Resurrection of the Dead*, trans. H. J. Stenning, 1933, 202.

13. For what follows see J. Moltmann, *Theology of Hope*, 1967, ch.III, sections 5–9; also B. Klappert (ed.), *Diskussion um Kreuz und Auferstehung*, 1967; C. F. D. Moule (ed.), *The Significance of the Message of the Resurrection for Faith in Jesus Christ*, 1968. W. Pannenberg in 'Dogmatische Erwägungen

zur Auferstehung Jesu', *Kerygma und Dogma* 14, 1968, 105–18, advances rather more cautious and well-considered comments on the historical problem of the resurrection of Christ than in earlier theses.

14. G. W. F. Hegel, *Philosophy of Right*, trans. T. M. Knox, 1942, Preface, 13: 'When philosophy paints its grey in grey, then has a shape of life grown old. By philosophy's grey in grey it cannot be rejuvenated but only understood. The owl of Minerva spreads its wings only with the falling of the dusk.' M. Heidegger, *Holzwege*, 76: 'Because history, as research, outlines and objectifies the past as an explainable and observable nexus of effects, it requires source criticism as an instrument of this objectification. The standards of this criticism change to the degree in which history approximates to journalism.' 'All history calculates what is coming on the basis of its images of the past, which are determined by the present. History is the continual destruction of the future and of the relation of history to the coming of destiny. Not only has historicism not been overcome today; only now is it reaching the stage of its expansion and consolidation. The technical organization of world publicity through radio and the press – which is already lagging behind – is the real dominating form of historicism (301).'

15. H. Plessner, 'Conditio Humana. Einleitung zur Propyläen-Weltgeschichte, 1961', *Opuscula* 14, 1964.

16. Cf. W. Benjamin's 'theses on the philosophy of history', *Illuminationen*, 1961, 268–81.

17. G. W. F. Hegel, *Glaube und Wissen* (1802–3), (PhB 626), 1962, 123f.

18. E. Käsemann, 'Die Heilsbedeutung des Todes Jesu nach Paulus', in: F. Viering (ed.), *Zur Bedeutung des Todes Jesu*, 1967, 13–34: esp. 30. F. Rosenzweig, *Der Stern der Erlösung*, ³1954, 170: 'The world is not yet finished. There is still laughing and crying in it. The tears are not yet wiped away from every face. This state of becoming, of being unfinished, can only be understood if we reverse the objective structures of time. The past, what is already finished from its beginning to its end, can be recounted – and all counting begins from the top of the column; what is coming, however, is precisely that and therefore can be understood only through anticipation. If one wanted to recount what is coming, one would inevitably turn it into the petrified past. What is coming wants to be prophesied; the future is experienced only in anticipation. In thought, the last here becomes the first.'

19. K. Barth, *Church Dogmatics*, II/2, 162. For the interpretation of this statement cf. E. Jüngel, *Gottes Sein ist im Werden: Verantwortliches Reden vom Sein Gottes bei Karl Barth. Eine Paraphrase*, 1965, 90ff.; also id., 'Vom Tod des lebendigen Gottes. Ein Plakat'. *Zeitschrift für Theologie und Kirche* 65, 1968, 93–116: esp. 105ff.

20. Cf. D. Sölle, *Christ the Representative*, trans. D. Lewis, 1967, 150ff.

21. E. Bloch, *op. cit.*, asks the same question to give the following answer: 'The simplest solution is that in the world there is always an exodus that leads out of a particular status, and a hope that is linked with dismay.'

22. For the understanding of the word as gospel and the gospel as a historical verbal prolepsis of the eschatological future, cf. P. Stuhlmacher,

Gerechtigkeit Gottes bei Paulus, 1965, 79 n.l. Also H. Schlier, *Wort Gottes. Eine neutestamentliche Besinnung*, 1958, 20ff.

23. Cf. *Theology of Hope*, 19ff.

24. This is the sense in which the Reformers spoke of the present event of justification as the *usus resurrectionis* and of the *fides justificans* as the *finis historiae Christi*. E. Bizer, 'Über die Rechtfertigung', *Das Kreuz Jesu Christi als Grund des Heils* (see n.10), 13–29; esp. 23, where Luther is quoted: '*Resurrectio a mortuis est nostra justificatio per fidem solam*' (WA 39, II, 237, 1ff.). This corresponds almost word for word to Augustine: '. . . *in illo vera resurrectio, ita in nobis vera justificatio*' (*Enchiridion*, 33.12). If, however, the resurrection of Christ is the ground and presupposition of the justification of sinners and if its reality is revealed in no other way than in this liberating action, then this action cannot be the only and final action of that reality.

25. E. Käsemann has worked out this double relation of the new obedience as an analogy to the liberating event in Christ and as the anticipation of his kingdom of freedom. Cf. most recently, *Jesus Means Freedom*, 1969, 81: 'If the freedom of the Christian man and the Christian church is centred on love, the resurrection of the dead is anticipated, because in it there appears the sovereignty of Jesus, which is perfected in the overcoming of death.'

26. For Moses Hess cf. E. Silberner, *Moses Hess. Geschichte seines Lebens*, 1966; E. Thier, *Das Menschenbild des jungen Marx*, 1957. For more recent anthropology cf. H. Plessner, *Lachen und Weinen*, [3]1961; F. J. J. Buytendijk, *Das Menschliche: Wege zu seinem Verständnis*, 1958; G. Marcel, *Being and Having*, trans. K. Farrer, 1949.

27. D. Bonhoeffer, *Letters and Papers from Prison*, [2]1967, 247.

28. Cf. N. O. Brown, *Life against Death: The psychoanalytical Meaning of History*, 1959, especially the last chapter, 'The Resurrection of the Body'. Also *Love's Body*, 1966.

29. G. W. F. Hegel, *The Phenomenology of Mind*, trans. J. B. Baillie, 1910, 9.

30. C. Blumhardt, quoted by E. Staehelin, *Die Verkündigung des Reiches Gottes in der Kirche Jesu Christi*, VII, 1960, 254.

31. H. F. Kohlbrügge, quoted by Karl Barth, *Die protestantische Theologie im 19 Jahrhundert*, 1947, 584.

3

EXEGESIS AND THE ESCHATOLOGY OF HISTORY

I *Historical criticism and tradition*

The historical-critical investigation of the past begins where traditions in which the past is preserved and is present are threatened or are said to be threatened. Historical reflection begins where traditions have no longer kept pace with the present and are no longer experienced as being unquestionably 'obvious'. 'Since Herder, historical meaning has been reflection on threatened order' (Heimpel).[1] Historical inquiry begins as early as the seventeenth century at the point and in the moment in which the dogma and ethics of traditional church doctrines, Catholic as well as Protestant, are no longer considered to be 'obvious', i.e. institutional, because these 'houses of history' have not grown with the new experience of the present. This experience includes confrontation with people in Asia and America who can no longer be synchronized with the Bible, discoveries in nature which can be revealed only through hypotheses alien to their origin, and social reformations by the rising *bourgeoisie* and its philosophies of life and the world.[2] Historical inquiry, therefore, begins where predeterminative factors are alienated from the present and results in a strengthening of the obsolescence of origin. For a 'historical' relationship to origin does not only presuppose that this origin is experienced as 'past' and obsolete but also brings about the irrelevance of origin for the conquest of the present and the future that dawns in it.[3] This process, therefore, occurs at the point when historical inquiry still believes that it is serving the apologetic consolidation of a tradition that has become insecure.

In the relationship of the present to its origins, history takes the place of tradition as the bringing into experience, examination and reporting on the past which has become understandable because of its distance from the event. This critique of the remoteness of tradition is part of the seventeenth-century bourgeoisie enlightenment in which historical explanation of time and history corresponds to physical explanation of space. Just as natural science and technology destroy man's traditional sense of the cosmos, the rising science of history destroys his traditional consciousness of tradition. Through both, the feeling of being embedded and at home in overarching ordinances is destroyed. In the seventeenth century, both sciences of enlightenment still had a deistic trait which endured for a long time particularly in the theology of salvation history and the 'theology of saving facts'.

If one wanted to express this process in a formula, one might say that the critical history of the present alienates the past. What happens in the historical relationship to the past is simply the emancipation of man from predetermining forces and from the influence of his origins. The historicizing of history frees man from history. 'The force exerted by tradition on our behaviour below the level of consciousness continually declines in history as a result of the progressive *science* of history'.[4]

This can be expressed in terms of the French revolution's sense of freedom: 'Historical consciousness breaks the last chain which philosophy and natural science could not shatter. Man now stands there completely free'.[5] It can also be expressed in terms of the final result of the industrial revolution as Hegel had expressed it in his *Philosophy of Right*. Modern society 'historically' leaves its beginnings and establishes itself on the unhistorical, constant nature of man's need. Such a society which is, so to speak, reduced to economy, thus becomes independent of the predetermining facts of history, for it establishes itself on the foundation of abstract unhistoricality. In it, so far as work or need are concerned, man passes for man in the uniformity of all men. Therefore neither beginnings, morals, nationality nor religion are necessary to guarantee man's sociality. All man's historical determinations, which earlier had been either socially necessary or obligatory, as for instance confession, nationality or class, are released from the bond of society and made optional for the individual. 'Precisely through its abstract unhistoricality, the society of subjectivity grants individualism its rights'.[6] The historicizing of man's origin so that it becomes the 'past' thus results in the freedom or the unhistoricality of the present. This is an apparently paradoxical consequence but one that is logical and can be verified everywhere. That this consequence is also deliberate becomes particularly obvious through the practical application of the science of history as sociology after the French revolution, and in the development of what is known as positivism.

Modern man's epochal experiences of history and of being sacrificed to the terrors of historical change in modern times have the earthquake of the French revolution in the background. All reflections on 'history' by nineteenth-century European philosophers, historians and sociologists proceed from this revolutionary and catastrophic aspect of history. It was here that the traditional shell of Western metaphysics was first broken. The intellectual and social maxims by which men lived were lost, and the radical historicity of existence was fully realized. For Saint-Simon, 'revolution' meant 'crisis'. 'L'espèce humaine', he wrote in 1813, 'se trouve engagée dans une des plus fortes *crises* qu'elle ait essuyée depuis l'origine de son existence'.[7] This concept of crisis in Saint-Simon and Comte is a new element in the history of the human intellect. Yet it became the central concept of the modern understanding of time. 'It (sc. the concept of crisis) means revolution, but penetrating its political foreground it opens up the prospect of historical-social reality in its totality. In other words, when Saint-Simon speaks of *crisis*, he is the first to mean *history* in a quite modern sense.'[8] What is more, he means 'history' in what has become the absolute use of the term. For Saint-Simon and Comte, the goal of the historical and sociological understanding of revolution is the 'conclusion of the revolution': 'terminer la révolution'. But if revolution is crisis and crisis is history, this means the 'conclusion of the crisis' through sociology as 'the science of anti-crisis' which, in turn, means nothing less than the 'conclusion of history'. Comte saw his epochal task in the following way: 'We have the immense task of bringing to an end what Bacon, Descartes and Galileo began. Only then will the revolutionary upheavals be at an end.'[9]

In terms of the aspects under which he himself announced and planned it, Comte's 'positivism' has a messianic and apocalyptic flavour. According to his well-known law of the three stages, the coming 'positivistic' phase leading to the conclusion of history has begun. In it, men renounce research for the causes behind the phenomena – that was the object of the age of metaphysics – and investigate and describe only the more regular relationships between phenomena. The goal of this 'positivistic' science is ultimately not in the establishment of facts in the 'examen du passé' but rather prediction based on the knowledge of their regular relationships: 'savoir pour prevoir'.

The French and English positivism stemming from Saint-Simon, Comte, John Stuart Mill and Herbert Spencer influenced the German cultural sciences from 1860 on and, in history, superseded the historical romantic school of Herder, Humboldt, Ranke, Droysen and others.[10] Whenever, in the following decades, an 'overcoming of metaphysics by historicism' is mentioned, Comte's philosophy of history and messianic law of the three stages is in the background, whether consciously or unconsciously. This is so even in the cases of Dilthey[11] and Troeltsch.[12]

From this point on it becomes very questionable whether there is a historical relationship between the Reformation and positivistic historical-critical method; whether there is an inner, objective relationship between the *sola fide* of the Reformation doctrine of justification and the historical-critical method; and, finally, whether Luther's struggle to free theology from (scholastic) metaphysics can in any way be said to be analogous to the historical and positivistic 'overcoming of metaphysics'.[13] The relationships here are very complicated. In any case, however, the distance of the Reformation faith from the autonomy and subjectivity of the individual which has been set free by the historical method and the abstract unhistoricality of society must be preserved at all costs.[14] Seen historically, the connection between the historical method and neo-Protestantism is found in the idea of the individual emancipated from history and society, and of his autonomy. This, however, more closely approximates to the spiritualism of the Anabaptists in the Reformation period than to the Reformation itself.

II Principles of historical methodology

As a critical science, historical investigation is still related to traditions, to dogmatic sketches of the relationship and meaning of history and also to definite representations of particular history in sermons, and represents their falsification or verification.

In this sense, apart from the apocalyptic-positivistic undertones which resonate in it, world history is indeed world judgment. Dilthey could write:

What obscurantism is found in those who overlook world history, in the delusion that they are the only possessors of the truth. These high priests of some metaphysic completely fail to recognize the subjective, temporally and spatially conditioned origin of every metaphysical system. For whatever makes up a person's spiritual constitution, whether it is religion, art or metaphysics, boasts vainly in its claim to objective validity. World history as world judgment shows every metaphysical system to be relative, temporary and transitory.[15]

In this sense, as D. F. Strauss declared, 'the real critique of dogma is . . . its history',[16] or, as Overbeck acknowledged, 'science executes a sort of last judgment on things'.[17]

In the framework of criticism, it is impossible to demand from historical research itself the construction of tradition and permanence, the discovery of what is lasting and constant, or of the comprehensive meaning of history. However, as criticism, historical research would be without an object if it were no longer related to some presence of the absolute in time, understood in some way. As criticism it is related not only to tradition but also to every possible historical image of the present, among others also to the historical understanding held by a positivistic conception of reality. Such understandings of history are historically conditioned, but do not arise from the foundation of historical research itself. They arise from the historical power of imagination – what used to be called speculation – and have to undergo historical criticism.

When one speaks of 'historical research' and 'the historical critical method', one must differentiate between:

(*a*) the *historical* criticism of specific traditional outlines and projections of the past;

(*b*) the early nineteenth-century romantic school of history which took over a more or less historical pantheism from Herder and Humboldt;

(*c*) historical positivism stemming from French and English positivism, which began to dominate the science of history after 1860.

If we omit the romantic school of history with its great artistic representations because of its cultural singularity, and investigate the principles of the scientific character of historical research, then after the fundamental 'methodizing' of the human experience of the world by *Petrus Ramus* and *Descartes* – the concept of 'method' appears first in these two men and supplants the scholastic logic of being – we arrive at the following principles:

(*a*) The historical accuracy of statements made by the science of history. The science of history is not art, poetry or legend. The concept of truth on which it is based is the concept of a verifiable factual truth, the *adaequatio rei et intellectus*, or 'what the evidence obliges us to believe' (Collingwood).

(*b*) The historical accuracy of knowledge and statements presuppose that they are in principle controllable. Adherence to the sources and critical examination of the sources is adherence to the controllability of that reality of which historical research speaks and which it wants to recognize.

(*c*) Controllability, however, presupposes that historical

events can be reconstructed. This in turn becomes the characteristic of the method as a method.

Historical research represents the 'rational disciplining of historical consciousness' (Heimpel) under these unavoidable principles. Over and above this, however, this methodizing 'objectifies' the historical reality that is historically recognized in this way. Historical science proceeds 'objectively' in the sense that it cuts through the relationships of the particular subject to its environment and its history and replaces it by relationships which are to be valid for every man. It seeks a certain freedom for the location of its knowledge. Only in this way does historical knowledge become reliable, i.e. verifiable at any particular time or at all times, and thus common property, i.e. verifiable by anyone who takes the trouble.[18] In this way it is differentiated from legend, poetry, experience or encounter in that its statements must be methodologically verifiable in facts that are available to all men at all times.

In this way, historical reality is 'fixed', 'ascertained' and 'seized'. It is imagined as an abundance of limited and orderable facts which may again be grasped at all times through the same methodological approach. It is established apart from the situation of the first discovery, apart from personal encounter, which is always unique.

This methodological objectification of historical reality is a quite singular way of representing the past. It is a representation by objectification, for the historical objects which are agreed upon in this way have become accessible and available at any particular time or at all times. That which is 'lasting' in the maelstrom of history, that which is sought in the terrors of history, is represented as something that is objective.

The fundamental concept of truth in historical accuracy, the possibility of control and reconstruction is the *adaequatio rei et intellectus*, and not a personal or existential concept of truth of any kind.

The critique of historical criticism which attempts to show the limitation of this method in man's relation to history and particularly the fatal consequence of the unhistoricity of existence which it causes, begins at two different points:

(*a*) The question can be asked whether the historical method does justice to the historicity of existence or whether it does not ignore and neutralize man's own historicity and the historical conditions of his standpoint. This would have to emerge in a critical illumination of the idea of the world underlying the historical methodizing of reality, and would begin with the subject of the observer, who would have to be made aware of his own position *in* and not *over* history.

(*b*) The question can also be asked, however, whether the historical method of the given form does justice to its object, 'history', or whether it does not rather lead to a naturalizing of the historical process. In any case, this would have to be shown in the presupposed idea for the world and this would still have to be tested against the reality of history.

III   *History and historicity*

1. Since the emergence of historical positivism and the application of a scientific concept of knowledge to historical research, it has been assumed that a 'closed nexus of effects' exists in history.[19] In his work *Über die Gesetze historischen Wissens*,[20] von Sybel remarks, 'The presupposition with which this security of knowledge stands or falls is that of absolute lawfulness in development, common unity in the continuance of earthly things.' Heidegger gave a similar explanation of the basic process of modern times in 'Die Zeit des Weltbildes': history as research objectifies the past in the sense of an explainable and observable relationship of effects.[21] Bultmann also begins from the assumption that the historical method incorporates the presupposition that history is a unity in the sense of a closed nexus of effects in which individual events are connected by the sequence of cause and effect.[22]

Let us now leave the question whether the investigation of such a 'nexus of effects' does not presuppose a clear decision on what the effective powers in history are. In any case, the presuppositions of such a closed nexus of effects of whatever forces makes possible the objectification of history. This objectification of history then gives rise to the abstract subjectification of the human being, and the well-known separation of subject and object in man's relationship to world and history is the consequence. The ethos of regularity in theoretical reason dialectically produces an ethos of spontaneity in an unperceived area of man's inmost self-being for practical reason. Historicism and existentialism are two sides of the same process.

2. In the face of the success and the unsurpassable finality of modern science under this presupposition of the closed nexus of effects in historical reality, theology, which is now dependent on a particular historical origin, finds itself in a desperate state. Within the closed nexus of whatever historical forces there may be, which historians investigate, Jesus does not appear to be the ground of faith in such a way that he could be the ground of faith.[23] As long as one accepts the historical method with its inclusions as final, Christian theology must look for other approaches to that special history which is founded on faith, or it must attempt to establish faith in another reality which cannot be attacked by historical criticism and does not enter into the 'closed nexus of effects'. The accepted principle of historical positivism, that the framework of nature or the closed universe are inviolable (even for God, if there is one), and that the scientific method, which explains the world of things, cannot be rejected, runs through the history of theology in the nineteenth and twentieth centuries like a thread, against which theology measures its scientific nature and the binding character of its statements as *theologia civilis*. Faith, on the basis of this, searches for access to a special history that gives a basis to faith (God in Christ) by means of the categories of the closed relationship of effects, of unaffected subjectivity, by means of 'personal experience', 'inner experience', 'intuition', 'conscience' or personal 'encounter'. Theological work is divided into a historical positivism and materialism on the one hand, which pointed to 'facts' of salvation in what it thought to be faith and found only

facts of the world in unbelief, and an unhistorical subjectivism on the other. This produced a double relationship to the person of Jesus: (*a*) a historical-critical, naturalistic or rationalistic relationship, and (*b*) over against this an 'inner' or 'higher' relationship – at any rate, another one. A supernaturalism of the Holy Spirit, or inner experience, a spiritual dissolution, personal encounter, involvement through direct address arose which accepted the naturalism of the science of history and the 'closed nexus of effects' in which neither God nor spirit appeared and only found itself in leaving them. Historical and theological exegesis fell apart to such an extent that there was a threat that theological exegesis could only be expressed by 'Niebergall in the fifth volume' (practical theology).[24]

This dualism of method[25] carried the division further into its object. The writings about the twofold Jesus, the 'historical Jesus' and the 'Christ of faith', are numerous and characteristic, from D. F. Strauss to the most recent collective work about 'the historical Jesus and the kerygmatic Christ' (1960). Which of the two was thought to be the 'so-called' one could change. There is no need to point out how deeply this dualism reaches into modern thinking from Lessing to Herrmann, from Kant to Bultmann.[26] It is simply the spiritual fate in which we exist. Here we need only add that a reality in two kingdoms is dogmatically inherent here in the light of which the doctrine of the two kingdoms in political studies appears harmless.

With this dilemma, theology participates in the universal intellectual problem of modern time, which is illustrated in the separation of science and existence, in the logical tendency of modern science towards a neutral truth of statements removed beyond all subjectivity and in the tenor of the modern self-consciousness towards an existential truth removed beyond all objectivity, commonality and communicability.[27] If, as Heidegger says, the historicizing of history corresponds to the concept of work held by a world dominated by technology, then one can understand the wish to connect that 'other' access to history with a new knowledge of education and salvation (M. Scheler) and the truth of existence with a radical contemporary critique of science, technology and the mass society.[28] However, such an existence finds its authenticity only in the leap from the forgetfulness of being into a world of facts which is experienced as being 'devoid of meaning', a word which is 'disenchanted' (M. Weber) by scientific rationalization. Demythologizing or existentialist interpretation may intend to be an interpretation 'without a world view', an interpretation which has neither mythical nor scientific objectivity,[29] but it is precisely in its negative character that it is imprisoned by the modern 'world in view' of objectivity, as the earlier religion of the soul and of self-consciousness was imprisoned in that world view in which the framework of nature was seen as being invulnerable. Much as they want to part from one another, objective scientific factual truth and – as they say – the non-objectifiable truth of existence remain problematically entangled in one another, for they arise with each other and are indebted to each other.

As long as one leaves historical research with its principles and ontological presuppositions where it has established itself, and searches for access to history apart from historical questioning[30] or sees existentialist interpretation as an alternative or supplement to historical critical research, the deplored separation of subject and object is not only overcome, but is radicalized.

3. Modern hermeneutical considerations in theology began precisely at that point where the separation of historical and theological exegesis of the Bible was felt by both sides to be an impossible state of affairs. The discussion began, leaving aside form criticism, the significance of which has been presented in various ways, with the debate on Karl Barth's interpretation of Romans (1918–21) – especially between Bultmann and Barth.

Barth began his first edition of *Romans* with the terse introduction:

Paul, as a child of his age, addressed his contemporaries. It is, however, far more important that, as Prophet and Apostle of the Kingdom of God, he veritably speaks to all men of every age. The differences between then and now, here and there, no doubt require careful investigation and consideration. But the purpose of such investigation can only be to demonstrate that these differences are, in fact, purely trivial. The historical-critical method of Biblical investigation has its rightful place; it is concerned with the preparation of the intelligence – and this can never be superfluous. But, were I driven to choose between it and the venerable doctrine of Inspiration, I should without hesitation adopt the latter, which has a broader, deeper, more important justification. The doctrine of Inspiration is concerned with the labour of apprehending, without which no technical equipment, however complete, is of any use whatever. Fortunately, I am not compelled to choose between the two. Nevertheless, my whole energy of interpreting has been expended in an endeavour to see through and beyond history into the spirit of the Bible, which is the Eternal Spirit.[31]

In the Preface to the Second Edition he declared these considerations with reference to Calvin: one must argue with it (the text) until the wall between the first and the sixteenth centuries becomes transparent, until Paul speaks there and man hears here, until the conversation between document and reader is totally concentrated on the subject matter (which cannot be a different one in each case!). Until this time comes, I, as the one who understands, must push forward until I almost reach the point of standing only before the riddle of the substance and no longer before the riddle of the document as such.[32] Finally, in the Preface to the Third Edition (1922), in response to Bultmann's friendly greeting[33] and Schlatter's friendly rejection,[34] the thought finally emerges that the interpreter stands before an alternative. Either he himself knows what the main concern is, enters into a faithful relationship with his author, wants to read him on the hypothesis that the author has known with more or less clarity down to the final word what the concern is, and then writes his commentary not *about* Paul, but rather, as much as possible, down to the final word, *with* Paul, because he feels himself to be responsible in this concern; or, as an irresponsible observer, he wants to write his commentary *about* Paul.[35] Barth feels that it is impossible to do justice to any author, to make any author speak again, without risking this hypothesis and entering into that faithful relationship with him.

There is no other way to the spirit of the scriptures than by means of the hypothetical anticipation which permits their spirit to speak literally through these words to our spirit. Only out of a faithful relationship with the author can there be a real material criticism of his statements.

Barth's course from a Platonic formulation of the hermeneutic problem to the clear representation of the circle between textual exegesis and material exegesis, exegesis of the text in terms of the subject matter, becomes clear from the development of thought in this Foreword. However, the question still remains open as to whether the hypothetical character of the faithful relationship which is to be entered into, must not always demand historical critical disengagement from the subject as a corrective. The observer who questions historically and self-critically what he really does in that faithful relationship with the author of the biblical writings must not be an 'irresponsible' one. The 'either-or' which Barth sets up is understandable both in terms of contemporary history and polemics. It does, however, keep presenting itself again in the course of exegesis as its own dialectical tension.

Bultmann suggested a way which was similar to begin with, but completely different in tendency.[36] For historical science, the subject of the observer of history and his position is left out of account. It is uninteresting because the observing subject must be interchangeable and his knowledge must be objectifiable, i.e. communicable and controllable. But is such an intended 'objective' observation of history or a corresponding 'neutral' exegesis possible at all when the observing man himself does not stand *over* history but rather *in* history? Exegesis is concerned with historical texts. The exegete himself stands in history, i.e. he exists historically in the question about himself, in those concrete decisions in which his existence is at stake. If we note both these factors, the interpretation of the text must be a historical one, i.e. an existential one, and cannot be made neutrally or objectively as perhaps might be possible in man's relationship to nature, a nature which he himself is not.[37] The historicity of exegesis means that the knowledge and representa-

tion of history through a historical being can only be an uncon-
cludable dialogue in encounter. Existentialist exegesis means
that the interpretations of both history and the self must
consciously correspond with each other. The interpretation of
history is the interpretation of self and the self-interpretation of
existence occurs in the interpretation of history. When this
expressly happens, the interpretation of the text does not
degenerate into subjectivism. Because the interpretation of the
text and of the self cannot be separated, historical and theological exegesis come together in the actual process of exegesis.
True historical exegesis is based on the existential encounter
with history. In this way, the solution of the modern dilemma
in theology comes within reach, namely, that historical and
systematic theology come together in a historical hermeneutic.

Yet what relationship still exists between really historical,
existential exegesis in encounter and objectifying historical-
critical exegesis at a distance? What relationship does the
'hearer' of history, who is affected in his existence, have to the
researcher of history and the 'observer' who methodically
refrains from his possible involvement?

If the 'hearer' gains his involvement which is no longer
demonstrable because it cannot be objectified, in the leap from
the disinterested, uninvolved conduct of the 'observer' or
investigator; if the kerygma of the biblical text, which is only to
be understood existentially, finds itself only apart from the
historical line of questioning, then the antipode to be overcome
will be stabilized rather than actually overcome.

At the basis of this hermeneutic are two anthropological presuppositions which must be considered. (*a*) Man stands *over*
nature but *in* history. (*b*) Existence cannot be objectified. I cannot talk *about* my existence but only *from* it. Its reality is not the
reality which is to be seen in objectifying observation, but
rather that of the encounter.

(*a*) But is it anthropologically valid to say that man stands
over nature but *in* history? Surely man stands *over* and *in* nature,
for he *is* body and he *has* a body. In his physical existence,

nature confronts him in the mode of being as well as that of having. Similarly, he stands *in* history as well as *over* history. He is not only historical but he also *has* history. History also confronts him in the modes of being and having. To be a man he must through observation and investigation be able to separate himself from history, to experience it in the mode of having as well as through hearing and acting to identify with it, to experience it in the mode of existing. He can neither blot himself out of this view and overview of history, nor can he find himself in his historicity. A mysticism of identity cannot resolve either side of this double relationship. Faith is not the unreflected immediacy of involved, concerned hearing and decision alone. Rather, it must critically ask both itself and its concern about its real involvement. It will seek a personal and objective relationship to that message which confronts it. On the basis of man's 'ex-centric position' (H. Plessner), there is no reason and no opportunity to 'overcome' the often-mentioned separation of subject and object, for this separation of subject and object is the basic structure of man as distinct from animals and angels.[38] The animal is so embedded in the environment characteristic of its species that it does not experience its objectivity and its own subjectivity. For man, however, an 'objective external world' comes from the environment that he experiences through spirit, knowledge, and love. One could perhaps even say that the 'objectification' of the environment and of what is experienced in it can be a form of love directed towards the intrinsic value of that which is experienced. In any case, love also has an objectifying tendency. The separation of subject and object as such is a dialectic that is necessary for man. Humanity and indeed the Christian faith cannot find themselves apart from it, but rather are only to be understood and found in it. Naturally it is a serious question whether the present form of this dialectic, as it is expressed in the incongruity between science and existence or specifically for theology in the lack of relationship between the 'historical Jesus' and the 'Christ of faith', can be its final or even appropriate form.

(*b*) The second presupposition of the non-objectifiability of existence means that only in personal being and in personal relationships do I have my authentic being. Accordingly we confront the text in the same way as we confront the man with whom we have daily relationships, in which we first find existence at all, namely, in the relationship between the 'I' and the 'Thou'. In that case it is clear that real history cannot be reconstructed any more than the relationship between 'I' and 'Thou', friend and friend, husband and wife, father and child.[39] This thesis concerning the non-objectifiability of existence does nothing less than challenge the dialectic counter-thesis that existence cannot be subjectified without its disappearing. Man can only indirectly hold on to a permanent relationship to himself and to others like him. He must find himself through sacrifice and objectification by a roundabout way.[40] According to Nietzsche, man is not only the 'unidentifiable animal' which, in the language of the philosophy of existence, corresponds to the 'non-objectifiability' of existence, but also the animal 'which is able to promise'. '. . . How much must man himself first have become *calculable*, *regular*, necessary, even to himself for his own idea, in order finally to be able to answer for himself *as future* in the same way as the one who makes promises'.[41] In 'promising' man speaks *from* his existence *about* his existence. He makes himself reliable and also calculable. He objectifies himself. This goes not only for promising in personal relationships but also for commitment in social institutions. The objectification of personal relationships, nevertheless, does not mean their 'dehumanizing'. Rather, without a certain amount of objectification, personal relationships find no permanence. One may characterize this as an alienation within the unreal character of existence – without such a sacrifice, life finds no continuance. In promising, man commits himself and spans his inconstancy and his historicity. Faithfulness in which he keeps and endures his promise is temporal, but has the character of spanning time. The institutions and organizations, professions, functions and roles in which life occurs and has continuance are found along the way of this sacrifice and objectifying commitment. Human existence cannot be subjectified without its disappearing. Hegel, speaking against the romantic consciousness of his period, described this very well:

It (sc. the self) lacks force to externalise itself, the power to make itself a thing and endure existence. It lives in dread of staining the radiance of its inner being by action and existence. And to preserve the purity of its heart, it flees from contact with actuality, and steadfastly perseveres in a state of self-willed impotence. . . . It becomes a sorrow-laden 'beautiful soul', as it is called; its light dims and dies within it, it vanishes as a shapeless vapour dissolving into thin air.[42]

4. Heidegger's existential analysis has long suggested a transcending of the positivistic observation of history. The concept of 'historicity' in *Being and Time*, §76 has been taken as the basis for an existentialist interpretation. Some of the important basic theses for this are:

(a) 'Higher than actuality stands *possibility*.'[43] The thesis of the ontological priority of possibility over reality permeates the whole work.[44]

(b) It follows from this presupposition that existence is not temporal because it is 'in history' but rather, conversely, that it can only exist historically because it is temporal in the very basis of its being.[45] *History is rooted in historicity*, as time is rooted in the temporality of existence.[46] As a consequence, history as a science is based on the historicity of existence.

(c) Heidegger emphatically puts the question of the 'essence of history' and gives as the 'essence of history' historicity as the constitution of the essence of human existence.[47] Now however one wants to put the question of the 'essence' of something, there is an inherent tendency towards abstraction. For the question of the essence fails to consider the many kinds of things and events, does not ask about their real connection or their reality at all, but rather asks about their essential character of making something possible. It looks at the one matter of the origin of what in truth is really there.

(d) The root of the historicity of existence is that there is an 'ability to be' as a being to death, the possibility of existence that cannot be overcome. In this way, the real event arises from the future of existence, and history as a mode of being has its root essentially in the future, in the ontological priority of possibility. The central topic of history is thus not the real individual event or the regular connection of events, but 'the *possibility* of existence which has-been-there'.[48]

But when historicality is authentic, it understands history as the 'recurrence' of the possible, and knows that a possibility will recur only if existence is open for it fatefully, in a moment of vision, in resolute repetition.[49]

History becomes a return to possibility, to the repetition of possibility and the return of that possibility for existence which existed. On the other hand, the 'they' evade making a choice.

Blind for possibilities, it cannot repeat what has been, but only retains and receives the 'actual' that is left over, the world-historical that has been, the leavings, and the information about them that is present-at-hand. Lost in the making present of the 'today', it understands the 'past' in terms of the 'Present'. On the other hand, the temporality of authentic historicity, as the moment of vision of anticipatory repetition, deprives the 'today' of its character as present and weans one from the conventionalities of the 'they'.[50]

The late Heidegger,[51] on the other hand, no longer expects the 'primary-historical' from history, but rather considers it as the science of fallenness into the common-historical. His opinion on Dilthey's work, which *Being and Time* attempted to adopt, also changes.[52] Scientific existence tries to grasp the pure reality of being, i.e. purified by that which is possible. 'Thinking about being', however, searches for the authenticity, the possibility, the temporality and the futurity of existence. The following judgment stands in contrast to the thematizing of 'history' in *Being and Time:*

All history calculates what is coming from its images of the past, which are determined by the present. History is the continual destruction of the future and of the historical relationship to the arrival of destiny. Historicism today has not only not been overcome, but is only now entering into the stage of its expansion and strengthening. The technical organization of world publicity by radio and the press, which is already lagging behind, is historicism's real form of domination.

But how can we introduce and represent the early hours of an age other than through history? Perhaps historical research is for us an unavoidable means of making the historical present. However, this in no way means that history, taken by itself, can acquire an adequate relationship to history within history.[53]

If one holds fast to this alternative, which becomes increasingly difficult, then it follows that science, particularly historical research, is based on fallenness and an irresolvable gulf emerges between thinking, the thinking of being, and science. 'Science does not think.' A way thus ends in that aporia which theology hoped that it would overcome. This gulf is spanned by oracles of the philosophy of history, following Nietzsche and Spengler, which deal both with an all-enveloping night of the world in the scientific forgetfulness of being and with the announcement of an eschatology of being.

5. *On the theological use of the existentialist concept of history.* As long as one proceeds from the ontological priority of possibility over reality, the interpretation of history can only be an existentialist one and must be directed towards a return to repetition and to the experience of the possibility of the existence which was there. In that case, however, there is no conceivable transition or continuity between the kerygma which is seen as the understanding of existence and the historical Jesus; between the Easter faith and the reality of the resurrection; between the gospel and Old Testament history. In that case, one must concentrate the 'phenomena' of the historical Jesus on Jesus' 'understanding of existence' (Robinson), on the 'inner life of Jesus' (Herrmann) or on that 'which is expressed in Jesus' (Ebeling). The historical-critical question of what really happened there must be rejected as inappropriate. Only when the 'possibility of that existence which has-been-there' is asked about in this way can that understanding of existence which reveals itself in confrontation again become the 'possibility' of man's own potentiality for being. An exclusive circle then arises between Jesus and one's own understanding of existence, between that which was expressed in Jesus and one's

own faith, a circle between word and faith which, by being indismissable by either side, hangs 'in the air'[54] and finds contact with reality only to the extent to which the naked 'that' of the historical Jesus and the naked 'that' of man's own unique existence is presupposed.

One such sublimating existentialization of the truth of faith by sophisticated delimitation over against any objective – and that also means common and communicable – factual and objective truth doubtless meets the confusion of modern man whose soul is alone and speechless in a technically controlled and disenchanted world of facts. Precisely at this point, however, a fateful alternative arises: either the modern absolutism of subjectivity disappears before objectivity, before the self-evidence of the concern of Christianity; or Christianity is destroyed in the whirlpool of modern subjectivity. Christian faith has constantly attempted to demonstrate the truth of statements which are in no way to be developed only as illuminations of existence but rather at the same time touch upon the factual state of affairs. Every theological statement, like 'Christ is Lord' or 'He is truly risen' contains a factual as well as an existential reference, a certainty of existence as well as a recognition of a factual state of affairs – however that may be understood. It seems as if New Testament proclamation does not only oppose a historical-critical reduction to that which, in the historical sense, could be regarded as factual truth and which then will really concern no one. It also opposes a reduction by existentialist interpretation to its truth about existence whose reference to reality would be uncertain. This modern dualism is alien to the New Testament, although it stems from the confrontation of Christianity with Greek thought. In order today to understand the content of truth of its statements, the separated and conflicting concepts of truth must be connected. The alternative which is always posed in this dualism, as to whether the gospel is to be read as a historical source or is to be understood as a kerygmatic call to decision, is an alternative in which the gospel does not reveal itself. According to its intention, the gospel is neither source nor call to decision; rather it narrates proclamation and proclaims narration and in this way expresses the certainty of existence in the factual state of affairs and factual affairs in the illumination of existence. If we are to understand this, we must approach the reciprocal relationship between existential and factual truth in a new way.

Every theological statement made in the New Testament belongs to a definite, unique situation as witness, *kerygma* and concrete address. This does not, however, mean that the subjective certainty of existence, which causes it, was itself a guarantee for the truth of that which was proclaimed. Existential truth is not directed towards itself but rather towards an outside truth. The truth on which existence is founded has, at the same time, to be universal, for true human existence can be satisfied with nothing less than that truth itself.[55] The characteristic quality of the biblical statements of proclamation is that they reach out beyond the historical situation in which they were spoken and heard into the universal. The Bible does not only belong to its situation but rather claims to belong to that universal human situation which is found in the future. Otherwise there would be no need to translate these statements into other situations, traditions and times. Precisely when proclamation expresses concrete existential truth, through the factual relationship of its statements, it also contains 'universal truth', namely, the claim of 'truth' itself. This change is found in the '*eph'hapax*' which means both 'unique' and 'once for all time'.[56] This is not the change from an 'accidental historical truth' to a 'necessary' universal 'truth of reason', but rather the change from historical uniqueness, givenness and irreversability to eschatological and universal significance whereby apocalyptic eschatology, in the light of which the unique history of Jesus is told, represents the first expression of this universal and general significance.

That shift of theological-exegetical work to the material reference of New Testament statements, to the reality which is expressed in them and is given for understanding, would mean the exact reversal of the Heideggerian concept of history, and must proceed from the ontological priority of reality to possibility. Only then is it possible to say that our possibilities are pre-formed through the historical reality in which we live and which we have, that through the events which precede our present, possibilities are first opened up for us and others closed off, and that, in an analogous way, our possibilities of belief and unbelief are disclosed in the givenness of a particular reality.[57] Now that would mean that our possibilities of existence are related and indebted to a reality which in factual truth must be addressed *ad extra nos*. In the end, this would mean a reversal of Heidegger's next thesis, namely that history is not based on the historicity of existence and made possible from it, but rather that the historicity of existence is based on that history which is real, has happened and is given, and is made possible by it, since existential truth is not based on itself but on a truth which is found outside it and is directed towards it.

In that case, however, so-called 'objectifying thought' can no longer be characterized as the possibility of the decay of existential thinking. Rather, it becomes obvious that existential thought is always already directed towards a fact-related thought if it wishes to articulate at all the fact that Christian proclamation already continually exists within a projected and intended horizon of universal truth and claim anticipatory universality.[58] This relationship to 'universal truth' can be dialectic, protesting and denying, but it cannot be liquidated and is in fact nowhere liquidated *de facto*, not even by Kierkegaard nor in the end, by Bultmann.[59] This historical-critical investigation of history and existentialist interpretation remain related to one another in the same way as the 'authenticity of existence' and 'fallenness into technology, industry and mass society', even if existential thought is achieved only in the leap from objectifying thought, when concrete proclamation is achieved only in the leap from the so-called universal truths. The so-called separation of subject and object continues and keeps reappearing. Its dialectic cannot be disposed of, but can be 'transcended' in a greater, more comprehensive context.

IV   History and eschatology

We are thus led back to the question whether the historical method together with its presupposition of a 'closed nexus of events' in historical reality correctly does justice to its object, 'history'. Does the method which historicizes reality into a series of facts correspond to the reality that is questioned by it?

1. Historical research in no way sets out to produce a distillate of 'naked facts'. Certainly the datable and fixable facts of the final selection that stands the test are concerned with a reality which can be seen. But only that which is significant, i.e. that which is found in a context of relation and reference, can be observed and stated at all. *Individuum est ineffabile!* A 'naked fact', an individual event, is unrecognizable and cannot be stated. So historical thought cannot be concerned with the ascertaining of facts as such, but rather with the ascertaining of one fact in relationship to others. All historical knowledge is a perceiving of relationships. Only in definite relationships with others does an event appear and can it be classified, whether it is in a 'process' or a 'development', in a 'style', a 'structure', a 'situation' or an 'understanding of existence'. Without ontology, nothing factual can be opened up for us.[60] Here significance, interest, lines of questioning, methodological observances, etc., arise from ontology.

The 'objectivity' of scientific results is based on objectivity, but the universal validity of the result is based on previous agreement between men concerning the line of questioning which one uses, and the angle from which one attempts to see the problem.[61]

2. The 'closed nexus of events' of positivism is only one attempt to characterize more precisely the correlation (Troeltsch) which takes place between historical process for definite parts of his reality. The same holds for the idea of development, the anthropological typology of cultural processes and the idea of style, of structure and of situation. It is characteristic of the selective

tendency of positivism that within it the theory could develop
that philosophy, art and religion, strictly speaking, could have
no history.[62]

What is individual does not appear without an understood
relationship, but all developed relationships must be verified in
what is individual. At this point, the problem of the knowledge
of history arises. 'If a man surrenders himself to real history, the
idea disappears; if he constructs from the idea, real history
disappears.'[63] Constructed universal concepts cannot be united
with a concrete, individual, historical form, and historical
appearances can only be observed in those over-arching rela-
tions for which they have meaning. Ranke may have objected
to Hegel, 'I, however, maintain that every epoch is immediate
towards God and that its value is not found in what proceeds
from it but rather in its existence itself, in the immediate self',
but the continuation of this sentence ought not to be omitted:
'Yet if every epoch has its justification and its value in itself and
for itself, then what preceded it cannot be overlooked', namely,
the 'inner necessity of the succession of events'. This inner
necessity of succession arises from the relationship of the events
to the whole or to the final goal of history. It does, however, pose
the problem, 'If one wished to provide a definite goal for this
(world history), one would obscure the future and fail to
recognize the limitless range of the movement of world history'.[64] Ranke's solution for the recording of history by a
'teleology without telos', as Masur has called it, at least holds
the dialectical process of understanding open in the circle
between contingency and continuity, individuality and generality. An appointed and fixed goal of history would reduce that
history, which is full of everything that is possible and unfore-
seeable, to a natural process. Renunciation of all teleology,
however, would dissolve history into inexpressible individualities.

Knowledge of the 'relationships' arises each time from an
understanding of relevant facts and the ongoing processes in
history. Positivism, which counts on a closed nexus of effects,
fixes its concern in history and, according to its conception,

brings it to light. Even Troeltsch's reference, over against the dogmatic method, to the general relationship of the correlation of all events in which everything is conditioned and relative, and his comment that it is the 'correlative relation of the phenomena of the human spirit',[65] is a dogmatic fixation of the substance of history, which is hidden, if history is to be history and not just a natural or intellectual interweaving of correlates. Both the 'planned goals of history' and the 'planned substance of history' make history an event which is still accidental. Historical positivism and materialism and an idealistic interpretation of history in their own way present the resolved puzzle of history. This, however, means that ultimately neither reckons any longer with 'history'; but are rather 'neutralized' in the direction of a partial relationship of the effects of developed substances. This, however, is on each occasion a kind of 'conclusion of history' and results in the transference of society into an unhistorical condition.

3. At this point, the question of the nature and 'essence' of history must be discussed. There is no 'history' in the absolute sense. History is always a history *of* something; history of culture, history of religion, world history, etc. That this something is found in 'history' means, however, that it is the not-yet-definite, open, unconcluded, disputed. The history of the 'something' has not yet appeared, but finds itself in the process of appearing and of definition, that is, in becoming, and because of this, is at risk. It only appears definitively when history is at its end. When it shows itself to be something definitive and can be decided upon, history has arrived at its goal. Until this time, however, the case is still pending and its truth, its apocalypse, is still outstanding.

In anthropological terms, this means that the essence of mankind is hidden and has not yet appeared. 'Mankind' – the realized generic concept – is becoming, is still in process, has not yet acquired a fixed 'nature'. One could say with Droysen, 'What the generic concept is for animals and plants . . . history is for men',[66] if one does not understand this, as did Droysen, as participation in the divine, but rather understands history as the open process surrounding man's becoming man. Every determination and every definition of man's essence is an apocalypse of the force towards concealment which constitutes his history and that process in which he must find himself. It is an anticipated *eschaton* of history. Man loses his mystery and his open history with a natural law which presupposes a *natura hominis*, however that may be described.[67] Every universal-anthropological definition of what being human really means is basically eschatological; a final, i.e. ultimately valid conclusion of that openness which drives the history of man, which first must be brought to a conclusion and which is therefore also at stake. Nor should one contrast concrete existence in the here and now with man as a 'generic example', as the 'individualization of the general', for in the concrete decisions of existence, what is involved is truth and universal human nature. World history is the adventure, the open process of struggle in regard to 'unknown humanity'.

Applied to religion, this produces the problem of the absoluteness of Christianity, as Troeltsch saw it:

Before the end of history, one cannot speak of an absolute religion. There must be absolute twilight before the bird of Minerva can begin its flight into the land of the realized, absolute concept. . . For this reason, the construction of absolute religion never tries for long to cling to a historical religion and of its own accord becomes the contradiction of a religion of the future.[68]

Put in positive terms, this means that only that religion which is concerned with and announces the end of history can represent itself as the 'absolute religion'. The 'absoluteness' of Christianity is found in the eschatological horizon of the Christ-event and the apostolic process of proclamation. On this point, it can be asserted against Troeltsch that it is eschatology which first gives history a meaning for theology and does not close it. Eschatology stimulates historical research which is not satisfied with ascertaining the probable and the real, but also wishes to understand the processes.[69] For such an understanding of history as that which is still in the process of developing, the object of historical research is not the 'petrified, coagulated fact' of a concluded past, but rather the still unconcluded open *fieri*, not a collection of facts but interwoven processes in a still unfinished world. The question 'What has happened?' presupposes that what has happened is *passé*. Bultmann was correct when he said that phenomena which kept still got objective observation. But the alternative, that existential events do not keep still and do not allow themselves to be produced and to become objects of observation, means a split in reality.[70] Historically, phenomena comprehended in the process must be understood in terms of the significance of their process. Here, the historical 'process of inquiry' is itself in the process-event. 'Objective' ascertainment is always an investigation into a suspended process and, as such, must be accounted for. Objective observation and research is an undertaking to be accounted for existentially and the existential responsibility is found in the struggle for that truth which is to be discovered. As long as there is no 'final end', there is no *rebus sic stantibus* but rather only the *rebus sic fluentibus*.[71]

The dating and computing of reality in terms of facts in a closed nexus of effects have the character of making a judgment in a suspended process. They are a 'conclusion of history' which poses a threat to our age through precisely this modern positivistic process, in the departure from history (A. Weber) or through dreams of the immanent 'perfectibility of history' (H. Freyer) which has now been brought into the realm of the possible. The historical-positivistic fetishism of facts understands how things stand and lie, but does not understand in what direction they are moving. Yet anyone who does not measure things by their intended meaning sees them not only superficially but also incorrectly. The following profound insight appears many times in Bultmann's later writings:

Events or historical figures are not historical phenomena 'in themselves' at all, not even as parts of a causal relationship. They are phenomena only *in their relationship to the future* (italics mine) for which they have meaning and for which the present has responsibility. It can also be said that every historical phenomenon has its own future in which it first shows itself for what it is; or, better, in which it shows itself *more and more* (italics mine) for what it is. For it will show itself finally for what it is when history has reached its end.[72]

Here the truth of history, to gain which historians work, becomes a special problem of apocalyptic. What slips through the transitory is shrouded in impenetrable darkness. The historian attempts to uncover it. If he wants to say how things 'really' were, then at the same time he anticipates the end of history in which historical phenomena no longer appear in changing forms but rather appear as that which they really are. Historical work takes place, then, within an eschatological horizon of anticipation, because what history and the individual event really are is only recognizable when history has reached its end. Conversely, history reaches its end when historical phenomena show themselves for what they really are and, as such, are uncovered.

Here some common ground is found despite all basic differences between Christian proclamation, which reveals and publishes the 'mystery of God' in Christ, and the attempt of historical research to discover how things really were, down to historical positivism which concludes history because it believes that it can recognize the end (cf. Comte). Yet Christian revelation is not revelation of history in the sense that it would have to replace historical research or, on the other hand, that historical research replaces kerygmatic communication. The Bible is not the divine commentary to divine activity in history, as could be said in the theology of salvation history. In that case it would only be the revelation of providence or a divine plan of history and not the revelation of God. No history is of its own accord the revelation of God. The revelation of the special history in Christ that gives faith its basis occurs in that word of election, calling, justification and mission which affects history. The reality in which this special salvation event takes place, becomes visible precisely through this as the reality of the lordship of the one who gives life to the dead and tells that which is not that it is (Rom. 4.17). It becomes understandable as 'history'. History thus becomes not revelation, but the sphere of action of revelation. The Lord who is recognized in revelation is made known as the first and the last over all reality. World history in its eschatological impenetrability is understood as the sphere of action of its still impenetrable rule. That does not mean that salvation-event and world history would be severed in a Marcionite way. Rather, through the revelation of God, through proclamation, witness and faith, reality is brought into an eschatological movement, into a dynamic process. It becomes 'historical' in the real sense. God's revelation is not the 'disclosure' of this historicity, but it effects and provokes this historicity. Eschatological proclamation effects and provokes the experience of reality as history. It revives interest in history and the question about its final meaning. It arouses the eschatological conscience in all recognizing knowledge of history. The proclamation of the eschatological mystery of 'God in Christ' produces a reality in which men live with each other, a trial of history, a judicial process of the truth of God. As the Dutch say, the apostolate 'historicizes' reality.[73] But in that case – what is 'history'?

In that case, history cannot be understood positivistically as a closed area of events which can be dated and fixed in a calendar. Nor can history be understood as an existential. Rather, history must be seen as the sphere of action of revelation, in which the judicial process of truth takes place. Bultmann has correctly said that scripture is what it is only when considered together with its history and its future.[74] The 'opening of the scriptures' was once a special problem of salvation-historical apocalyptic. It was thought that the events of the final drama 'open up' scripture in its hidden prophetic meaning. These are speculations for a period when men attempted to read the Bible as a handbook for world history. But in Paulinist theology, Rom. 16.25–7; Col. 1.25–8; Eph. 3.1–3, speak of a revelation of the mystery of Christ through the apostolate to the Gentiles among the nations. Scripture belongs together with this history of the apostolate and with the future of the pantocrator. The one who is always calling the word of proclamation 'witness' and designating believers as 'witnesses to Christ' in the world, and does not understand this as a lyric testimony of the heart, is saying that history is God's judicial process against the gods or the legal process of truth against lies. This happens not only with Israel but also with the nations *through* Israel (Isa. 43.8–13), not only with the church but also with humanity *through* the church. In this process of history the Christian witness is materially bound to the truth of Christ and is to be accounted for existentially by coming to grips with every other observation of truth. Christian faith is then held responsible in this process and, therefore, is directed towards holding open both this process and the future.

4. But where does that history, in which truth is fought for, reach the end in which truth shows itself for what it is? For Bultmann, from whose statements we began earlier, the meaning of history reveals itself always in me and in my own present which is called to responsibility for the future. The question about the meaning of the whole course of history, towards which this quotation is directed, has become a meaningless question, but the question about the meaning of history, from which – as from our history – we come, is meaningful.[75] The future in which historical phenomena show themselves for what they really are would in that case be synonymous with the 'meaning' which they have for the present understanding subject. But this would mean that history 'ends' in its own unique historicity and the 'historicity' of existing is the apocalypse of history, the content of Christian revelation and that which is 'disclosed' in it. Faith itself would be the 'coming to its goal of what came to expression in Jesus'.[76] World history would then be 'exhausted' in the existential dialectical circle between 'word and faith'. Faith would be synonymous with perfection.[77] This, however, would mean that faith, in its historicity, can no longer have history.[78]

Now the question is – and it is faith that asks it – whether the *telos* and *eschaton*, the future of the history of Jesus, have already been reached in faith itself. Does Jesus show himself here for what he is? Faith observes that it itself is not yet this future, that it is not yet the present of the absolute and the end of history, but rather, in the great not yet, in the face of that which the announced meaning of the event 'Christ the Lord' still contradicts, it is full of eschatological impatience. It awaits the future in which that which has already broken in with the revelation of the risen one reaches its goal and its apocalypse.

The 'meaning' of an eschatological event is not yet exhausted in the fact that, through question and answer, it calls the present to responsibility for the future, though this is a part of it. 'Meaning' is – to use E. Bloch's phrase,[79] something which draws and moves ahead towards what it intends to signify, announce and exhibit, and the shape of which is not yet fully there. 'Meaning is not only to be interpreted existentially as the relation to existence and the truth of existence, but also historically, eschatologically, factually and typologically[80] as a relationship to coming events. We recognize events. We recognize events only when we observe their meaning in terms of 'their' future and not only in terms of our unique present and future. Only on the strength of this does the observation of their significance arise for our future and the observation of our significance for their future.

Certainly we are only required to remember the past in its meaning for our existence when it is not a matter of the distant past in the sense of the conclusion, satisfaction, care of and finishing of events and the order of events, but rather when it, so to speak, is a matter of a 'waiting' past which in this way is still standing there, waiting. There is future in the past (E. Bloch). The proclamation of the resurrection of the crucified Christ means that in this event there is future in the past, that something is contained in the reality of the exaltation of Christ which has not yet been realized, which is still possible, which is directed towards a future. There is hope in the mode of remembrance and remembrance in the mode of exhortation to hope. We can characterize the still outstanding and unsatisfied meaning of this event as *promissio* and say that the promise constantly overtakes the past of its way of thinking. Only in fulfilment does it become transitory, when it becomes clear that promise does not first come to the event but rather is nothing other than the explication, which is only possible in this form, of the eschatological openness of this event itself.

At this point, the question arises as to what endures in the quicksand of time and keeps a tradition alive in changing spiritual landscapes and times. Tradition is not kept alive by the 'connection of numerous accidents' (E. Meyer) or even by continually new actualization. For what is necessary for repeated actualization? Certainly the idea of a *theologia perennis* which grows like a tree from the roots of historical origins does not correspond to reality. There is, however, a *spes perennis*, and historical tradition remains alive through that moment of hope inherent in it, through 'waiting for history', in the same way that the words of the prophet are preserved and obeyed 'as a witness for the coming day'.[81] Hope, as a waiting for history, enters, actualizing itself, into every new situation and, at the same time, still reaches out beyond every situation.

5. For the Reformers – at any rate according to the usual understanding of the confessional writings, especially those from Melanchthon's pen – the *telos* of the *historia Christi* was the *fides justificans*. The *remissio peccatorum* and the *fides* were given as *telos* and *finis*, as *effectus* and *legitimer usus*, as *causa finalis historiae Christi*. The question, however, is, whether justifying faith does not belong together with the eschatological righteousness of God, in which God claims his right in that world in which the believer lives. The future and the meaning of what has happened in the resurrection and the exaltation of Christ are not yet exhausted in the realization of faith itself, but only eschatologically in what is universal resurrection of the dead, universal judgment, universal new creation of heaven and earth or by the fact that 'God is all in all' is addressed as the designation of the tendency and the intention of God's activity in Christ and as the designation of what is still hidden in the exaltation of Christ as Lord. Therefore, the promising and the future which are found in the exaltation of Christ are not yet satisfied by faith.

The believer, rather, recognizes the peculiar future of this event and enters into its universal, eschatological horizon. His present does not yet become the present of the absolute, but rather the foyer in the arrival of the anticipated *novum*. The proclamation, which interpretatively expresses the Christ event which has still not been completed by God, becomes the initiation of the witness in that process of history which is determined and opened up by this event. The historicity of existing in faith then understands itself as 'participation in the history of Christ' within the community of Christ which leads to 'suffering with him', 'dying with him' and 'arising with him'. The past of the resurrection, which has not yet been completed by God, and the exaltation of Christ, makes faith a 'hope against hope' and a 'confidence in things which one does not see', and a patience which bears the afflictions to come because it looks forward in hope to the promised future. The remembering of the resurrection of Christ leads to an anticipation which can be quieted with nothing but a new heaven and a new earth, or, in the words of Johannes Herrmann's Easter hymn: 'Here what he brought out of his grave has not yet been fully revealed. . . . The last day will show what he has really done.'

The proclamation of Christ becomes, in faith, a truth which gives ground to existence when it expresses a material truth that bases the believer's existence on something outside itself. In regard to existence, it takes place within a horizon of intended universal truth, for the proclamation of Christ occurs in 'eschatological openness' (E. Käsemann), in anticipatory generality and forward-looking universality. It explains the history of Christ in such a way that the future is announced and uncovered in it. It can only proclaim this certainty of the future by expressing the history in which the future lies in the past. '*Narrantur praeterita ut futura etiam praedicantur*', remarked Augustine.[82] This history is to be proclaimed because and in so far as it is eschatological history. Interest in its historical research arises from the hope that is remembered with it. Therefore, historical research must continually check not only its results but also its eschatological presuppositions.

*V   Conclusion: the origin of history and apocalyptic
in the question of permanence*

The basic question which arises in the face of the flowing
stream of time is the question about that which has permanence
and may give permanence, or, as Meinecke once put it as an
expression of Troeltsch's particular problem, combining sayings
of Heraclitus and Archimedes: πάντα ῥεῖ – δός μοι ποῦ στῶ.
Where is there a standpoint in life if all the contents of life are
historically determined and, therefore, also historically transitory?[83]

This question expresses itself in historical science in the
search for the permanent, the continuing, in the context of
ever-changing events. Whatever repeats itself is constant and
typical, whatever is already there and can be compared becomes
the basis on which the unique, the diverse and the changing are
reckoned. One must, however, continually be aware of the fact
that the typical, that which is at the foundation of all change,
is not a substance which is unhistorical itself. Rather, everything
that can be determined as continuing and typical is itself within
the process of history as something open and contested. 'The
genus "man" melts in the process of history', said Dilthey.[84]
Indeed, the process of history is the process involving true
humanity, the truth and the revelation of the true man.

The question of the 'relationship' of entities in the sense of
the unity and connection of events has its foundation in the
experience of impermanence and of being sacrificed in the flow
of time. It finds its meaning and its intention in coming to grips
with that process. World-historical plans seek the universal and
unitive meaning of history; without the knowledge of that
meaning that process would lead to anarchy among men.

The question of history arises for Christian faith also from the
contestation of its ability to continue, from the contradiction of
contestations and persecutions or simply from the experience of
its own confinement in history and its transitoriness. It comes
from the question of the *perseverantia fidei usque ad finem*.[85] It
is not accidental that both historical remembrance, which

confronts God whether in praise or lament with his historical faithfulness, and the prophetic and apocalyptic future promise of his activity in history, still open, consistently join in the paraenesis to the 'patience of hope': 'He who steadfastly continues to the end will be blessed.' The enquiry about history and the goal of his activity arise in the onslaught on hope based on God's faithfulness.

For the existentialist interpretation of existence, the question of 'connectedness' and what is permanent is not appropriate for past, present and coming history.[86] For it, the origin and the possibility of this horizon of questioning in the absent-mindedness, undecidedness and lostness of the self are found in man and in the history of the 'world'. This type of being loses itself in such a way that later it must draw itself together out of its dispersion and must devise a comprehensive unity for its 'togetherness'. The longing for an objective demonstration of the relationship which is found outside one is seen to be a product of the fallenness of the original longing for the collected wholeness of existence itself. The 'world'-historical contextual question results from a 'flight from death' and deterioration into 'inauthentic historicity'. Provisional decisiveness only brings this being unto death into authentic existence, into 'authentic historicity'. And precisely here is found the original, unforfeited prolongation of all existence, which is not in need of relationship. 'The Self's resoluteness against the inconstancy of distraction is in itself a *steadiness which has been stretched along*.'[87] This collected resoluteness is not meant to be understood in actual terms, nor is it meant to be limited for the duration of the act of decision. Rather, the permanence and steadiness which are found existentially in the decision 'preserve' themselves in every possible instant which may first arise from them. Permanence is not acquired from a sequence of moments and decisions of the moment. Rather, 'these (sc. the moments) arise from the temporality of that repetition which is futurally in the process-of-having-been – a temporality which has *already been stretched along*'.[88] Thus permanence does not arise from a succession of what is temporarily new, from an arrangement in a supposedly overlapping, objective relationship. Rather, that which is lasting 'exists' in 'resort to the sources', 'nearness to the origin', in the 'parousia of being'. 'What lasts is founded by poets.' Thus in place of permanence in the horizontal extension, a sort of consistency in vertical intensity of being appears. Permanence presupposes a time which is torn open in present, past and future; consistency, on the other hand, presupposes an entanglement of being and time which appears in the origin.

This existentialist interpretation of 'permanence' is, for its part, inappropriate if the historicity of human existence is found in its participation in the reality of history, if historicity is not existential but rather means the concrete interweaving of life by guilt and destiny, suffering and love, physical existence and society. In that case, the question about what is really continual arises, about what persistence is first possible; about what endures upon which one can 'depend'; about the permanent element upon which hope can be directed. Then contested faith asks about the faithfulness of God to his covenant, his election and his promise in the midst of the riddle of history. It does not ask about his faithfulness in order to examine and estimate the divine plans of history in advance. It not only intends to repent and return the past possibilities of existence, but also looks for the faithfulness of God in order to surrender itself in love and to leave itself in the perseverance of hope. The meaning of the historical books of the Bible and the apocalypses, however they are constructed, is their *anamnesis* and their apocalypse of the faithfulness of God and the overcoming of the *tentatio de infirmitate fidei*, which is made possible through knowledge in the 'ability to live with the darkness of history' (R. Wittram). The vital interest in horizontal remembrance of history and in the horizontal anticipation of history arises here. The two do not allow themselves to be drawn together into a vertical immediacy of the present of faith to God without this faith being delivered over to the danger of spiritualistic dissolution.

NOTES

This article was first published in *EvTh* 22, 1962, 31–66.

1. H. Heimpel, 'Geschichte und Geschichtswissenschaft', *Vierteljahrshefte für Zeitgeschichte* 5, 1957, Part 1, 15.
2. Beside the well-known work of P. Hazard, *The European Mind*, trans. J. L. May, 1953, cf. particularly B. Groethuysen, *Die Entstehung der bürgerlichen Welt- und Lebensanschauung in Frankreich* I, 1927), which points out this tremendous reshaping in its pre-ideological period, at the beginning and in the middle of the seventeenth century, in which the world-view was not yet articulated.
3. Cf. G. Kruger, *Studium Generale* 4, 1953, 322ff.
4. M. Scheler, *Die Stellung des Menschen im Kosmos*, 1947, 42.
5. W. Dilthey, *Gesammelte Schriften* VIII, 225.
6. J. Ritter, *Hegel und die Französische Revolution*, Arbeitsgemeinschaft des Landes Nordrhein-Westfalen, Heft 63, 1957, 43. Cf. Hegel's *Philosophy of Right*, §§ 182ff.
7. N. Sombart, 'St-Simon und A. Comte', in: Alfred Weber, *Einführung in die Soziologie*, 1955, 87.
8. *Ibid.*, 88.
9. A. Comte, *Die Soziologie* (Kröners Taschenausgabe 107), 1933, 15. The first detailed contextual information about Saint Simon's and Comte's positivistic messianism and the combination of apocalyptic hope with technicratic, sociological and nationalistic thinking, unique in European history and following the French revolution, is given in J. L. Talmon's great work, *Political Messianism. The Romantic Phase*, 1960.
10. E. Rothacker, *Einleitung in die Geisteswissenschaften*, ²1930, 190ff.
11. *Ibid.*, 256.
12. Cf. C. Antoni, *From History to Sociology*, trans. H. V. White, 1959, 60: 'Troeltsch could detach the modern world and make of it a type in itself only by eliminating every religious element, making of it a schema. And here an unconscious influence upon him is manifested: his "modern world" is nothing but Comte's "third stage", the civilization of science and of positivistic interests, immune from theological and metaphysical influences. This was a positivistic residue inherited by Troeltsch from Dilthey.'
13. Dilthey and Troeltsch already sought this connection, but did not find it in the proclamation of the Reformation itself; they only saw it in 'Luther's individualism'. G. Ebeling, 'The Significance of the historical-critical Method', *Word and Faith*, trans. J. W. Leitch, 1963, 17ff., has sought with great care to stimulate a 'deep objective relationship' between the 'affirmation of the historical critical method' and the 'Reformation doctrine of justification'. He mentions as an example of this material relationship the understanding of representation in the sola fide as historical, personal encounter. As a result, historical-critical theology is a necessary means of reminding the church of that freedom that has its roots in the *justificatio impii*. The question remains open, however, as to whether the relationship

of faith to the word of promise is identical with a 'true, personal confrontation' with history. Even with Gogarten's thesis (*Verhängnis und Hoffnung der Neuzeit*, 1958, 164) that 'this metaphysical thought (sc. of the dogma of the early church) was overcome in Luther's theology, at least in principle' and that Luther's faith relates to a 'purely personal event, as to that history which occurs between the person of God and the person of man' (*op. cit.*, 160), the question remains open whether the 'overcoming of metaphysics' in F. Ebner's personalism (*Das Wort und die geistigen Realitäten*, 1921) is identical with the Reformers' criticism of scholastic metaphysics or whether this personalism, which is critically directed against modern subjectivism, does not rather remain imprisoned in the unhistorical abstract social situation of modern subjectivity.

Cf. also H. G. Drescher, 'Das Problem der Geschichte bei E. Troeltsch', *ZTK* 57, 1960, 186ff.

14. Drescher, *op. cit.*, 220.

15. Dilthey, *Gesammelte Schriften*, VIII, 12.

16. D. F. Strauss, *Die christliche Glaubenslehre* I, 1840, 71.

17. F. Overbeck, *Selbstbekenntnisse*, 1941, 129.

18. This is the main point of Adolf von Harnack's letter to Karl Barth, *CW* 37, 1923, 8: 'If the person of Jesus Christ stands as the centre of the gospel, how else can the basis of a reliable and common knowledge of this person be achieved other than through *critical historical study*, in order to prevent the confusion of an imaginary Christ with the real one? What else but scientific theology can attempt this study?' Barth retorted by saying that the reliability and availability of the knowledge of the person of Christ as the centre of the gospel could only be that of faith aroused by God. The horizon of christology is not the Christian, scientific world, but rather the community in its mission and its witness in the world (*CW* 37, 1923, 244ff.).

19. Even in the romantic school of German history writing, the possibility of historical criticism seems to be based on the philosophical presupposition that the history of the universe is a 'closed nexus of events' which is meaningful in unity, connection and rational consistency. For Ranke, the periods follow one another in such a way that 'there happens in all what is impossible in any single one, that the whole fullness of the spiritual life breathed on the human race by the deity comes to light in the sequence of centuries'. They follow one another in a definite divine order whose laws cannot be formulated but whose connection may be 'guessed'. Here the idea which holds hidden sway in history is not discarded in the dialectical process of historical development to find itself and be manifest at the end, as with Hegel; rather, like a sun resting in itself, it remains behind all limited, incomplete manifestations which come and go historically, so that each of them can be understood and evaluated in a relationship of immediacy to the supreme idea or 'immediately to God'. Ranke's theology of history thus acquires a panentheistic character. Cf. C. Hinrichs, *Ranke und die Geschichtstheologie des Goethezeit*, 1954, 164ff. The question is, however, whether historical-critical research is really dependent on this panentheistic conception for which history itself becomes the changing, transforming, unending fullness of the epiphanies of the eternal presence of being. Further,

the question is whether this idea does not obstruct historical understanding of the eschatological revelation of God. F. C. Baur, whose kinship with the theology of history of the Goethe period has been pointed out by K. Scholder in his article 'F. C. Baur als Historiker', *EvTh* 21, 1961, 435ff., explained the effort of the historian as 'to bring the still firm substance into the universal stream of historical becoming, in which, in the unending linkage of cause and effect, the one is always the presupposition of the others and *everything holds and keeps itself together*, and only that must remain always uncomprehended that could make the claim of standing outside all historical connections while being in the midst of history' (F. C. Baur, quoted *op. cit.*, 444, my italics). Yet again the question arises as to how the theological presupposition that historical connection is equivalent to the universal substance of the cosmos of history can be justified. On these presuppositions, F. C. Baur subjects the history of the gospel not only to historical criticism but also to a historical world view.

20. *Über die Gesetze historischen Wissens*, 1864, 16.

21. *Holzwege*, ³1957, 76.

22. *Glauben und Verstehen* III, 1960, 144.

23. Cf. W. Pannenberg, 'Redemptive Event and History', *Basic Questions in Theology*, trans. G. H. Kehm, 1970, 15ff., esp. 33ff.

24. Karl Barth, *Romans*, trans. E. C. Hoskyns, 1933, Preface to the second edition of 1921, 9; taken up again by R. Bultmann, 'Über das Problem einer theologische Exegese des Neuen Testamentes', *Zwischen den Zeiten*, 1925, 357.

25. Cf. the discussion of E. Troeltsch, 'Über historische und dogmatische Methode in der Theologie', 1898; C. A. Bernouilli, *Die wissenschaftliche und die kirchliche Methode in der Theologie*, 1897; M. Reischle, 'Historische und dogmatische Methode in der Theologie', *Theologische Rundschau* 4, 1901, 261ff.; G. Wobbermin, 'Das Verhältnis der Theologie zur modernen Wissenschaft', *ZTK* 10, 1900, 375ff.; F. Traub, 'Die religionsgeschichtliche Methode und die systematische Theologie', *ZTK* 11, 1901, 301ff.; L. Ihmels, *'Die Selbständigkeit der Dogmatik gegenüber der Religionsphilosophie*, 1901. This debate over method in theology was analogous and contemporary to the 'debate about value' in sociology unleashed by Max Weber: cf. Max Weber, *Gesammelte Aufsätze zur Wissenschaftslehre*, 1922.

26. On this see R. Niebuhr, *Resurrection and Historical Reason*, 1957; H. Ott, *Geschichte und Heilsgeschichte in der Theologie R. Bultmanns*, 1955.

27. W. Kamlah, *Wissenschaft, Wahrheit, Existenz*, 1960, 56ff.

28. E. Topitsch, 'Soziologie des Existentialismus', *Merkur* 7, Part 6, 1953; C. Graf von Krockow, *Die Entscheidung, Eine Untersuchung über E. Jünger, C. Schmitt, M. Heidegger*, 1958, 68ff. Here is a reason for the frequent alliance of existential thinking in philosophy and theology with the criticism of time made by F. Tönnies, O. Spengler, Ortega y Gasset, etc.

29. R. Bultmann, *Kerygma und Mythos* II, 1952, 187.

30. R. Bultmann, *Kerygma and Myth*, 1960, 35: 'The facts which historical criticism can verify cannot exhaust, indeed they cannot adequately indicate, all that Jesus means to me. How he actually originated matters little, indeed we can appreciate his significance only when we cease to worry about such

questions.' Cf. also F. Gogarten, *Demythologizing and History*, trans. N. Horton Smith, 1955, 77f.

31. Karl Barth, *Romans*, Preface to the first edition, 1.

32. What follows is quoted from *Romans*, 7.

33. R. Bultmann, *CW* 36, 1922, 320–3, 330–4, 358–61, 369–73.

34. A. Schlatter, *Die Furche* 12, 1922, 228–32.

35. *Op. cit.*, 18.

36. What follows is deliberately taken from Bultmann's article 'Über das Problem einer theologischen Exegese des Neuen Testamentes', *Zwischen den Zeiten*, 1925, 334ff., when he had not yet found the hermeneutic key of 'existentialist interpretation' as he presents it in 'The Significance of "Dialectical Theology" for the Scientific Study of the New Testament', *Faith and Understanding* I, 1969, 145ff.

37. R. Bultmann, *Jesus and the Word*, trans. L. P. Smith, 1958, 11ff.

38. H. Plessner, *Die Stufen des Organischen*, 1928; id., *Lachen und Weinen*, ³1961, 47ff.; F. J. J. Buytendijk, *Das Menschliche. Wege zu seinem Verständnis*, 1958, 39ff.; A. Portmann, *Biologie und Geist*, 1954, 64.

39. R. Bultmann, *CW* 34, 1920, 452; *Faith and Understanding*, 144, 147; *Glauben und Verstehen* III, 116 and frequently.

40. A. Gehlen, 'Über die Geburt der Freiheit aus der Entfremdung', *Archiv für Rechts- und Sozialphilosophie*, 1952, 350. There is no access from the thesis of the non-objectifiability of existence to an adequate understanding of social institutions and organizations. Bultmann's article 'Forms of Human Community', *Essays*, 1955, 291ff., shows the alliance, mentioned above, between existentialist theology and F. Tönnies' criticism of society: 'There is a threat to the genuine nature of historical community through convention and organization' (*op. cit.*, 294), and W. H. Riehls' criticism of the metropolis ('The cities play us false . . .', Rilke, quoted on p. 295), and O. Spengler's dark prophecies, as they re-echo in Gogarten (cf. the quotation on p. 296). Cf. also F. Lieb, 'Geschichte und Heilsgeschichte in der Theologie Rudolf Bultmanns', *EvTh* 15, 1955, 507ff.

41. Cf. F. Nietzsche, the first two aphorisms of the second discussion on 'Genealogie der Moral'. For the anthropological significance of promising cf. O. F. Bollnow, *Wesen und Wandel der Tugenden*, 1958, 168ff.: 'Becoming oneself in keeping promises'. For the social and political significance of promising and of the theory of the state contract cf. H. Arendt, *Vita activa*, 1960, 239ff.: 'The incalculability of facts and the power of the promise'.

42. *The Phenomenology of Mind*, trans. J. B. Baillie, 1910, 667f.

43. *Being and Time*, trans. John Macquarrie and Edward Robinson, 1962, 63 and frequently.

44. For the origin of this thesis in romanticism and its significance for contemporary political and social romanticism see C. Graf von Krockow, *op. cit.*; for philosophical discussion see W. Müller-Lauter, *Möglichkeit und Wirklichkeit bei M. Heidegger*, 1960.

45. M. Heidegger, *Being and Time*, 428.

46. *Ibid.*, 433.

47. *Ibid.*, 429f.; similarly, R. Bultmann, *Faith and Understanding*, 149f. and F. Gogarten, *Demythologizing and History*, 38.

48. *Being and Time*, 447.

49. *Ibid.*, 444.

50. *Ibid.*, 443f.

51. Cf. *Holzwege*, 1957.

52. *Ibid.*, 92.

53. *Ibid.*, 301.

54. The expression 'put oneself in the air' comes from F. Overbeck and was a favourite expression of early dialectical theology. F. Overbeck, *Christentum und Kultur*, 1919, 77, thinks: '. . . we men only advance at all by putting ourselves in the air from time to time and by living our life under conditions which do not permit us to avoid this experiment'; 286: 'He who really and rigorously puts himself on himself in the world must also find the courage to put himself on nothing.' Cf. Max Stirner's phrase, 'I have put my concern on nothing.' Karl Barth, *Romans*, 98f. (on 3.22): 'Faith is . . . a leap into the darkness of the unknown, into empty air, . . . the most hazardous of all hazards.' F. Gogarten, *Die religiöse Entscheidung*, 1921, 21: Before God one enters on the unconditional: 'Here man puts himself in the air . . .'; R. Bultmann, *Kerygma und Mythos* II, 207: 'The man who wants to believe in God as his God must know that he has nothing in his hand on the basis of which he might believe, that he is so to speak put in the air and can require no proof for the truth of the word that addresses him.'

55. W. Kamlah, *Wissenschaft, Wahrheit, Existenz*, 1960, 70.

56. Cf. E. Käsemann's apt interpretation, *Essays on New Testament Themes*, trans. W. J. Montague, 1964, 30f.

57. E. Käsemann, *op. cit.*, 15ff., esp. 32ff.

58. This is what Luther means in *De servo arbitrio* (WA 18, 606ff.), when in scripture he finds the *public* proclamation of the mysteries of God and, therefore, speaks of the *claritas scripturae*. Cf. H. J. Iwand's comments in: *M. Luthers ausgewählte Werke*[3], suppl. vol. 1, 1940, 317ff.; W. Pannenberg, *op. cit.*, 33ff.; K. G. Steck, 'Verlegenheiten der Theologie heute', *Unter der Herrschaft Christi*, 1961, 14: 'We can only really follow Luther's thought if we relate the biblical testimony to Easter to a – *horribile dictu* – general truth; not go back to, but relate.'

59. W. Kamlah, *op. cit.*, 65: 'No one, not even Kierkegaard, would be satisfied to lead a successful life by himself, privately, but here everyone thinks in anticipatory terms and once again, in an astonishing way, "universally".'

60. E. Rothacker, 'Die dogmatische Denkform in den Geisteswissenschaften und das Problem der Historismus', *Abhandlungen der geistes- und sozialwissenschaftliche Klasse der Akademie der Wissenschaften Mainz*, 1954, no. 6, 56.

61. E. Rothacker, *op. cit.*, 48.

62. One of Bultmann's early statements takes this line, *CW* 34, 1920, 451: 'There is no history of religion. There cannot be, if the life of religion is not present in objective forms but in individual life. There are no problems in religion in the sense of historical problems and solutions, of progress, etc., but always one and the same problem, which must always be given a

new individual solution: to find the power in the face of which free self-sacrifice is possible.'

63. *Der Historismus und seine Probleme*, 1922, 131.

64. Cf. C. Hinrichs, *Ranke und die Geschichtstheologie der Goethezeit*, 1954, 165; F. Meinecke, 'Deutung eines Rankewortes', *Zur Theorie und Philosophie der Geschichte*, 1959, 117ff.

65. E. Troeltsch, *Gesammelte Schriften* II, 1922, 734.

66. J. G. Droysen, *Historik* § 82, ³1958, 357.

67. P. Ehrenberg, 'Every formulation of natural law is a self-portrait of man. It is the structure that he acknowledges for himself and his life. . . . Tragic man wears a mask and embodies a mystery that no one, himself included, understands; but the man of natural law, who is the measure of all things, is portrayed in the self-portrait.' Quoted by E. Wolf, *Gottesrecht und Menschenrecht*, Theologische Existenz Heute, NF 42, 1954, 11.

68. *Die Absolutheit des Christentums*, ²1912, 30.

69. Cf. M. Kähler, *Dogmatische Zeitfragen* I, 1898, 252: '. . . eschatology discloses the meaning of history for theology. As surely as a scientific understanding of Christianity, i.e. the biblical revelation, is impossible without an understanding of history, so surely, in its eschatology, theology protects a tremendously important treasure for its own prosperity and for the fructification of all anthropological and historical research, which is not satisfied only to ascertain the probable and the real but also wants to understand the processes.'

70. *Glauben und Verstehen* III, 119.

71. E. Bloch, *Philosophische Grundfragen* I, *Zur Ontologie des Noch-Nicht-Seins*, 1961, 15.

72. *Glauben und Verstehen* III, 113; similarly 'Die christliche Hoffnung und das Problem der Entmythologisierung' (part of a broadcast discussion subsequently published), 1954, 54; *Glauben und Verstehen* III, 148ff.

73. Cf. A. A. van Ruler, *Theologie van het Apostolaat*, 1954, 43ff.; 'Apostolaat en Geschiedenis'.

74. *Glauben und Verstehen* III, 150.

75. *Glauben und Verstehen* III, 14.

76. G. Ebeling, *Word and Faith*, trans. J. W. Leitch, 1963, 298. Where is the support for the thesis, so often to be found in Bultmann, on the meaninglessness of world history and the consequent restriction of meaningfulness exclusively to the history or historicity of the individual? Is this a reaction against Hegel, following Kierkegaard's example, or the feeling of resignation so common in the twenties? How is each man to find meaning for himself and his history without orientation in his social and world-historical situation, without a fixed location in the present? How is he to find meaning in the history which he *is* in his own particular unique and present historicity, if not through orientation to that history which he *has* and will have together with others? Besides, Bultmann's existentialist concept of history represents a quite definite fixed location for man in modern times which does not conceal its culturally critical and ideological elements.

77. Cf. J. Körner's analysis, *Eschatologie und Geschichte: Eine Untersuchung des Begriffs des Eschatologischen in der Theologie Rudolf Bultmanns*, 1957.

78. G. Ebeling against E. Käsemann, *ZTK* 58, 1961, 240f.: 'To think
of God and history together in the name of Jesus necessarily leads to a
criticism of apocalyptic, but not necessarily to a reinterpretation of apocalyptic as a universal historical concept of revelation, of Hegelian proven-
ance. Rather, it means that through the word, God shows his power over
history by bringing the power of history to an end by liberating it for his
present. In this way, the eschatological tension which apocalyptic produces
is radically established, as is the case in Luther's doctrine of the two kingdoms, which forms the basic structure of his theology.' Behind this thought
lies the idea of Kierkegaard that in confrontation with the absolute there is
only one time, namely, the present. But with this concept one comes very
close to the Greek way of thinking about the epiphany of the eternal present.
Certainly apocalyptic stands under the symbol of the 'distance of God'. But
the situation of the believer, so long as he lives 'in the body', is the situation
of 'being away from the Lord' (II Cor. 5.6). That makes faith into hope and
the spirit in which God is present becomes the 'pledge' and 'guarantee' of a
coming present in glory.

79. E. Bloch, *op. cit.*, 12f.

80. For the question of typology cf. especially H. W. Wolff, *EvTh* 16,
1956, 356ff.; 20 1960, 225ff.; and O. Weber, 'Typologie', *Evangelische
Kirchenlexikon*, 1959, cols. 1523–6. I understand typology to be the question
about the context of meaning that eludes the observation of the plain
actuality of events by searching for the finality and intentionality of the
event. It is not satisfied to report accidental facts. But at the same time it is
not the method for a metaphysical philosophy of history. It does not result in
an unbroken chain of all events, but rather emphasizes only those which are,
at the same time, the proclamation of coming events.

81. H. W. Wolff, *EvTh* 20, 1960, 220.

82. *De civitate Dei*, X, 32. Cf. A. Wachtel, *Geschichtstheologie des A.
Augustinus*, 1960, 27ff.

83. Cf. E. Fülling, *Geschichte als Offenbarung*, 1956, 64 and *RGG³*, III 370.

84. Dilthey, *op. cit.*, VII, 6. Cf. O. F. Bollnow, *Das Lebensphilosophie*,
1958, 40ff.

85. For the dogmatic aspect of this question cf. J. Moltmann, *Prädesti-
nation und Perseveranz*, 1961.

86. The following account draws on M. Heidegger, *Being and Time*, 441f.

87. *Ibid.*, 442.

88. *Ibid.*, 443.

PERSPECTIVES OF CHRISTIANITY
IN MODERN SOCIETY

PART TWO

PERSPECTIVES OF CHRISTIANITY
ON MODERN SOCIETY

4

THE UNDERSTANDING OF HISTORY
IN CHRISTIAN SOCIAL ETHICS[1]

I   *The disclosure of the reality of man*

1. Possibilities for a sociological concept of reality

The question of God's commandment in the real human situation always presupposes a definite understanding, a specific disclosure of reality in the horizon of which the question can be raised and the answer found. However, the reality of man and his world, as it appears within the phenomenon of existence, is continually the object of very different human modes of consideration. Consequently, the question arises whether sociology and theology even have the same reality as the object of their consideration and whether, if this is the case, a co-operation or even an interdependence can be shown to exist between the two. Theology will always have to start from the fact that it speaks about the very reality of man that also confronts sociology. Were this not the case, the statements of theology would only be the arbitrary and non-binding agreements of a religious group. But if theology speaks at all about 'the true man', destiny, justification, the demands made on man and his destiny, then its statements ought to be valid apart from faith. It must stand the test in the reality that has been entrusted to man. In other words, that which surrounds man and that reality with which he has been entrusted are one and the same.

In that case, the question arises whether from a methodological point of view the scientific aspects of sociology and theology may be separated from one another, so that in the comprehension of the one reality a reciprocal complementing of

both aspects is possible. In the discussion which was started by
H. Schelsky and has been carried on since about 1957 in the
Zeitschrift für evangelische Ethik,[2] the ground has been prepared,
at least on the part of sociology, for such a differentiation:

That the tendency towards statements of faith, i.e. ideology-free
statements, is today a fundamental value of social science and one by
which it measures its scientific character is to be accepted in the same
way as the tendency of theology to understand itself more than other
disciplines in terms of faith and being founded on faith . . . the compulsion to extend the various aspects of *all* disciplines into their
scientific legitimation leads to an awareness of an interdependence
and co-operation between the sciences which cannot be documented
by a universal claim or by faith and value judgments.[3]

Schelsky therefore speaks of parallel statements of a sociological
and a theological nature, and in so doing asks sociology to
abstain from making confessions of faith and value-judgments.[4]
The question is, however, whether theology can accept the
place assigned to it. The 'confession of faith' slips into the sphere
of subjective arbitrariness and the secondary evaluation of
conditions which have been demonstrated by sociology. However, the real question does not arise first in the confrontation
of sociology with religious groups in the social realm, groups
whose particular views and practices the sociologist makes the
subject of an analysis; on the contrary, the question already
arises where the sociologist has to understand that concept of
reality which he has accepted, i.e. in the problem of the particular horizon of disclosure of reality in which he can identify,
designate and understand social conditions and processes. If
sociology is the 'science of reality' (H. Freyer), then the question
of the context of the meaning of the conditions which are to be
pointed out must necessarily be asked, if they are to be understandable. Otherwise sociology will be confronted with the task
of analysing a meaningless world of unrelated facts or uncontrollable processes. Here the problem of understanding arises
with urgency for sociology as it had already developed within
the science of history in the trend towards historicism. The
dilemma arises in which the peculiar structure of understanding

is illustrated of which Troeltsch said: 'If one surrenders oneself to real history, the idea vanishes; if one constructs from the idea, then real history vanishes.'[5] Thus, though Western sociology even today thinks that it must oppose its ideological past and follow the tendency to 'de-ideologize', note must be taken that sociology, precisely through the freedom from value judgments for which it has striven, defames the social process as being a world of facts which is devoid of meaning and consequently is itself in danger of becoming an 'instrument of conformism' (Sontheimer).[6] The social function of sociological analysis itself remains in a vacuum, free from social pressures, in which the problem of understanding is not considered, because human activity in its possibilities is always connected with the understandability of activity – otherwise it has no social relevance.[7]

This statement is not an attempt to provoke a new ideologizing of the social sciences. However, the thesis ought to be presented that the common ground between sociology and theology is found not only in the common reality which confronts both but also in the problem of the way in which the understanding of this reality is to be experienced. In what context does sociology identify the social processes and interpret them? In the horizon of which context of meaning and promise does Christian theology understand the history of these processes? For sociology the concrete question is whether it will find a path between neo-positivism on the one hand and the Marxist (or Marxist-type) science of society on the other; between an abandonment (however hypothetical) of such a context of meaning in order to grasp the unique and unrepeatable quality of the situation, and an ideologically comprehensive view of the social processes in order to be able to understand the individual facts.[8]

2. The theological concept of reality

(a) *The eschatological disclosure of reality as history.* For a biblical, Israelite Christian theology, the reality of man is understood through an eschatological disclosure to be 'history'. The course of history is determined and directed by a once-for-all, radical, unique, unrepeatable event. God's action is not seen in that which is repeatable or which remains the same, or in that which is taken from time and history, as for example in the eternal laws and regularity of nature. Rather, it is seen in the unique and unrepeatable quality of temporal contingency. Israel did not flee from the terrors of history into natural eternal laws, the cyclical time of the eternal return. On the contrary, she recognized and expected the coming of God with the incalculable events themselves.[9] The Greek man stands in 'the epiphany of the eternal present'; the Israelite-Christian man stands in the 'apocalypse of that which is coming'. He expects truth to come out of the future of God and not out of the appearance of that which is always in the present of eternity.[10] He experiences a truly 'open', namely an eschatologically open, world and he experiences his reality as a history which is unique and unrepeatable, irreversable and oriented towards a goal; he does not experience his reality as eternal nature which always remains the same in the cyclical pattern of its process.[11]

Thus a singular historical consciousness develops out of the Israelite-Christian understanding of reality. In Luther this bursts out again so to speak in the form of an intuitive recognition, when he says in regard to Rom. 8.19:

Aliter Apostolus de rebus philosophatur et sapit quam philosophi et metaphysici. Quia philosophi oculum ita in presentiam rerum immergunt, ut solum quidditates et qualitates earum speculentur, Apostolus autem oculos nostros revocat ab intuitu rerum presentium, ab essentia et accidentibus earum et dirigit in eas secundum quod future sunt. Non enim dicit 'essentia' vel 'operatio' creaturae seu 'actio' et 'passio' et 'motus', sed novo et miro vocabulo et theologico dicit 'expectatio creaturae',[12]

and elsewhere he writes:

Christ has a strange language and grammar. . . . Because we are to become new men, he wants us to have new and different thoughts, understandings and feelings, and to see nothing according to reason as it is found in the world, but rather as man perceives it, because he wants us to direct ourselves towards that coming and invisible new being for which we can hope and which is to follow this suffering and miserable being.[13]

This specific historical consciousness was powerfully developed by Hegel and the philosophical school which followed him in the nineteenth century. However, only now has knowledge of the biblical disclosure of reality as history, as opposed to the Greek question of essence and the Greek idea of the cosmos, established a new direction in Protestant theology. Our task is to be that of thinking theology through in terms of the ethical problem of 'order and decision'. In order to do this, we must, however, first ask what kind of effect this knowledge could have for Christian anthropology. Seen theologically, the axiom of historicism – 'man does not have a nature but a history' – can be accepted when we define what man's history is.[14] According to the biblical conception, man is identified and determined in and through that history in which he is incorporated by God's covenant and promise. His 'essence', and that means his identity and continuity, is determined by the call of God, by his being called to a partnership in the covenant, by the event of justification.

In this call, man recognizes himself as himself in this one continually new and never recurring hour. Identity in calling is not continuing identity; it is rather a unique condition which cannot be repeated.[15]

But is man then conditioned by the fortuitousness and instability of those events which happen to him and is he, therefore, in the end no longer identifiable at all, but rather a conglomerate of reactions and functions? Certainly not. If man is constituted through God's call, then he is also determined by that faithfulness of God in which through the events of coming history God shows himself to be the same God and, in a surprising way, nevertheless acknowledges faithfulness to his convenant and to those men whom he has chosen (Ps. 146.6).[16] God shows himself within the history of Israel as the God of Abraham, Isaac and Jacob by remaining faithful to his unique promises and fulfilling them. God is proved to be the Father of Jesus Christ in the apocalypse of history. In such faithfulness, continuity and stability occur within the unsteadiness of historical events. Similarly, man's humanity can be found only in this faithfulness

which is controlled historically and eschatologically by God.
These events include man's faithfulness to himself. Continuity
and identity, that is, man himself, may be acquired by man in
history only in acceptance of his past, in confession to himself
(e.g. in the confession of sins), in faithfulness to promises and in
thankfulness (e.g. in praise). This is a continuity which is
acquired through each new act of identification. Man 'remains'
alone here. But he does not 'remain' through a forfeiture of
history or a denial of his historicity. Man cannot be identified
by abstracting permanent characteristic traits from his concrete
history which may be found at all times and in all places because they are presumably at all times and in all places the
foundation for his historical appearances. The man who is
determined by eschatological revelation does not stand in the
epiphany of that which is timeless and eternal, but rather in the
apocalypse of that which is 'temporal and coming'.

(b) *The christological disclosure of reality as world.* It follows that
a Christian theology sees the reality of man as a godless, worldly
reality, disclosed by the revelation of God in the cross of Christ.
If the whole of man's reality is accepted by God in the cross,
then at the same time man's reality is revealed to him in the
cross as a reality which is both directed and forsaken by God.
God's reality in the reality of the world is a hidden event, hidden
in the figure of the crucified and rejected one. The worldly
reality of man is revealed in the dialectic of the God-forsakenness of the Son of God. For this reason, Christianity can never
lend itself to a supernatural religious glorification of the world,
because this cross of God, which it proclaims, discloses the
radical worldliness of the world, disenchants the cosmos trans-
figured by the 'gods' and destines man to live and to suffer in
the present *'etsi deus non daretur'.* Free from the law, free from
the στοιχεῖα τοῦ κόσμου, he finds himself in a godless world
which is borne and taken up only in the cross of Christ. This is
not the world on which one can depend. It is the world in which
God has suffered; only the cross makes it possible to accept it in
its total worldliness, through self-abandonment and sacrifice.[17]

Secular consciousness as well as *historical consciousness* has its roots in the Israelite Christian tradition. An understanding of the worldliness of human reality is based, in a radical way, on the event of the revelation of God in the cross of Christ. Again, Protestant theology has only recently realized this knowledge of the profanity of human reality as opposed to a Greek glorification of the cosmos by holy orders and institutions. Its importance, however, has as yet not been fully recognized.

(c) *The pneumatological disclosure of reality as confrontation with God.* Nevertheless, the above-mentioned historicization and secularization of human reality cannot be equated with relativism and secularism, for the events of history and the world are disclosed in the confrontation with God through the spirit. Here history is truly 'open', and man's protective casing will keep being shattered, in that a new, promised and yet surprising encounter will occur and must be expected in the dawning future. This fundamental eschatological openness and unfinished quality of reality makes relative those ordinances in which human behaviour becomes habitual, so that they become open processes of the integration of God's history. The human desire to shape things cannot be completed in history, and is continually challenged to produce new answers through the openness of the future. This and the human desire to escape from such 'terrors of history' can be explained both on the basis of 'the constitution of man as being at risk' (Gehlen) and of man's character as a 'utopian being' (Ortega y Gasset) that is continually directed ahead of itself. However, in that case one will be able to interpret these utopian powers of man in terms of the sociology of knowledge and to speak of an increasing atrophy of man's ability to be critical of existence in the emergence of a perfect society (K. Mannheim).[18] Theologically, we may say that man is an eschatologically determined being and that his history is controlled by eschatological transcendence in its unique aspects. Determined by eschatological revelation, he experiences the future of truth as history. As a result, there can be no chiliastic perfection or perfection in history. Man always expresses the risk of his constitution in those utopias and ideals in which he attempts to master the future. Every utopia is true 'because it expresses the essence of man, namely, the inner goal of his existence', declared Paul Tillich.[19] But in this way every utopia is untrue and turns truth into lies by transforming the promise, which occurs in the word, into an image. The Old Testament prohibition against the creating of false images is pre-eminently valid against man's eschatological expectation. This prohibition of false images is not an arbitrary ceremonial law, but rather corresponds profoundly to the reality of God's history. The petrifying of the history of human societies within a status which negates the future will always be shattered by man's eschatologically unfinished quality. It appears either in boredom or in revolutions, to which the Spirit is provoked by all the attempts to negate history.[20] Consequently, nothing can be acquired from Christian faith for the stabilizing of normative conceptions of order in an unstable world. There is, however, the wider horizon, an eschaton of all history which is itself historical and yet no longer historical. There is no security in history, though there is an eschatological horizon for all historical processes.

In a similar way, this worldliness can hardly be endured without illusion or resignation unless in and under it one expects and believes in a confrontation with God in the Spirit. It is the life in the Spirit which holds this freedom open to man. Only the certainty of being kept in openness, in the flowing relativities of history, communicates the courage to be in this history and the freedom for sacrifice in it. Conversely, it is not a part of man's timeless essence to transcend the reality of the present in the Spirit; rather, this essence is constituted by the preservation in the Spirit of his historicity that is to be expected from God's faithfulness. In the hidden faithfulness of the Spirit, man is directed ahead of himself; he acquires future – not an automatic future but rather a historical future – in the departure from the ever-tempting subterfuges of history into nature and its cyclical pattern or an artificial nature produced by technology and its rhythms. He acquires continuity in the midst of changing conditions in as far as he acquires future. He acquires future in as far as he is at no point raised above history into that which is timeless; he does, however, precede everything into the future.

II   Order and decision

1. The sociological criticism of today's cultural values

Out of the abundance of modern sociological analyses of our situation, we have chosen a particular orientation. The reason for this will become clear when we go on to discuss the theological doctrines of ordinances. The following tendencies in our present situation are often mentioned:

(a) We find ourselves today in a rapid transition from an agricultural to an industrial society. With the progress of automation in industrial societies, we find ourselves in a 'second technical revolution'. Those communities which bind man in his whole humanity are being replaced by social, artificial and organized bonds. Man is forced to forsake the security of the rhythms of nature and falls into the uncertain ground of the historical process with its prospects and its catastrophes. Conditions become unsteady; man becomes manipulable. His countryside becomes a milieu. In place of permanent obligations, he is asked for an unlimited capacity to conform. His concrete and immediate experiences are replaced by vicarious and artificial experiences in films, television, etc. The place of organically developed orders is taken by organizations; the business or the industry takes the place of the parish-based market. Vocation for life is replaced by a job for a particular space of time. Man acquires a freedom which hitherto was inconceivable and, at the same time, loses the ground under his feet. All ordinances become unstable and lack both certainty and driving force. Man creates for himself, so to speak, a second, artificial nature within the technically organized system of goals.[21]

In establishing and identifying what really is happening here, sociology is in part strongly influenced by evaluations that are critical of culture. F. Tönnies, whose influence may be seen down to H. Freyer and others, attempted to comprehend these events in his concepts of 'community' and 'society':

The relationship itself, and therefore man's obligation, is understood either as a real and organic life (this is the essence of community) or as an ideal and mechanical formation (this is the essence of society). . . . Community is permanent and authentic life together, while society is only a temporary and fictitious life together. Accordingly, it is the community itself that ought to be understood as a living organism and society as a mechanical aggregate and artefact.[22]

This can be shown to be a theory which has developed from a spontaneous reaction to the high capitalism of the period of promoterism, to a German class-differentiated society at the turn of the century, by youth movements and nationalism. If 'nation' and 'nationality' were at that time the entities in which men hoped to find natural unity and organic wholeness, the lost experience of community which was to weld the classes together again, this hope was altered by Tonnies' students and is today mainly directed towards a regaining of 'Western humanity'. H. Freyer describes 'society's' mode of being as a 'secondary system' in the following way:

An existence in a totally artificial world which reduces life to the factory, freedom to free time, happiness to comfort, humanity to a humanitarian social programme which scarcely conceals the cruelty of the system. . . .[23]

He still, however, has the following hope:

In fact humanity is, in each individual case, an island – an island of meaning in a world which is certainly not meaningless but is non-human – an island which, whether it has been reached by calm sailing, by adventure or by shipwreck, must now be preserved. . . If it were possible . . . to establish a humanity which was a match for this secondary system, then that ground would be given back to this system which it has itself dug up.[24]

For Freyer, it is conceivable that European nations have expended their energy in the production of the industrial system and that, in the course of generations, human powers will be available for new industrial areas which could meet the needs of the industrial situation in a surprising way.[25] If Freyer hopes that 'the artificial' can be transformed into 'the human', pro-

vided that the secondary system could acquire a human foundation at some point, Mackenroth thinks that 'in the realization of
his ultimate form, the self-sacrificing man himself . . . (becomes)
wholly form, a receptacle for the influx of transcendent power',[26]
while D. Riesman wants to contrast his 'lonely crowd' with
an 'individualism reconsidered'. In these Western circles the
expectation is evidently of a personalistic ek-stasis from the
senseless demonic determinations of a technological world,
which is possible only for the élite. Demands for 'abstinence
from consumption' and 'partial non-communication', for
instance, take over the role of catharsis in this gnostic religiosity
of the late European spirit – if one does not give oneself over to
a mood of destruction.

(*b*) At the same time, an unsuspected freedom has developed
for man with the increasing mechanization and organization of
life. The new compulsions of matter and forms of life are no
longer conceived of as 'a complete expression of an inner
quality' (Freyer); they only encounter man, subsume him and
are 'thrown over him like a net' (Freyer). Consciousness is
unburdened by automated processes and man, released from
them, reaches out for hobbies and other games. On the other
hand, the quasi-automatic compulsion of circumstances is
matched by a growing pluralistic arbitrariness of projections of
meaning with a non-binding character that is so typical for our
time; no world view or religion is binding in the positivism of
technological intelligence.

It is plain how, in these sociological representations of both
tendencies, whether consciously or unconsciously, a theory of
descent that is critical of culture is up to its tricks. Such prejudices from the philosophy of history are, however, inadequate
for anthropological understanding of what really happens in
industrial concerns and consumer society.[27]

If one can cautiously extract one thing from this analysis of
the cultural movement today, it is certainly the fact that man's
natural strata are increasingly carried over into the historical-
social process. Man and his conditions become more mobile,
changeable and movable than they ever were before. Today

man can no longer find that which is eternal and continuing, that which gives him a firm foundation, either in his nature or in his circumstances – but could he ever find it? He must find himself within the continuity and the process of history itself.

2. The theological concept of ordinances and the problem of history

For a long time theology has attempted to understand God's commandment in terms of the dialectic of 'order and decision'. This dialectic is inappropriate in terms both of the basic intentions of its biblical foundation and of the reality of history. For that reason, it is relatively unimportant whether a theology of ordinances develops from a doctrine of ordinances of creation or from a christological foundation. The concept of order which is both presupposed and sought for is, as such, rooted in the Greek structure of thought and logically always leads to unhistorical, naturalistic conceptions. The New Testament offers no metaphysical doctrine of ordinances. It does not refer the 'historical and unique' to universal prototypes. It does, however, offer a historically dated reality which is to be appropriated anew in every generation.[28] A theological departure from the question of stable hypotheses of order in the world and in history thus seems to be necessary and a search for pointers towards surrenders to the relativities of history to be desirable. Man and human society must acquire an eschatologically determined historicity rather than a lasting nature. The theological question is associated, usually in an unreflected way, with the universal, religious and cultural question, 'How can stable institutions develop in an unstable world and prove to be directive ethical constants?'[29] It is fatal to read immediately afterwards A. Gehlen's comment that 'man has an elementary need, instinctively rooted in his "risked" constitution, to read a maximum of order, coherence and regularity into the half-ordered interpenetration of the course of events and the world of experience'[30] and to find P. R. Hofstätter regarding as a 'superstition' towards which every man is inclined the over-estimation of the degree of order in the stream of events.[31] To what extent, then, is man's historicity included or concealed within the traditional theology of ordinances?

(*a*) The doctrine of the *ordinances of creation* is based on Luther's social and ethical understanding of the three main authorities or conditions of Christianity (church, state and society), though at the same time it is also of more recent date. Paul Althaus sees the ground being prepared in ethics for a move away from individualistic limitations to a 'theology of ordinances' after G. C. A. Harless, the founder of the Erlangen school of Lutheran ethics. The similarity of this concept of the ordinances of creation to Tonnies' 'mature communities' shows that here we have, *inter alia*, a theological answer directed against modern industrial conditions. Here is a search for preservation from the decay of ordinances and a nihilism which accompanies this decay which is found chiefly within those nationalistic thoughts that are supposed to overcome the segregation of classes. When, in his *Theologie der Ordnung* (1934), Althaus based the task of the church on these ordinances by saying that juridical thought has fundamentally turned away from positivism and looks for a metaphysical basis for the law, its authority and contents; when he hears a call for an 'ethics of ordinance' in the fact that the state stands on the ground of positive Christianity; when, finally, he takes the subject of such an ethic to be not only the action of the individual Christian or the church in the ordinances, but the ordinances themselves, then, despite his links with Luther, the modern character of this attempt becomes obvious. Althaus specifies the following almost classical principle for any theology of ordinances: (1) Ordinances are forms of man's common life, which are *indispensable conditions of human life*. (2) They are both given and enjoined. (3) They present themselves to the conscience as holy law. Nevertheless, fallen humanity is only able to hear this witness correctly through God's revelation in salvation history. (4) Faith in Christ points past the natural knowledge of ordinances because it sees these ordinances in the light of the kingdom of God. Faith recognizes the provisional character of these ordinances, their function of preservation and their didactic character. It sees in them

parables and hints of the constitution of the kingdom of God.[32]
This theology of ordinances is not thought of in terms of natural
law, but rather finds divine ordinances within the movements
of history itself. While it is superior to natural law in regard to
a certain proximity to reality, it is at the same time inferior to
natural law in regard to a certain occasionalism. Nevertheless,
there can be no question of a perception of the eschatological
significance of history when, for example, we read, 'There is no
unconditional form of marriage, but there is an unconditional
essence of marriage. There is no unconditional constitution of
the state, but there is an unconditional vocation, an unconditional essence of the state – and every constitution is to be
measured critically against this essence.' As with Tonnies, this
seems to present an unconscious escape from the terror of
history, from relativism and nihilism, into the stability of
supposedly real organisms.

(*b*) For Brunner, the ordinance of creation is connected with
the naturalism of the Western European tradition.

By this we mean those existing facts of human corporate life which
lie at the root of all historical life, as unalterable presuppositions,
which, *although their historical forms may vary, are unalterable in their
fundamental structure*, and, at the same time, relate and unite men to
one another in a definite way.[33]

As such basic structures he lists the 'communities' in which
inhuman egoism and collectivism are said to be overcome: communities of life (marriage, family, home), work, culture and
faith.

Here we see not merely particular spheres of life *within which* we are
to act, but ordinances *in accordance with which* we have to act, because
in them, even if only in a fragmentary and indirect way, God's Will
meets us. Hence we call them 'Divine ordinances'.[34]

Such a determination of man's essence and his constitution
through continuing basic structures can only be acquired
through abstraction from historical experience. It is therefore
necessary to make the history of human society into a more or
less successful image and epiphany of its eternal unchangeable

presuppositions. Karl Barth rightly objected that, according to Brunner, God's historically revealed will and the ethical event of the command are relegated to the realm of individual ethics which is itself limited by the given and natural 'basic structures'. To put it in an exaggerated way, for Brunner, the main concern is a 'fairway' ethics with individual degrees of variation.

(c) After the many difficulties to which a theology of ordinances of creation led, W. Künneth and H. Thielicke emphasized the concept of 'ordinances of preservation'.[35] With this concept, on the one hand the attempt is made to avoid an erroneous ontology of the ordinances of creation and to take seriously the reality of human sin and human blindness. On the other hand, an attempt is made to consider the theological relationship between historical ordinances after the fall and Christ and salvation, without falling directly into a christological ethic of revelation. Within the chaos of sin, God's good order is the original remembrance of God's intention for creation and, at the same time, a means for God's eschatological goal. These writers therefore speak of 'interim ordinances' between the fall and the eschaton or of Noachite emergency ordinances. Now a certain historical element has been incorporated into this concept of ordinances. At the same time, however, man's authentic eschatological historicity is hidden. Here world history runs, so to speak, in great steps and through mutations of salvation history, which contain their time and their cosmos in themselves: ordinance of creation – ordinance of preservation or interim ordinance – ordinance of the kingdom of God. One evidently acquires possibilities for the stabilization of ordinances from the 'not yet' of the eschaton. The Noachite emergency ordinance remains in force until the 'last judgment'. This eschatology of the 'last judgment' means, however, that the eschatologically important elements in our age are bracketed off and put in suspension. The eschatological Christian element here appears only in situations of conflict; symbolically it appears each time on the frontiers of firmly established orders.[36]

(d) In his *Ethics*, Dietrich Bonhoeffer replaced the concept of ordinance with that of the mandate. He wanted to overcome the deplorably unrelated juxtaposition of imposed order and decisions made in the face of the real command and understood the mandate (marriage, state, work, culture, church), like the decalogue, as that law of life of the one lordship of Christ which encompasses all of human reality. All possible statements about worldly ordinances are based on Christ and, for that reason, must be related to him as the origin, essence and goal of everything that is created.[37] Mandates are not eternal structures of human existence but rather are historical functions of God's active lordship. They are, nevertheless, not historical and transitory, but rather 'extend to the borders of time' and continue up to the end. Bonhoeffer selected the word 'mandate' because it 'refers more clearly to a divinely imposed task rather than to a determination of being'.[38] The concept of the mandate is directed at true obedience. In consequence, the 'ordinances cannot be the second divine authority alongside the God of Jesus Christ, but must rather be understood as the 'place in which the God of Jesus Christ obtains obedience'. God's word is concerned not with the ordinances in themselves, but with the obedience of faith within these ordinances. One might say that the ordinances of the world fade into secular spheres before the real event of command and obedience. They lose that normative character that is attributed to them by the unconscious force of tradition or by religious glorification and become the concrete places within, on and against which the 'temporal future' represents itself and within which history takes place. This, then, is somehow in line with what Paul says in I Cor. 7.20ff., where his concern is the relationship between the divine word and the social sphere. Still, the normative character of natural law remains in Bonhoeffer's concept of the mandate, when the mandates are referred to as that particular historical form in which God gives his command,[39] and when the selection and elimination of the mandates established by him cannot be founded either anthropologically or biblically, but rather only historically, on the basis of the process of Western history.

(*e*) Since 1945, an attempt has been made in the Commission for Church Law to reconcile the problem contained within the dialectic of foundation and shaping acceptance by the choice of the concept of institution (H. Dombois):

(i) Institutions are the *expressions of typical forms of relation* which are thoroughly capable of being shaped but are given in their outline. (ii) The realization of the institutions needs an act of acceptance. Institutions are not first created through the realization of acceptance and sacrifice. . . (iii) The reality of institutions is not only a condition but a process. The unity between condition and process is resolved in the character of the institution as foundation.

So run the 1956 theses.[40] But the foundation of this 'outline' givenness remains uncertain. The institutions which are understood as fundamental human traits seem to elude any material grasp although their given and enjoined character asserts itself in every human confrontation. So the commission's final discussions return more than before to the historicity of the institutions.

Institutions, however they may be conceived as fundamental human traits, stand within the history of human existence. . . . This is true above all of their change in nature with the transformation of social conditions in connection with which the question remains open as to whether this change embraces the totality of their essence (perhaps even their membership in the category of institutions), or whether a lasting contour in them escapes transformation.[41]

Partly anthropological elements (degrees of existentiality) and partly biblical and salvation-historical elements (supralapsarian or infralapsarian foundation) are presented for the identification of the institutions.

In my opinion, a tendency to conceal real history keeps recurring in the applied image of the theology of ordinances. Whether one speaks of the 'island of natural law in the ebb and flow of positive law' (Ellul), or of 'unchangeable basic structures' (Brunner), or the 'conditions of man's historical life' (Althaus), or 'interim ordinances', or of 'God's fundamental structures for the preservation and ordering of human society', of immovable starting points which are determinative for the Christian social ethics of all ages and under all social systems (H.- D. Wendland),[42] one can always stumble upon a timeless foundation under the quicksand of history which is to give a lasting foundation to the house of human society. The question of stable orders in an unstable world can never be answered by denying their historicity in small points. The recognition that man does not have nature but history means an overcoming of all the naturalistic or quasi-naturalistic ways of thinking. That which is lasting, about which questions are asked, can be neither that which is timeless and eternal beneath the flood of appearances nor an uncontrollable frame, outline or archetype to which one can refer back for repetition and illustration in order to transcend concrete time. Rather, it must be an influential continuity which is understood in terms of the goal and the end of history, within history itself. The order itself is not lasting. What is lasting is rather that which is endured (by God) and is to be endured (by men). Corrective constants are not to be found as 'islands' in the rough sea of history, but rather as waves which point the ship towards the mouth of the river. Therefore we do not need to ask about the eternal ground to the degree that we need to ask about the eschatological goal and the historical openness of those traditional institutions and organizations which are directed towards the coming event which is grasped in the promise of God.

III   *The ethical decision and the problem of continuity*

1. The other side of the problem

By refusing to accept the traditional theology of ordinances we now seem to have gone to the opposite extreme, that of an individualistic decisionism – there is no fixed order, no lasting relationship, no institutional foundation under man's feet; man is thrown into the stream of history and can only make decisions at the moment in question. He finds himself placed in a chronic state of alarm in which he must continually shape and find himself. Although all possibilities are infinitely open to him, his decision never becomes reality, because he must continually overcome every decision once more. He stands over against a flood of seemingly meaningless facts and is able to acquire meaning for himself and for the present goals of his concrete, private sphere only through his own decision.[43] This permanent decision in the permanent questionability of existence is an unreasonable demand. The ethical 'concretism' of the sceptical generation remains abstract.

For the theologian, this dilemma certainly arises when he no longer reads God's commandments in the Bible as expressions of timelessly valid norms for all men – the decalogue as a new version of natural law (Melanchthon) – but rather as the historical will of God at particular points in history, when historical research shows him that all commandments and instructions in the Bible are determined by the particular situation and so emphatically warns him against taking over the Bible directly, as it abandons him at that point where a 'translation into our situation' is demanded. To the degree to which the 'there and then' is ascertained in his unique historical character, the 'here and now' becomes open and arbitrary. Where can a constancy of divine spheres in history be found? Where do the commands point out beyond themselves into history and become binding for the time to come? If no answers can be found here, the radical historicizing of human existence leads to a short-term unhistorical existence.

2. The overcoming of decisionism in Karl Barth

It is Barth who, in his doctrine of creation (*Church Dogmatics* III 4, 3ff.), first attempts to move from the ethical punctualism with which he began in his early period, to an ethical field theory, without falling again into a static unhistorical consideration of ordinances. For Barth, as for Brunner, God's commandment is not a law that hovers over given reality without having any relationship to it. It is God's commandment which has created, redeemed and saved this reality. Christ's command is not ultimately foreign to human reality, for it is 'the reality' ('he came to his own') that is hidden under the offence of the cross. His command corresponds to reality in a parallel which is, however, concealed by suffering in a world alienated from God but which, nevertheless, appears in the apocalypse of history. If this is correct, then between the God who commands and the man who is called there can only be a sporadic point of confrontation, a tangent-like contact, which has no effect, and the field on which this confrontation takes place. Its field, its text, its material principle is the context, the arrangement and the differentiation of history in which, according to God's word, the ethical event is found, in which it forms a moment. As I see it, man's reality here is no longer addressed as a relatively intact cosmos of order which encompasses certain areas of freedom for obedience, but is consistently 'history'. We must therefore ask about the continuities and relationships of the history of both the divine command and human fulfilment and transgression. We need not, however, ask about eternal norms, outlines, islands or foundation-stones.

This *history* is the reality in which the ethical event takes place, to which we look from the event and from which we must look back to the event in order to see it in its concreteness (III 4, 28).

Barth's special ethics attempts, therefore, to be 'more the narration of his history or description of his way than a definition of his being' (25). The main concern, seen from every step of the way that man takes in his history as the creation of God, a pardoned sinner, or a child of God confident of his future, is accordingly to point to 'the mystery of the encounter' in a way that matches its character. Here ordinances do not emerge in human reality as laws and imperative, but rather as 'spheres in which God commands and man is obedient or disobedient' (29f.). We see the historical content of the ethical event which produces no more – but also no less – than 'a definite lead in the direction of the answer' which 'is finally asked of each of us individually in his relationship to God and his fellows' (30). The determination for being in history, for being in encounter with his fellows, for the unity of body and soul and that being which is limited both by time and by God as the hope of his existence, constitutes one such contour, perhaps, for the form of man as a created being. Barth uses the image of the intersecting point between the horizontal and the vertical. The vertical, the perpendicular from above, is the moment of the encounter with the God who commands. The horizontal is the relationship of this event with history, in the past and future of God's activity, effect and revelation: the historical moment in its incalculable and surprisingly unique quality is always a moment of God's beginning, continuing and fulfilling guidance of the whole of history, a moment within the context of divine order, of the divine plan for history. Although this plan of guidance is not clear to the man who lives in time, we still have to 'take into account this connection and therefore the constancy and *continuity* of the divine command' (17). Correspondingly, human activity occurs in many single decisions. Man, in the time given him, keeps choosing a new possibility determined on the way and in this possibility he chooses and realizes himself in a new and different way. However, the activity is that of the same subject – of man. Who this man is in his identity and continuity is determined by God's activity in him:

Concrete human action thus proceeds under a divine *order* which persists in all the differentiations of individual cases. It, too, takes place in a *connection* which is *sure*, though it can seldom if ever be demonstrated. We have to take this connection into account and therefore the *permanence* and *continuity* of human activity as well (17).

The aspects which Barth considers here are at any rate a progress beyond a 'staticizing' of the historical process in the theology of ordinances and beyond decisionism. But does Barth maintain these new aspects? Does he not have an actualism which is anti-institutionalist? Can history be understood correctly in terms of the image of the vertical breaking-in and the horizontal relationship, if, first, the confrontation with God is to be understood as one in which each person must find the ethical answer for himself and, second, the contour of this event is to be understood in anthropological terms? It seems as if Barth retains this vertical breaking-in as 'a mysterious reality', certainly evident not only as an incommensurable fact in Christ but also as word and, therefore, recognizable yet still only accessible and describable within this contour. An actualistic tension continues to exist with the horizontal, historical relationship which does not allow for the correct understanding of the ethical event. There is a subjective radical obligation in the ethical decision, but the social context with the continuities and stability of human activity in history remains unclear.

3. An attempt at a historical ethic of hope[44]

If we consider the *structural ethics* sketched out above in terms of its eschatological horizon, we shall find that hope directs itself towards that which will remain, what is and was, at least until the last judgment. If one considers the decisionism of *situation ethics* in this regard, one finds that hope in the pure futurity of God is placed in each individual realization of historical existence. In both cases, the character of history as process and the present of the future are not properly understood in hope. However, one only does justice to the disclosure of reality as history sketched out above if one designs an *ethic of moral process* and if Christian ethics understands itself (like Schleiermacher's moral doctrine) as a *science of history*. What in this context is to be understood as 'process' stems from Barth's comments in regard to the 'instant' and the 'moment'. In his pedagogy, Schleiermacher realized that the temporary pedagogical decision must be completely related to the present *instant*, to the child's present historical situation and that this decision must at the same time point beyond the situation and therefore be understood as *moment* in the child's development.

Similarly, one could say that the giving of oneself to the historical *novum* of the moment is part of the ethical process. At the same time, however, a part of this process is the opening up of the horizon of the future and the observation of the past, from which the present is determined. The synthesis between the instant and the moment is found in the present of the future. The ethical decision is always related to the instant and yet still points beyond it in hope, in self-surrender to and belief in a certain future. If, however, the future is not to be made unreal as empty openness for the arbitrary character of every new plan, one must talk about a concrete future. Only in terms of a concrete future do ethical instants acquire continuity, does history become a process within the context of its events.

Definite hopes arouse definite remembrances. The past is preserved in the present by remembering when the present reaches out beyond itself into the future through hoping. Traditions are alive when hopes are aroused. When he gives up his future, man also loses his past and, therefore, his historicity and his history. 'In terms of its end: history is shaped by that which has not yet become history.'[45]

On this basis, let us examine the biblical commandments. All biblical commandments are related to a historical fact, to God's covenant at Sinai, to the coming of Jesus, to the coming of faith, to the historical event of baptism, etc. They therefore do not express timeless and eternal norms; rather, the intention of God's covenant is expressed in them. The historical fact of the covenant with that life which is offered and promised in it is not, however, merely a historical point. It is a historical event which points beyond itself into the future. The covenant is a 'historical process' or, as Ellul explains with a juristic analogy, a 'successive contract' which is not exhausted in a unique process, but whose effects continue until the time of eschatological fulfilment. To this extent, the promise of the covenant and the commandment of the covenant have lasting significance 'until the fulfilment'. To this extent, the commandment of the covenant, which is nothing but the other, ethical side of the promise and of hope, places man's reality in a tension between history and the *eschaton*. Seen in terms of the historical datum of the covenant, an eschatological horizon opens up before the present, from which historical processes are determined.

One can then go on to say that covenant and commandment are always given in history to particular men and groups (through election and calling), men and groups which, through the historical covenant and its promise, are ripped out of their previous attachment to home, nation, habit etc. and are placed in a new historical process, namely, in the history of the promise. The commandments acquire universal significance only indirectly, in as far as God sees and elects his people in Abraham. the nation in Israel; the new humanity in the church of Christ; Election and covenant always involve representation and destination for sacrifice, service and apostolate to others. In eschatological expectation and historical sacrifice, all nations and men are included in the community of the covenant of God, in the demand of his commandment and the light of his promise.

What provides direction for the community is thus included in God's history, in that society in which it exists? Promise and commandment destine the community for an eschatological fellowship, i.e. for the assembly of those who live from the hope in that future which is determined by the historical event of Jesus Christ. The characteristic is excluded from sociological analysis, at least in the way in which sociological analysis has been carried on up to now. The eschatological community of God cannot be absorbed or fitted into a social structure. Since this community only becomes what it is within the movement of hope, it fulfils its significance, which is indirectly bound up with its existence, for society – light of the world, salt of the earth. The eschatological conscience came into the world through the Bible,[46] and the church must keep it alive.

What significance for social ethics can be gathered from this?

(*a*) The people of God who travel in hope become a source of eschatological unrest within a society which attempts to save itself from history through a dream of technological perfection. The *eschatological* impatience (Claudel) of the community, however, basically corresponds to the messianic character of God's history in the world. A community which could not be assimilated could hold the social process open through its existence and its witness. That is, in this community, it can become clear that social institutions cannot overcome their temporality and relativity, their historicity. They cannot perpetuate themselves either mythically or ideologically.

(*b*) By the particular hope through which they live, the people of God who travel in hope not only become a source of unrest but also provide a *directive* for that society which, confronted with unavoidable institutional diversity, sinks into the trauma of resignation in the face of meaningless determinism. Here that future is grasped which seems to enclose man in a 'mammoth society'. Here social institutions can be made obsolete by being questioned about their final purpose and their eschatological justification.

(c) It is clear, however, that eschatological impatience and hope relate not only to man in himself, but to the whole man, to soul and body, to the individual in his social condition, namely, to a salvation which includes man in and with his conditions and his conditions in and with him. The dilemma of Christian social ethics is decisively attached to the fact that theology dares to give man hope for himself but not for the conditions in which he works and suffers, in which love requires that he sacrifice himself. The eschatological salvation, the New Testament *soteria*, must therefore be interpreted more strongly than previously in terms of the Old Testament *shalom* and the concept of the kingdom of God. In its social ethics, the community does not only have to save lost sentimental values in the midst of a rationalized society and private personal integrity in a functionalized society. In the expectation of the *shalom*, of the kingdom of God which comes to earth, of the new heaven and the new earth, one can find and give hope and courage for a life which is now, for the most part, determined only by functions.

The kingdom of God does indeed embrace not only the consummation of the church but also at the same time the problems of the 'new world', that is, the eschatology of civilization and nature[47].

An eschatology of culture and of nature would, however, contribute to a decisive historicizing of both. One would view cultural and natural processes eschatologically. The state, for example, would have to be seen as a 'process of the formation of political intention' and no longer as a naturalistic order on the one hand, or as a decisionistic institution of power on the other. The 'process of the formation of political intention', however, must be critically questioned in regard to its historical purposes within the horizon of the coming righteousness and must be shaped in creative love by Christians co-operating, working and suffering together.

Between the illusion and resignation generated by the technical process of reshaping society, hope must find its way in faithfulness to that earth on which stood the cross of Christ. God's commandment summons historicity, worldliness and determination for an answer and, in this way, profoundly corresponds to man's reality.

NOTES

1. This lecture was given at a meeting of the Evangelische Akademie in Berlin on 8 January 1960, to the study group for 'Sociology and Theology'. The topic under consideration was 'Human Reality and the Commandment of God'.

2. H. Schelsky, 'Ist Dauerreflexion institutionalisierbar?', *ZEE* 1, 1957, Part 4, 153ff.; 'Religionssoziologie und Theologie', *ZEE* 3, 1959, Part 3, 129ff.; cf. esp. W. Schweitzer, 'Menschliche Wirklichkeit in soziologischer und theologischer Sicht', *ZEE* 3, 1959, Part 4, 193ff., and H. Schelsky, *Ortsbestimmung der deutschen Soziologie*, 1959.

3. H. Schelsky, 'Religionssoziologie und Theologie', *ZEE* 3, 1959, 131.

4. *Ibid.*, 135.

5. E. Troeltsch, 'Der Historismus und seine Probleme, I: Das logische Problem der Geschichtsphilosophie', *Gesammelte Schriften* 3, 1922, 131.

6. T. W. Adorno, 'Soziologie und empirische Forschung', *Wirklichkeit des Menschen: Plessner Festschrift*, 1959, 250, makes the pertinent comment: 'Public opinion polls deal better with men where under the pressure of circumstances they are reduced to the "reaction pattern of an amphibian", e.g. as the enslaved consumers of the mass media than does, say, an "understanding sociology", for the substratum of understanding which is there in harmonious and meaningful human action is replaced by a mere reaction in the subject itself.' The present move towards sociometry, public opinion research, statistics, etc. is in that case only the ideological reflection of an atomized and manipulated society.

7. C. Graf von Krackow, *Die Entscheidung: Eine Untersuchung über Ernst Jünger, Carl Schmitt, Martin Heidegger*, 1958, 149.

8. K. Sontheimer makes a similar remark in his report of the sociological conference in Berlin, *Frankfurter Hefte*, 1959, 332, about the 'continually increasing contradiction in German sociology between an empirical positivistic analysis of society and the desire for a theoretical permeation of the whole complex of social problems'.

9. For the development of a theological concept of history see W. Pannenberg's summary and heuristic article, 'Redemptive Event and History', *Basic Questions in Theology* I, trans. G. H. Kehm, 1970, 15ff. Cf. also M. Eliade's examination of mythical and concrete time in *The Myth of the*

Eternal Return, trans. W. D. Trask, 1955, and G. Picht, *Die Erfahrung der Geschichte*, 1958; cf. also the works of K. Löwith, Auerbach, etc.

10. G. Picht, *op. cit.*, 20. The question arose in the discussion whether epiphanic and apocalyptic thought can be contrasted so strongly, since the biblical concept of revelation employs both.

11. In this regard it is interesting to note that orthodox Marxism, in defence of Ernst Bloch's 'religious eschatologism', finds itself inclined to make Engel's materialistic theory of cycles binding over against any form of future expectation and open experience of history. Cf. F. Engels, *Dialekt der Natur* (Bücherei des Marxismus-Leninismus 18), 1959, 27: 'Matter moves in an eternal cycle . . . we have the certainty that matter eternally remains the same in all its changes.' Cf. also R. Rochhausen, *Ernst Blochs Revision des Marxismus*, 1957, 89: 'Every consistent materialist rejects the conception of a directed development. A truly materialist conception is therefore the theory of cycles. . . . The process of the development of matter is therefore never a one-sidedly directed process of differentiation. It leads forwards, i.e. to complicated forms . . . and finally . . . it also leads backwards to less differentiated forms of matter. . . . Bloch attacks the theory of cycles with the utmost asperity and in so doing agrees with most idealists. Instead of the cyclical pattern, he calls for a 'world-confidence' that is to be directed towards 'an ever again of entropy'. M. Eliade, *op. cit.*, 141ff., has shown very well that the present reawakening of the myth of the eternal return in the sphere of national economy develops from a longing for the annihilation of concrete time and escape from the 'terrors of history'. These features, which emerge in Marxism with the divergence of the Lukacs-Bloch line, should warn Christian apologists against regarding Marxism only as 'secularized eschatology'.

12. M. Luther, *Romans*, ed. Ficker, II, 1908, 198. Cf. also Luther's anthropological theses, WA 39, I, 175-7.

13. WA 34, II, 481, lines 1f. and 12-16.

14. Cf. Dilthey, *Gesammelte Schriften* IV, 529: 'Only history says what man is'. O. F. Bollnow, *Lebensphilosophie*, 1958, 41, rightly observes: 'The statement that man knows himself only in history means not only that the knowledge of man in this indirect way is connected with the knowledge of his historical manifestation, but more profoundly, beyond this, that there is no fixed "essence of man" which existed as something similar before history and independently from history; rather, this essence itself is change in history.'

15. G. Picht, *op. cit.*, 37.

16. Compare O. Weber's fundamental article 'Die Treue Gottes und die Kontinuität der menschliche Existenz', *Ecclesia semper reformanda*, Sonderheft to *EvTh*, 1952, 131ff.

17. In addition to Bonhoeffer's theology of the 'true worldliness' of the Christian, the works of Bultmann and Gogarten ought also to be noted.

18. K. Mannheim, *Ideologie und Utopie*, 1929, [4]1965, 213ff.

19. P. Tillich, *Die politische Bedeutung der Utopie im Leben der Völker*, 1951, 52ff.; further, 'Kairos und Utopie', *ZEE* 3, 1959, Part 6. Cf. also E. Bloch, *Das Prinzip Hoffnung*, I-II, 1959.

20. At this point in the discussion, the question arose as to whether one can attribute historical processes of this kind to the effect of the Holy Spirit. By modifying Calvin's doctrine of the Spirit and drawing on theocratic thinking in Dutch theology, I think that one can do this.

21. For this prognosis cf. A. Gehlen, *Die Seele im technischen Zeitalter*, 1957.

22. F. Tönnies, *Gemeinschaft und Gesellschaft*, 1887, [8]1935, 3ff.

23. H. Freyer, *Theorie des gegenwärtigen Zeitalters*, [2]1956, 247.

24. *Ibid.*, 243f.

25. *Ibid.*, 258.

26. G. Mackenroth, *Sinn und Ausdruck der sozialen Formenwelt*, 1952, p.200.

27. The investigation by Popitz, Bahrdt, Jüres and Kesting, *Technik und Industriearbeit*, 1957, is significant and full of surprises.

28. E. Wolf, utilizing Rosenstock-Huessy's thesis, *Königsherrschaft Christi* (Theologisches Existenz heute, NF 64), 1958, 49ff.

29. Cf. W. Schweitzer, *op. cit.*

30. A. Gehlen, *Die Seele im technischen Zeitalter*, 47.

31. P. R. Hofstätter, *Sozialpsychologie*, 1956, 110ff.

32. P. Althaus, *Theologie der Ordnungen*, 1934, 20: '. . . hope for the kingdom of God is learnt in political hope, although it points beyond all political possibilities. That is the *usus symbolicus* of ordinances for the knowledge of the kingdom of God.'

33. E. Brunner, *The Divine Imperative*, trans. O. Wyon, 1937, 210 (slightly altered). My italics.

34. *Ibid.*, 291.

35. W. Künneth, *Politik zwischen Dämon und Gott*, 1954, 138ff.; H. Thielicke, *Theological Ethics* I, trans. W. H. Lazarus, 1968, 434ff., esp. 439f., where Thielicke speaks of 'ordinances of history' as 'emergency ordinances' of the Noachite covenant under which the world is to reach the 'longed-for Last Day'.

36. One concrete example of this is H. Thielicke, *Die Atomwaffe als Frage an die christliche Ethik*, 1958, where atomic warfare is really confronted with 'Noachite ethics' rather than Christian ethics.

The theology of ordinances, which seeks standards for the shaping of the historical stream of events, is manifestly always in danger of suspending the eschatological theme of this shaping. The application of the eschatology of the 'longed-for Last Day' leads to the justification of the opposite to that which is expected here in history. Thus in the stabilization of the 'two kingdoms', any crossing over of the dividing line is regarded as 'chiliasm' – even in the allegedly eschatological justification which the South African Reformed Church has given for the policy of apartheid: any communion of the races in Christ is rejected as utopia and chiliasm.

37. For a discussion of Bonhoeffer's concept of the mandate cf. J. Moltmann, *Herrschaft Christi und soziale Wirklichkeit nach D. Bonhoeffer* (Theologisches Existenz heute, NF 71), 1959.

38. Bonhoeffer, *Ethics*, [2]1964, 207.

39. *Ibid.*, 344ff.

40. H. Dombois (ed.), 'Recht und Institution', in *Glaube und Forschung 9*, 1956, thesis 72. My italics.

41. Unpublished report of the conference of 19–20 October 1959.

42. H. D. Wendland, *Botschaft an die soziale Welt*, 1959, 167. On the other hand, Wendland is concerned to bring out 'the effect of eschatology on social ethics' (cf. *ZEE* 1, 1957, Part 4, 145ff.) and to embrace the eschatological and salvation-historical finality of the institutions. But the two sides remain in hiatus, unless the significance of history itself is taken into account.

43. R. Bultmann, 'Gedanken über die gegenwärtige theologische Situation', *Glauben und Verstehen* III, 1960, 190ff. Bultmann bases his negation of all the church's judgments on politics (*a*) with an individualism in principle: '. . . the church which is said to give advice here in fact consists of church officials, and these men can only make a personal judgment' (195) and (*b*) again in principle, with an apolitical dimension of the word of God: 'It (sc. the church) is to proclaim the word of God, but it is not to give political judgments. A political judgment in a concrete political situation is not the word of God' (195). In conclusion, he mentions the task of theology today: 'It is to make clear that Christian faith in no way provides security in the world; faith, however, as faith in God's revealed grace, bestows freedom to come confidently through darkness and mystery and to venture and bear the responsibility for action in the loneliness of man's own decision' (196). Bultmann here seems to want to overlook the fact that Word and Spirit of God are social events within history and cannot only be understood correctly in ecclesiastical terms. The community finds expression as a community between the 'church officials' and the individual Christians in presbytery and synod, and finds ethical direction here in the 'fellowship of the brothers and the fathers'. The word of God encounters real man, and always has a political dimension. The 'solitary man' is an abstraction, and action in the loneliness of man's own decision, as Bultmann describes it, has no social and therefore no historical relevance. Cf. J. B. Souček, 'Politisierung der Theologie?', *Communio Viatorum*, 1958, Part 4, 210ff.

44. The remarks coming at the end of this lecture necessarily have the character of an attempt which tries to point in a definite direction. They cannot present a complete concept. The plan of a *general ethical field theory of Christian hope* would also be conceivable. Christian action and suffering are the 'fruits of hope'. Good works do not build the kingdom of God, but hope in the coming kingdom assumes ethical forms within history. Between optimistic chiliasm and apocalyptic lethargy Christian life stands in the dawn of hope (Rom. 13.11–14).

45. H. Freyer, *Soziologie als Wirklichkeitswissenschaft*, 1930, 305.

46. E. Bloch, *Das Prinzip Hoffnung* I, 254.

47. D. Bonhoeffer, *Sanctorum Communio*, translation revised by R. Gregor Smith, 1963, 199.

5

THE 'ROSE IN THE CROSS OF THE PRESENT'

Towards an Understanding of the Church in Modern Society

I *The concept of religion in industrial society*

The social position which society accords the Christian church today is most clearly illustrated in the sociology of religion or the sociology of the church congregation. Sociology is always a reflection of that society in which and from which it is derived, even when it attempts to be positivistic and free of value judgements. The sociology of religion always throws a characteristic light not only on the church or on religious groups which are the subject of its investigation but also on that society in which the church exists and in which the sociological investigation takes place. In this way, the sociology of religion shows how society sees the church, in what roles it understands the church and how it 'defines' the church. It therefore points out the limits which that society marks out for the church which exists both in and with it. The sociology of religion establishes the roles in which the church lives socially and in which it is operative. It calls attention to those role-expectations which society places on this church. On the basis of this, we must therefore ask: which situations and which roles has present society assigned to religion in general and to the Christian church in particular? In which areas today does society 'expect' the church to be operative? Further, we must ask where and how the church ought to respond to the command of its Lord and be operative. In what direction is it pointed by its calling? Where does God, who grants it faith, 'expect' the church to be active?

1. The change in the social concept of religion

During the last hundred and fifty years, the modern society in which the church exists today has fundamentally changed and revolutionized its traditional form: as a 'civil society', since the French Revolution; as an industrial society, or, as was said earlier, a 'society of need', since the beginning of the first technical revolution.

From the time of Constantine up to the collapse of the empire in 1803, the church, in spite of the reformation, puritanism and pietism, possessed a public and social character which was hardly questioned. As a result of the modern transformation of society, however, the church has become homeless, socially speaking, inasmuch as positions that are enjoyed over a long period tend to be accepted as home. Since about 1800, church and society have no longer known what to do with each other; their relationship, or lack of it, has become fluid. *Society no longer has a concept of the church and the church no longer has a concept of society.*

Seen in the light of church history, before modern times the church's public claim was derived from the *public character of Roman state religion.*[1] Beginning with Constantine and then consolidated by the legislation of the Emperors Theodosius and Justinian, the Christian religion became a *cultus publicus*, the administrator of the *sacra publica*. According to the ancient conception of the state, the highest duty of the πόλις was to grant its gods the reverence due to them. In the ancient definition, the public cult was to the benefit of the *societas* in determining the purpose of the state and was a permanent and indispensable feature of the πόλις. From the time of the decline of the Roman Empire, in the internal disorganization of the empire, the Christian church emerged as the 'reconciling centre' of society. The transference of the religious title of the emperor to the pope (*pontifex maximus*) and the medieval legal construction of the *translatio imperii* are characteristic of this. In Melanchthon's Protestant humanism, without which the reformation would not have come into being, princes and magistrates were appealed to on the basis of this ancient religious obligation of the state. The principal aim of society is true reverence of God in the sense of the first commandment. However, the effecting of the reformation of the church is designated as 'the true worship of God'. A magistrate who only wants to be responsible for 'peace and customs' is represented as a bewilderment.[2] Thus in the early, Western concept of *religio*, there is always a 'public' element, because a religious goal is always envisaged in the early, Western concept of society.[3]

Hegel was one of the first to see the development of the new, modern society, which destroys all originating factors and, therefore, seems apocalyptically monstrous in its significance for world history, and analyses it as a 'system of needs',[4] i.e. as a system of the reciprocal satisfaction of need through common and shared work. 'The necessity and the work which go to make up this generality form a monstrous system of sociality and mutual dependence, a self-enclosed system of the dead . . .'[5] Here he means to say that, for the first time, society established itself on man's constant and uniform nature of need and his work for the satisfaction of needs; in this way, it becomes independent of the predetermining forces of history which otherwise shape the sociality of men. Neither intellect, morals, customs, nation, tradition, race, position – nor even religion – are necessary in order to make the sociality of men possible. Men associate themselves solely as representatives of production, commerce and consumption. All other human values and relationships come out of the context of society and are placed in the individual freedom of man. In the new society, man now necessarily associates with man only as worker and consumer. All other determinations of human being are eliminated and released from the necessary requirements of sociality. The commerce of society becomes 'abstract', as Hegel says. The necessary communication of society is made technical and in that way is selectively limited. A 'morality of commerce' (A. Gehlen) appears, which overcomes confessional barriers.

Now Hegel saw well that a society which in this way is to be called 'abstract', which makes the system of work and needs the single social determination of man, is a fatal threat to the human quality of man.

Civil society is rather the tremendous power which draws men into itself and claims from them that they work for it, owe everything to it, and do everything by its means.[6]

But, at the same time, Hegel recognized the other side of this process, that this society releases and frees the individuality and the authentic power of man to be himself in spirit, morality and religion in an unsuspected way. The modern discovery of the category of subjectivity as man's power to be himself, from Kierkegaard to existentialist philosophy, is based on and inescapably bound up with the development of modern society, as Hegel described it. The revolution of modern industrial society realized in its own way the French Revolution's conception of freedom, for both revolutions are only two sides of one and the same historical process. For this reason, the age of the 'great factory' (K. Marx), of 'crowding together' (G. Le Bon, J. Ortega y Gasset), of 'society' (F. Tönnies), of 'conformism and of levelling' (D. Riesman, A. Gehlen) is, at the same time, still the 'personal age' of individuality and of an increasingly intimate and refined subjectivity.[7] It is therefore meaningless to break into a one-sided, romantic lament against society. The one question is whether everything freed in this way from groups of associations and given over to freedom of subjectivity must not necessarily deteriorate because and in so far as it no longer has social relevance. This question applies particularly to religion and the Christian church which has now turned into the religiosity of man. For through this development, the Christian church has become what it never was and, according to the New Testament, can never want to be, i.e., *cultus privatus*.

If in the first centuries of persecution the Christian church had yielded to the possibility which existed in the Roman Empire, of becoming a tolerant and tolerated *cultus privatus*, it would hardly have been persecuted. But the claim of the exclusivity and the absoluteness of God, who was present in

Christ, would also never have been expressed.[8] In the nineteenth century, however, religion was private, internal and
subjective. For Kierkegaard, this meant, 'Everyone ought to
consort with others only with great care and speak of essentials
only with God and himself.' Sociologically this can be expressed
in the following manner: 'Through the influence of Christianity,
this private realm contains a transcendental point of reference
which is symbolized by the church, as bearer of the faith.'[9] In
this connection we must consider a point made by Bonhoeffer:

> It is thought that a man's essential nature consists of his inmost and
> most intimate background; that is defined as his 'inner life', and it
> is precisely in those secret human places that God is to have his
> domain.[10]

The public validity of Christianity declines in proportion to the
emancipation of the 'society of needs' from the religious needs
of human society, on the one hand, and the growth in the church
of liberal, pietistic or existential inwardness, on the other.

It cannot be said that the modern division of man into
'private' and 'public', the problem of the twofold man, was seen
at all in the ethical work of nineteenth-century theology,
although since Rousseau (*bourgeois* and *citoyen*), Hegel and Marx
it had been a recognized problem in philosophical anthropology
and the critique of society. The church, rather, slid practically
unaware into the modern *cultus privatus* and produced in its
theology and its social ethics a corresponding self-consciousness
as the shelterer and protector of personal, inner freedom.

2. Religion as *cultus privatus*

If we now try to set the intellectual theological positions over
against their corresponding social situations, we run up against
the first concept of religion in industrial society – religion as
cultus privatus. Subjectivity is truth (S. Kierkegaard), a free-
floating, spontaneous, creative subjectivity which, in the face
of a 'meaninglessness' in the world of things and relationships,
decides for God, the one who completely changes conditions, a
subjectivity which would like to be understood in terms of God.

Historical and social situations no longer contain a coherent meaning. For this reason, they are taken to be the *occasio*, occasion, pretext and motive for the individual decision of faith. Faith wanders into the sphere of a subjectivity which is a matter of opinion and preference. 'Love' parts company with law and becomes an esoteric I-Thou relationship, while law is understood positivistically. As a subjective, occasional 'decision', faith becomes transcendent over every – socially communicable – context of meaning. Faith is not experientially demonstrable, nor can it be refuted. Unbelief, the contra-decision, is its sole enemy. This subjectivity of faith can still be sociologically comprehensible as 'man's total reflection on himself'[11] or as a 'permanent reflection' (H. Schelsky). The question is whether faith can be 'institutionalized' in such a manner.[12] Such a concept of religion can be advocated very movingly. It does not, however, disturb in the slightest the limits of that social realm in which society has placed the *cultus privatus* in order to emancipate itself from this concept of religion. In the literal sense, it is socially irrelevant because it stands in the social no-man's-land of individual unburdenings, that is, in a realm which society has otherwise freed from subjective preferences. This subjective decision of faith, therefore, hardly continues to provoke the contra-decision of unbelief; it no longer struggles with unbelief over reality but rather continually provokes its own voluntary character, i.e. the notorious non-decision in this question: 'religion without decision'.[13]

The transcendent point of reference in the private realm, which the church is meant to symbolize, has already been neutralized in social terms before it can be considered in faith. A theology which represents the decision of faith as non-accountable and non-demonstrable certainly makes this decision unassailable, and also completely irrelevant. It puts faith 'in the air' (F. Overbeck).[14]

3. Religion as community

The second sociological concept of religion and the second place assigned to the church in today's society is the idea of religion as 'community'. It has often been said by sociologists and critics of culture that modern society is in no way moving toward a totalitarian anthill, in which each and everything is regimented, but rather that the period of so-called crowding together and unification is, at the same time, a 'personal age' of small special groups, of relationships of familiarity in small circles, etc. In other words, the fluctuating groups, societies, clubs, sects, etc., as micro-structures of society ('informal groups'), correspond to the super and macro-structures of organizations and factories. Alexis de Tocqueville already observed this in the American democracy of the last century.

The first thing that strikes the observation is an innumerable multitude of men, all equal and alike, incessantly endeavouring to procure the petty and paltry pleasures with which they glut their lives. Each of them, living apart, is a stranger to the fate of all the rest; his children and his private friends constitute to him the whole of mankind. As for the rest of his fellow citizens, he is close to them, but he does not see them; he touches them, but he does not feel them; he exists only in himself and for himself alone.[15]

The inhumanity of men in the outside world is practically forgotten in circles of friends, intimate colleagues at work, children, in choral societies and parish halls. Perhaps, A. Gehlen suggests, all these small connections together constitute something like the cement of the total structure of society.[16] Here the church has its place and its function among others and alongside others. Here it can provide a refuge of inwardness from 'unfettered desires', from those overwhelming conditions which are intellectually so incomprehensible and can no longer be dealt with morally. Here the church provides – and the demands for the reform of the local congregation occasionally run in this direction – human warmth and understanding, neighbourliness and a home, without a specific purpose, but still a meaningful 'community'. To sum it up with one word – a modern magic word – 'contact'.[17] In this formless, unorganized, non-public vacuum of society, sects, communities and clubs of all types are rapidly spreading. Here the church could (or rather, congregations and small groups in the community could) become a

Noah's ark for socially alienated men – become an island of humanity and fellow humanity in the rough sea of those conditions in which the 'little man' can 'change nothing'. Here congregations could become assembly points for 'integration with men's fellow-men and in so doing, would, without doubt, fulfil a social goal.

It is entirely in accord with this social vacuum in modern society when in theology, from some directions of the public and legally constituted church, the true congregation is contrasted with the church as 'church of the spirit' (R. Sohm), as the 'spiritual fellowship of persons' (E. Brunner) or as the 'pure event' of 'the community of faith' or 'the community in the transcendent' (R. Bultmann).[18] We must be quite clear, however, that one such congregation as 'community' and as an 'event' on each particular occasion can neither disturb, change, nor heal the public activity of society, but rather leads to an existence which is below the threshold, so to speak, of the public domain. This subliminal existence of the congregation is very helpful for society because it can give a certain balance to the economic destructive powers in man's spiritual composition. The harsh reality of the society's problematic present is, however, hardly affected by it, let alone conquered by it.

4. Religion as institution

The third concept of religion is sociological use and the third social context for the church today is again, surprisingly enough, the institution, with all the public character and public claims which that possesses. Modern post-enlightenment culture again supports the 'institutional' church.[19] After the hectic years of the first industrial era in which men became unsure of their behaviour as a result of the great social pressures to which they were subjected, industrial society consolidated itself in new institutions, and these institutions, by set behavioural patterns, released men from the permanent pressure of decision and gave them security, permanence and community. A new treasure of unvarying usages, habits and precepts is in the process of being developed in work, commerce and the consumer world. The institutionalizing of social life arises, one could say with Gehlen, from man's need for security as he experiences himself in history as a 'being at risk'. This new institutionalizing, however, with a certain inner logic, at the same time suspends the question of meaning. 'Anyone who raises the question of meaning has either lost his way or consciously or unconsciously expresses the need for others as existing institutions.'[20] These are things which must happen 'naturally' and without question. Institutionalization brings about a disappearance of ideology which can be observed everywhere today in the highly industrialized countries. It is not Christian faith that overcame the ideologizing of the human soul, though a certain clerical apologetic is inclined to count this as gain; if anything, this very institutionalization of the human soul is itself the cause of its de-ideologization. Rather, faith has a certain proximity to ideology in so far as it is directed towards something other rather than towards the accepted presuppositions of present existence.

The tendency towards institutionalization and the fact that the arts and sciences have become so abstract[21] that only caricatures of them can be used ideologically, now forces theology to remain alone and without opponents in the arena of the philosophy of life. It can assert things in a neo-dogmatism or a positivism of revelation which can neither be verified nor denied on the basis of a reality which can be experienced, because they are now too little related to this reality or because institutionalized man is no longer confronted with a reality which is expressed theologically. A conflict over the Apostles' Creed like that which affected people – or at least educated people – round about 1900 is hardly conceivable today. An archaic liturgy no longer seems objectionable, but rather only increases the unique splendour of the institutional church which even for modern man is apparently the competent authority for the extra-empirical or whatever on the basis of common experience is out of the ordinary. On the other hand, there doubtless remains on the periphery of modern consciousness a remnant of insecurity, uneasiness and dread of the terrors of history. In normal times this is not articulated, but it is nevertheless reflected in the consciousness of the critical character of even stable conditions. Finally, in this context of archaic religious needs, the institutional church, with all that is connected with it, seems to be an institution towering above other institutions in institutional security because it seems to promise certain securities against the ultimate terror of existence.[22] The attempt at an *ecclesia semper reformanda* is hardly realizable in a church which is desired and held back by society as a non-obligatory but omni-present institution.

If we summarize the attempt – which can certainly be expanded into a whole variety of elements – at defining the social context of the church and theology in today's society, we find (1) a subjectivity of faith which is not capable of being communicated, (2) a community of faith which can no longer play a part in society because it is subliminal, and (3) an institutional church.

Common to these social limitations and the forms of Christian self-consciousness which correspond to them is (1) the terrifying decline of social love, a love which takes up and endures the pain of the present and (2) the no less terrifying decline of Christian hope, a hope which has in view 'totality' (Blumhardt), i.e., the kingdom of God, the new heaven and the new earth, *shalom* and life for this earth. This de-eschatologizing of Christianity shows itself in the loss of hope for the real outstanding future.

Finally the question arises whether the social captivity of the church mentioned above would also apply to the Marxist sphere of influence. Certainly Marxism takes the Christian religion seriously because it wants to inherit the church socially and ideologically and, in this way, provokes the Christian's public decision of faith, something which hardly ever happens in non-Marxist areas. But the trend obviously moves in the same direction. Marxism in its Leninistic form is the logical end of the process 'in which the tension with transcendence is itself constantly snapped, in which the attitude of man towards transcendence, man's reaching out beyond himself towards something higher, is intercepted and absorbed by the abundance of this-worldly possibilities and pressures, an abundance which has reached gigantic proportions'.[23]

II The sociological misunderstanding of the church or the church's misunderstanding of sociology[24]

Society attempts to understand the church in the sociology of religion, and that always means also to limit and to incorporate it. A sociology of religion which works with general social conceptions always finds the church only in certain social roles. The role-less church does not appear. As the church exists in certain social relationships, if it exists at all, it is necessarily the victim of sociological misunderstanding and social misuse.

Theologically, one can explain in various ways the mirror which sociology holds up to the church. One can say that the church as *corpus Christi* is 'more than' a social group. The church represents values which transcend experience and the sociology of religion points out how these values, which, as such, are not subject to historical change, are realized in socio-historical contexts. The sociology of religion then offers the church 'help for adjusting' to modern society on a scientific basis.[25] It is, however, a historical fact that the eternal values are not adapted to time but to an obsolete past of the changed present, and that 'adjustment' – like an exchange office of values – then threatens to become the basic value.

One could even say that only the 'human nature' of the church is revealed by the sociology of religion's method of investigation.[26] The question then is whether (1) this distinction does justice to the early church's doctrine of the incarnation from which this differentiation is taken (*una persona?*), and (2) whether it is theologically permissible to extend the doctrine of the two natures unreservedly to that church which, while most certainly the 'body of Christ', is not 'another Christ', whose structure is the *unio mystica* but not the *unio hypostatica*.

Because the sociology of religion up to now has been so untheological, because of its uncritical attitude, it can hardly do justice to its subject. 'He who does not measure things according to what they intend to mean, sees these things not only super-ficially but also incorrectly' (M. Horkheimer). This practical positivism of the sociology of religion corresponds to a 'sociology without society' or a 'psychology without a soul', and could be characterized as 'sociology of the church without a concept of the church'. Statistical and numerical evaluation remains abstract. The critical consciousness is lost when one finds no idea of the matter under consideration. 'Indifference to an idea in theory is a symptom of cynicism in practice,' is the just comment of M. Horkheimer,[27] and T. W. Adorno. This also applies to the positive effect of sociology on religious literature.

The sociology of religion as 'enlightenment' must become the theological critique of the church. For theological thinking about the church, the basic question is not how the church adequately adjusts or how it forms its human nature so that its eternal divine nature shines through it into time. The question is, rather, how does the church become *true*?

The sociology of religion cannot, therefore, be approved as a social report of the church, but rather only as the church's self-judgment in the question *vera aut falsa ecclesia*. In that case, such criticism does not mean subjective arbitrary displeasure, but rather requires that the subject (the church) be confronted with its own concept. Only in the criticism of the church in regard to its own concept, to its theological definition, does the con-sideration of love arise. This love is not blind, but rather 'critical', in that it tests what is correct and incorrect by the goal of being 'pure and blameless for the day of Christ' (Phil. 1.10). Such love suffers in the church because the church 'may suffer' it. What, however, is the 'concept' of this 'subject'? We turn now to a second question – Where and how does the Lord, who calls the church into life, expect the church?

III Towards a concept of the church

1. The questionableness of a dialectic of complementarity

The concepts of religion in industrial society mentioned above – the free subjectivity of faith, the community of faith as event,

the institution preserving tradition – suggests a series of extremely attractive additions for ecclesiology today. Attempts
are made to reconcile the unresolved tensions between subjectified faith and established ecclesiasticism, between 'institution and event' (J.-L. Leuba), tradition and charisma, institution and movement, institution and free society, by means of
a dialectic of complementarity.[28] This dialectic of complementarity of the not-only-but-also variety can then be applied
at will to all tensions in the church. In this way, Old and New
Testament Israel and church, state church and free church,
Lutheran and Reformed and finally even Catholic and Protestant can be complementarily supplemented, as if in these
differences the confessional question *vera aut falsa ecclesia* had
never existed! Here ecumenical integralism turns into the
universal dream of supplementation. Certainly the tensions
between personalism and institutionalism are social realities.
But the dialectic of complementarity which is used today
presents these tensions as necessary supplements to each other
and, in this way, justifies them. The tension can only be resolved
when we ask together about the 'true church' or the church in
truth.

(2) The concept of the church, in a traditional way, is usually
thought of in spatial terms as house, space, realm, place, etc.
We now want to attempt to think about it in a historical-
temporal way. The subject of discussion ought not to be the
space or the place of the church but rather the time and the
history of the church. In this way, the geographical components
of the church (mission to the Gentiles) should not be excluded.
Indeed, historical-eschatological elements of the church shed a
particular light on its geographical elements. If we ask about
the time of the church, then we must talk about the apostolicity
of the church or of the church of the apostolate.

*Christianity is the apostolic action involving Jesus within the
universal horizon of the expectation of the eschaton.* The expression
'Christianity' (*Christenheit*) (Luther) means not only the 'congregation' in the special liturgical exercise of office but also

Christian existence in all spheres of life. What is meant is therefore not only 'Christendom' as the embodiment of developing tradition and the Western world's approach to life. Christianity is the *ecclesia spiritualis*, the hidden body of Christ in which Christ *in nostra imbecillitate* exercises his power in the world. Christianity does not live only in the liturgical assembly but also in mission, and in conspicuous love within the horizon of the commonplace. Christianity is not in the church but rather the church in the world. This expression 'Christianity' reckons with a 'charismatic congregation'.[29] Perhaps there is no 'unconscious Christianity' as cultural Protestantism would have it; but there is certainly an abundance of unconscious and unaroused charisma in Christianity.

This Christianity is not to be understood as a perennial institution nor as an ever-new event of a free community of activity. Assembly and sending, the election, call and preservation of Christianity are ongoing elements within an action. Through spirit and word, Christ assembles, protects, and preserves his community. This constitutes the *historical action of Christianity*. It is certainly not the process of the church growing out of the *depositum fidei* and, like a growing tree, little by little filling history and the earth (the romantic picture of church history). But neither can this history of the church, on the other hand, be described as a series of unrelated situations, each one new. What we have, rather, is the *action*, the 'realizing' of the church, i.e. the apostolic action in prosecution, and defence in the testimony for truth. The whole of church history is almost an action in the legal sense. This character of the church is observed in synodal activity. Resort to an institution of decision at the summit of a church or to the irregular spontaneity of faith is a defection from the σύν–ὅδος of Christianity. Accordingly, church ordinances ought to retain the character of Christianity's historical action by being formulated as initiation into the apostolate.

The apostolate of Christianity is likewise such an action about the truth in, with, and against the world. Furthermore, the New Testament, in the multiplicity of its testimony, is a sign of that action which is involved. A dialectic of complementarity would only mask the apostolic action between Peter and Paul, Luke and Paul, between apocalyptists, enthusiasts, Gnostics and Jewish Christians. We need not mention that the doctrines of the Holy Spirit, justification and the eschaton, have a juridical character.

These historical-juridical proceedings are concerned with truth and falsehood about the history of Jesus, true and false witness. About the resurrection of Jesus and the new life which is revealed in the resurrection, there is only one truth; there are not various subjective judgments of faith. Faith is a lived interpretation of being and of the world in the horizon of the resurrection. As every human life is a lived interpretation of being and the world there comes into being antagonistic action over truth. Christianity must demonstrate, preserve and account for the truth which is revealed in Christ. It cannot withdraw into the calm realm of subjective choice, nor can it talk supernaturally about faith. The lived-out testimony of the raising of Jesus must stand the test of the historical, anthropological and sociological illumination of reality, since it calls into question all other conceptions of reality, even the thesis about the subjective choice of these understandings, because it sees the world in the horizon of divine judgment.

This action does not have an uncertain outcome, but stands in the horizon of the expectation of the divine eschaton. The data for the action over the resurrection of Jesus discloses the true horizon of the expectation of all history. Therefore, the much sought-after 'meaning of history' is found in this very action. If, however, this action conveys the meaning not only of the history of the human soul but rather, in universal terms, of *all* history, even social and political history, then it is a public action. Eschatology not only represents the future of believing confrontation with God but also reveals, in blessings and curses, an eschatological meaning for the whole of humanity and even in the non-human creation (Rom. 8.19) – in poverty, suffering, the search for righteousness, confession, acts of love, etc.

Christianity understood in this way would be the wave of the eschatological events of history, borne on by it in word and spirit. Its administration of messianic hope is that future which is accounted for in the present. It might be described as the community of service in the apostolate of Jesus. It might be the process of the apostolate itself. In that case, however, is the church functionalized, actualized and dynamically volatilized? Only if one understands the apostolate as a missionary experiment to the nations, and not if the function of the church is to be set in the eschatological history of God. All being has its horizon of meaning, is ek-sistent, points towards something, has a tendency and an interpretation in the direction in which it ought to go. We cannot talk about Christianity if we do not talk about that towards which it is directed, if we have nothing to say about that which constitutes the eschatological content of its history. That is all that is meant when the church is characterized as an instrumental function of the apostolic process of God's history.

The continuity of the church in history is the consequence of the hope that it lives out. If one sees the church historically as the function of the eschaton, then naturally the question arises – in what does its continuity and continuance, its permanence, exist? Instead of the emphasis on the church's historicity in the process of the *semper reformanda*, reference is normally made to tradition, succession, firm confessional commitment and the necessity of fixed orders, that is, to its institutionalism. The 'true church', however, does not achieve the desired continuity in this way; its permanence has a different character from that of an institution. There is a continuity of grace, but it is not historically demonstrable or metaphysically verifiable, but rather results in the history of the divine Word in which the proclamation stands its ground. Hebrews 13.14 says, 'For here we have no abiding city, but we seek the city which is to come.' This is obviously directed against Jewish expectations bound up with the City of God, Jerusalem. But it was also particularly important in a context where prayers were offered daily for the continuing existence of 'eternal Rome' (Roma aeterna).[30]

'Eternal Rome' promised men continuance against fleeting time. The institutions also promised a πόλις μένουσα, permanence and release. For Christians, who find their origin in the action of the raising of Jesus, there is no 'abiding city' here, for there is no such city in historical reality. The religious need for 'having', the 'having-with-oneself' and the 'having-in-oneself', indwelling in the 'abiding' is, in Hebrews 13.14, contrasted with the 'search for' (ἐπιζητεῖν) the 'city which is to come'. The coming πόλις is the city which has firm foundations (Heb. 11.10), the city which God had prepared for the fathers and towards which they were moving (11.26), the heavenly Jerusalem (12.22), the home, the promised rest, the new but not *re-newed* Jerusalem.

This 'searching for' means, rather, breaking out from what is given towards the future which is promised, but is not yet visible (in fact, on the contrary, it is concealed) and is contrasted to 'having'. It is not an uncertain searching in a limitless future as the empty direction of possible change but rather 'the searching of one who has already found' (O. Michel). Hebrews 13.13 connects this searching with confidence in what has been announced but has not yet appeared, with 'Let us go forth outside the camp' and in this way parallels it to the *exodus* of Abraham and Israel. The openness towards the future of the promise, the leaving-oneself and the emigration from the 'lasting city' implies that Christianity does not have its centre in itself but rather in the future. It is the community of hope. Its God is the 'God of hope' (Rom. 15.13), if you will, the *'exodus God'* (E. Bloch) who is powerful in history. Its apostolic process is then realized hope and its sacrifice in love is active expectation. Only as long as this hope is alive is it able to 'last', namely, in the 'steadfastness of hope' (I Thess. 1.3). Only hope has sustaining and enduring patience; only searching leads to continuance. The expectations that congregate around the concept of the institution are an escape from history. 'Continuing in hope', however, is continuing in Jesus, in his Word, in love and is nothing other than the life in the spirit who arouses to life. Faith has continuance and Christianity has continuity in history in as far as it, through hope, reaches out beyond itself. Not in self-preservation but in self-abandonment does Christianity acquire continuance in that which it abandons and in which it trusts.

Tradition has expressed this in the concept of the *ecclesia in perpetuum mansura* (Augsburg Confession VIII,1). The newer concept of an *ecclesia semper reformanda* means basically the same thing. For what is this remaining and continuing and being endured but the struggle of the spirit against the flesh, the true church against the false church, i.e. the apostolic process? The confidence of the church cannot rest on the perennial institution but rather on the fact that, like the phoenix from the ashes, it will again arise out of its charred form to hope, that it is 'persecuted, but not forsaken; struck down, but not destroyed; always carrying in the body the death of Jesus, so that the life of Jesus also may be manifested in our bodies' (II Cor. 4.9, 10).

The public effect of true Christianity is found in the acceptance of suffering. It is very obvious that, in Hebrews 13.13ff., the horizon of expectation into which Christianity is called is directly bound up with the call to go forth from the camp and bear abuse for Christ. The going forth in hope is bound up here also with the active acceptance of suffering. Christian hope, therefore, is not empty promises for another world; rather, it places those concerned here and now in the front line of the apostolic event, in the midst of the pain of love. The Reformation has, in this regard, spoken of the 'hidden church' whose hiddenness is not found in its invisibility, transcendence, inwardness or spirituality, but rather in its form of suffering – *tecta sub cruce*. Luther said that the *credo ecclesiam* means nothing other than this:

Haec est stultitia dei sub cruce latens, quam nemo principium potest accipere. Ideo in simbolo dicimus: Credo Ecclesiam sanctam Catholicam, quia haec sub cruce non videtur, ideo credenda.[31]

In suffering and abuse, in persecution and social contempt, patience and endurance stand the test. Suffering proves the search for what is to come and the eschatological impatience of Christianity which is hard pressed by the end. Conversely, this suffering certainly does not appear accidentally from outside, so that patience is left when 'one can do nothing else'. Hope leads forth from the camp into abuse. The expectation of the divine future prepares one to take upon onself the 'cross of the present' (Hegel). The place of sanctification which, through the raising of Jesus, becomes, so to speak, pregnant with the future, appears where, according to the laws of society, dishonour and disgrace are found. The peace of God bursts in where the discord of the world rages. Dietrich Bonhoeffer called this the great 'this-worldliness of Christianity': living in the midst of the multitude of tasks, questions, successes and failures, and taking seriously not man's personal suffering, but rather the suffering of God in the world.[32] This can also be characterized as 'pro-existence'[33] or as 'solidarity with the godless',[34] perhaps in the sense of the old rabbinical statement, that 'Every distress in which Israel and the nations participate is a distress. Every distress of Israel alone is no distress.'[35]

Suffering is found only where one loves. If Christianity loves the world with the world-transcending love of God, then it takes on itself the abuse of Christ. He who 'loves', suffers and endures. We must therefore add something further to the Luther quotation about the hidden church 'under the cross': '*Ideo sub nomine Amoris Vel charitatis semper Crux et passiones intelligendæ sunt.*'[36] Suffering springs from the passion of love and it is this love which directs the interest of Christianity outwards away from itself. The Christian does not shape life and the world out of the utopia of faith, but rather out of the fantasy of love. For this reason, the suffering of Christians becomes the form of Christ in the world. To live under the lordship of Christ means to take on oneself that suffering which the 'Yes' of real love brings into the world.

True Christianity is the 'Rose in the Cross of the Present'. We have seen the role of the church in the *theatrum societatis*. What role does the church play in the *theatrum gloriae Dei*? I would like to describe this with a simile used by Luther and Hegel.

Hegel in his preface to the *Philosophy of Right* has described philosophy as 'its own time apprehended in thought'. 'Since philosophy is the exploration of the rational, it is for that very reason the apprehension of the present and the actual.' For him, however, what is present and real is 'the substance which is immanent and the eternal which is present'. Here the decision is made on the fate of modern society. Either it successfully recognizes reason as 'the rose in the cross of the present' and so as 'the rational insight which reconciles us to the actual', or one must enter upon the retreat of resignation, search for the divine inwardly, in the piety of the past or in romantic dreams, and must surrender present society 'to chance and to caprice', and abandon it as god-forsaken and absurd, i.e. as not containing the truth in itself. Man, however, cannot live in absurdity. Either the changed social reality is successfully understood and, in this way, placed in relationship with the absolute, with the meaning of being, with God, or our destiny is the 'fury of disappearing'.

Now the song which Hegel's owl of Minerva has sung over modern society may not be adequate and in the nature of things represent the theory of his present age. The 'rose' of his philosophy may no longer be obvious at all in the light of the 'cross' of our present. But the task still remains. For Hegel, the rose is reason and the cross of the present is that present which is at hand, inadequate, and mediated in the pain of emotion. Hegel, however, also saw that what is involved is not only a *'theory of society'*, so to speak, a cognitive insight into this society's process of becoming. 'In order to gather the rose in the cross of the present, we must take that cross itself upon us', explains Hegel in his *Philosophy of Religion*.[37] Thus the 'rose' is essentially *'the spirit of society'*, a cognitive existence which takes upon itself the pain of the present and endures it and, in this pain, finds both itself and its future.

The life of mind is not one that shuns death and keeps clear of destruction; it endures death and in death maintains its being. It only wins to its truth when it finds itself in utter desolation. It is this mighty power, not by being a positive which turns away from the negative, as when we say of anything it is nothing or it is false, and, being then done with it, pass off to something else; on the contrary, mind is this power only by looking the negative in the face, and dwelling with it. This dwelling beside it is the magic power that converts the negative into being.[38]

A Christianity which does not resist the cross of reality but rather takes it up, communicates to society the power of the spirit – the spirit which, in the midst of temptations, ruptured relationships, pain and absurdity, gives the miracle of endurance and continuance; the spirit of hope where there was nothing to hope for, the spirit of him who gives life to the dead and calls into existence the things that do not exist (Rom. 4.17f.). Faith which stands the test in love, verifies the presence of this spirit. There is no other spirit in which the present social reality can be brought into relationship with the absolute, with God. Without this spirit, the 'fury of disappearing' confronts humanity.

Karl Löwith has shown[39] that this image of the rose in the cross comes from Luther's coat of arms in which a black cross is represented in the centre of a heart surrounded by white roses. Underneath is the inscription, 'The Christian's heart walks upon roses when it stands beneath the cross.' Luther interpreted this in the following manner: 'This is a mark of my theology: "*Justus enim fide vivet, sed fide crucifixi.*" '[40]

In this sense, Christianity, in the 'Yes' of faith to the cross of true love, bears the fate of the present and yet lives in the life-giving spirit of the resurrection. It does not soothe and calm the tensions of brokenness and the devastations of our society, but rather it brings these to a head and confronts them with the divine transformation. The church itself is not the home of salvation, where all contradictions are overcome and that which is torn is healed. But the church, in faith, love and hope, is the guarantee of the spirit, and the hidden appearance of salvation constitutes its world-transcending power.

For the ancient understanding of religion, the church was able to be the *crown* of society, the healing centre, the incarnation of the divine and the elevation of the human. Even today these conceptions are obvious to us. True Christianity, however, with its love in service, stands in the midst of the *cross* of society and, thereby, becomes this *hope* for society, a hope which is responsible for the present. Christianity will win the game of God in the wilderness of the world. In the process of history in our society, the kingdom of God itself is that which is both at stake and within the realm of possibility.

NOTES

This article was first published in *MPTh* 50, 1961, 272–89.

1. Cf. K. G. Steck, *Kirche und Öffentlichkeit* (Theologisches Existenz heute, NF 76), 1960.

2. R. Nürnberger, *Kirche und weltliche Obrigkeit bei Melanchthon*, 1937.

3. In periods following the collapse of the state or in the midst of a socially uncomprehended reality or on the occasion of an audible declaration of communism as *'hostis publicus'*, this concept of religion appears again in a restored form. Nevertheless, this makes very little difference to the fact that society has emancipated itself from the *cultus publicus*.

4. G. W. F. Hegel, *Philosophy of Right*, trans. T. M. Knox, 1942, paras. 190ff., taking up ideas from the English national economy of Adam Smith, D. Ricardo and others. This Hegelian analysis of society has influenced criticism of culture up to present times. F. Tönnies called this system 'society' as opposed to 'community'. H. Freyer speaks of the 'secondary system'.

5. G. W. F. Hegel, *Jenenser Realphilosophie* (ed. J. Hoffmeister) 1931, I, 239.

6. G. W. F. Hegel, *Philosophy of Right*, para. 238.

7. On this question, A. Gehlen, 'Mensch trotz Masse. Der Einzelne in der Umwälzung der Gesellschaft', *Wort und Wahrheit* 7, 1952, 579ff., is particularly informative. Cf. also H. Schelsky, *Die skeptische Generation*[3], 1958, 382f. The society of conformity and levelling places an unexpected diversity of individual varieties of taste, value and opinion at the disposal of the individual so that a most attractive variety of informal groups runs straight through that great organization which is always becoming bureaucratically more uniform; the age of a new uniformity of behaviour is, at the same time, that of a unique development of the spiritual and of the intellectual. 'Conformity and individualization . . . both have their roots in the fact that social relationships and connections become freer and less binding, that the external and internal mobility of industrial society makes the adjustment to uniform social standards of behaviour easier, just as it encourages the chance of the restraint of the private and personal realms before social conventions and pressures.' In this way, not only religion but also ideologies become 'private concerns'.

8. This has been formulated in a classic way in the Letter to Diognetus,

Ch.6. (The acceptance of the body-soul pattern for defining the relationship between church and world is, however, as deceptive here as its application to the early church's christology, because in this way the historical-eschatological aspect of the church is eliminated.) 'What the soul is in the body, that the Christians are in the world. The soul is spread through all members of the body, and Christians throughout the cities of the world. The soul dwells in the body, but is not of the body, and Christians dwell in the world, but are not of the world. The soul is invisible, and is guarded in a visible body, and Christians are recognized when they are in the world, but their religion remains invisible. . . The soul has been shut up in the body, but itself sustains the body; and Christians are confined in the world as in a prison, but themselves sustain the world. . . God has appointed them to so great a post, and it is not right for them to decline it.' (*The Apostolic Fathers*, trans. Kirsopp Lake, Loeb edition II, 1913, 361ff.)

9. Cf. F. Fürstenberg, 'Gesellschaft', *RGG*[3] II, col. 1508.

10. D. Bonhoeffer, *Letters and Papers from Prison*, trans. R. H. Fuller, 3rd ed. revised, 1967, 192 (8 July 1944).

11. F. Gogarten, *Der Mensch zwischen Gott und Welt*, 1951, 182, 187, 190.

12. H. Schelsky, 'Ist Dauerreflexion institutionalisierbar?', *ZEE* I, 1957, 153ff.

13. *Religion ohne Entscheidung*, the title of a sociological evaluation by H. O. Wölber, 1959.

14. This 'non-accountability' (ἀνευθυνία) is the basic concept of seventeenth-century political absolutism (Bodin). It appears again in C. Schmitt's decisionistic theory of sovereignty in the 1920's ('The political decision which is born out of nothing'). F. Gogarten's and R. Bultmann's theological decisionism of faith is obviously related to this. Cf. K. Löwith, 'Der occasionelle Dezisionismus bei C. Schmitt', *Gesammelte Abhandlungen zur Kritik der geschichtlichen Existenz*, 1960, 93ff.

15. *Democracy in America* II, Book IV, ch. 6; trans. Henry Reeve, rev. ed., 1948, vol. II, 318 [World's Classics ed., 1946, p. 579].

16. A. Gehlen, *Die Seele im technischen Zeitalter* (Rowohlts deutsche Enzyklopädie 53), 1957, 74.

17. Here the field even today is unconsciously dominated by F. Tönnies' differentiation (important for youth movements, the philosophy of life and personalism) between 'community', which is an indissoluble totality which is essential for the humanity of man, and 'society', which can be produced, organized and directed, and is no longer essential to men but rather only of arbitrary concern.

18. Here ecclesiological personalism has its sociological context. Cf., the article on social ethics by R. Bultmann, 'Forms of Human Community', *Essays*, trans. J. C. G. Greig, 1955, 291ff.: Considerations of purpose ruin the meaning of true human community (292). 'True human community is that between man and man; that is, that community in which man finds himself devoting himself to his fellow-men.' Bultmann sees the authenticity of this historical community threatened by convention and organization. The embodiment of man's illusionary existence in 'society' is the metropolis. To illustrate this, Whitman's vitalism and Rilke's esoteric are brought into play

('The cities play us false – they are beguiling. . . . Nought of that broader, real activity that is your prize as further you mature occurs in them . . .' 295). Even the church stands in danger of deterioration, as 'the church, which is in its essence invisible – organizes itself as an institution and, in so far as it appears in visible form, it is always real only as *event*' (303). Similarly F. Gogarten, *Die Kirche in der Welt*, 1948, 66. The church is simply an unworldly entity. It is not itself in the world as an organization but rather as the event of revelation. – Cf. also E. Brunner, *The Misunderstanding of the Church*, 1952, especially 10ff.

19. A. Gehlen, *Die Seele im technischen Zeitalter*, 43.

20. A. Gehlen, *Urmensch und Spätkultur*, 1956, 69.

21. A. Gehlen, *Die Seele im technischen Zeitalter*, 28.

22. Of course, one can understand the concept of institutions in another way, like that of Gehlen, who sees them more dynamically; the church, which has had to be an institution in a state of constant reform, can represent society as a 'paradigmatic institution'. Cf. W.-D. Marsch, 'Kirche als Institution in der Gesellschaft', *ZEE* 4, 1960, 73ff. The question is whether, in this way, one realizes the anthropological dimension of the institution.

23. P. Lutz in *MPTh* 49, 1960, 276.

24. Cf. W.-D. Marsch's excellent survey, 'Vom Dilemma des gedoppelten Menschen', *MPTh* 49, 1960, 423ff. and 491ff.

25. Cf., for example, the Catholic sociologists of religion. Cf. W. Goddijn in *Soziologie der Kirchengemeinde*, ed. D. Goldschmidt, H. Greiner and H. Schelsky, 1960, 28ff.; also L. Grond, *ibid.*, 65ff.

26. Such as W.-D. Marsch's attempt, *ZEE* 4, 1960, 73ff.

27. *Soziologische Exkurse* (Frankfurter Beiträge zur Soziologie 4), 1956, 19.

28. J.-L. Leuba's book *Institution und Ereignis: Gemeinsamkeiten und Unterschiede der beiden Arten von Gottes Wirken nach dem Neuen Testament*, 1957) which can hardly be verified exegetically but is, nevertheless, constantly quoted in regard to the sociology of the church, has had a misleading effect. Cf. for example, E. Stammler, *Protestanten ohne Kirche*, 1960; H. H. Schrey, 'Kirche als Institution und Verein', *Spannungsfelder evangelischer Soziallehre: Festschrift für H.-D. Wendland*, 1960, 183 and also many others.

29. Cf. G. Eichholz, *Was heisst charismatische Gemeinde?* (Theologische Existenz heute, NF 77), 1959.

30. Cf. K. Latte, *Römische Religionsgeschichte*, 1960, 323. Also W. Kamlah, *Christentum und Geschichtlichkeit*[2], 1951, 134: 'Here *religio* had the meaning of the devout veneration of those powers in which the divine eternity of Rome is represented, without which "Rome", in the full traditional sense, cannot exist.'

31. WA 31, II, 506, 15–8.

32. D. Bonhoeffer, *Letters and Papers from Prison*,[2] 1967, 201.

33. E. Adler, *Pro-existence: Christian Voices in East Germany*, 1964.

34. F.-W. Marquardt, 'Solidarität mit den Gottlosen', *EvTh* 20, 1960, 533ff.

35. *Deut. R.* II, 22 on Deut. 4.30. R. Akiba also said, 'Any distress which is limited to one individual is a real distress. But a distress which is not limited to the individual is no such (i.e., as intended here) distress.' Against

this exclusive individualism, R. Johanan (presumably R. Johanan ben Nuri) advanced the statement quoted above, which probably means: God listens to the petition of Israel in the distress which goes over Israel and the nations. In the light of Israel's early and later history, this statement comes from such a deep faith that it can only put to shame that church which understands itself to be a church of all nations.

36. WA 56, 388, 21f.

37. G. W. F. Hegel, *Lectures on the Philosophy of Religion*, trans. E. B. Speirs, 1895, Vol. I, 285. Cf. also E. Bloch, *Subjekt-Objekt*, 1952, 245, 255f.

38. G. W. F. Hegel, *The Phenomenology of Mind*, trans. J. B. Baillie, 1910, 30f.

39. K. Löwith, *From Hegel to Nietzsche*, trans. D. E. Green, 1964, 14ff.

40. Letter from Luther written to L. Spengler in Nürnberg on 8 July 1530, WA *Briefwechsel* 5, 445, 4, 10f.

6

THE END OF HISTORY

I The 'Resolved Puzzle of History'

To want to speak about the 'end of history' in the midst of history sounds like a presumption which, at any rate, one does not put past the theologian. We do not know what the future will bring, and we do not believe those who presume to know. Nevertheless, we do not need to be prophets or apocalyptists to think about the 'end of history'. We need only listen to those voices today which, from all sides, offer us an 'end of history' and suggest the way to its conclusion. We need only examine ourselves and our present conditions in order to ask the question whether we are not, consciously or unconsciously, attempting to annul, to render unconscious, and to bring to an end that history which increasingly tortures rather than delights man. At the beginning of the nineteenth century, Wilhelm von Humboldt said, 'The most common tendency of human reason is directed toward the elimination of chance.' Since then the means of achieving this elimination of chance have grown through developments of reason and science. The question for us today is therefore not so much how history can be concluded through enlightenment as how a history which is concluded and laid to rest can be newly and meaningfully reopened.

(i) In Karl Marx, we read: 'We recognize only one single science, the science of history.'[1] 'The history of all societies hitherto is the history of class conflict.'[2] 'It (Communism) is the solution of the riddle of history and knows itself to be this solution.'[3] Here the natural law of social movements is finally eliminated. The key to the puzzle of history has been found. Past history fades into the pre-history of its coming universal sulution.[4] In this way, Marxism is the last but extremely attractive progeny of German idealism's idea of the end of history, an idealism which undertook the grandiose task of overcoming, by means of a universal history and in a recognized history, the elements of chance and the agony of history.

(ii) Today we have the vague feeling that a science of history which lays claim to universal science has attempted too much. The owl of Minerva may have flown away in order to understand reality as that which is reasonable, but it has not returned. It has not brought us 'reason in history', but rather was devoured by the absurdity of the history of our century. Nevertheless, there remains all around us the 'onset of dusk' in which, according to Hegel, this owl can first begin its flight. To speak without metaphors, from the grandiose outlines of universal history in the nineteenth century, an uneasiness about history, a general weariness of history and a deep scepticism about the meaning, reason and ultimate end of history remained in the burned-out craters of European thought. This can be summed up as the flight of the spirit from history, as the dismissal and the loss of history. This 'end of history' looks different from the Marxist 'end of history'. Yet it, too, could be its end. There are good reasons for supposing that, over the horizon of modern industrial society, ahistorical conditions are dawning, and that in these ahistorical conditions the ending of history by men without memories may be able to replace the overcoming of history through universal memory. Neither reason nor meaning is found in what could be known and experienced as 'history'. Therefore, it appears to be meaningful and reasonable to convince oneself that history is no longer being experienced and to create conditions in which such a history no longer occurs. It could be that this solution of the problem of history, which is found where men solve the problem themselves and make the consciousness of the problem disappear, is the only solution, and that humanity will acquire the chance of survival only through abandoning history. Conditions could arise which would certainly contain infinite possibilities of development in every area but no longer allow alternatives in principle. In place of the experience of history in pain and in the work of the negative, a fatelessness as blissful as it was boring would envelop men in a culture of the general and total replaceability of all things. This, too, is an 'end of history'. The solution of the puzzle consists in making the puzzle disappear.

(iii) Finally, we hear in this chorus of voices the expression of that Christian theology which proclaims Jesus Christ and faith as the 'end of history'. God's revelation of eternity in the framework of time transcends time and history. The proclamation of the presence of God frees men from the power and the torture of history. Christian faith frees man from the world and practises the end of history where, in the fulfilment of the moment, he perceives the truth of existence. Man is freed from the shackles of world history by the discovery of the eternally authentic historicity of his existence as Christian faith reveals it. The one who complains that he can see no meaning in history and therefore thinks that his life is meaningless, must be roused:

Do not look around yourself into the universal history, you must look into your own personal history. Always in your present lies the meaning of history, and you cannot see it as a spectator, but only in your responsible decisions. In every moment slumbers the possibility of being the eschatological moment. You must awaken it.[5]

Having listened to the chorus of those who are bringing history to an end, we must ask:

(1) How and as what is history experienced in each of these cases?
(2) What history is being ended by the end that is being presented to us?
(3) To what extent and how far are we concerned with congruent statements about history and its end?

Along with such questions, we ought also to consider those limits at which a particular scientific discipline – in this case, history and theology – emerges from its normal concerns and tolerates critical reflection concerning the presuppositions and the consequences of its endeavours. Self-satisfaction and abstraction are certainly characteristic of the scientist. To consider the presuppositions and the consequences of his work interrupts the process of his thoughts. But just as Archimedes could not prevent his execution by shouting 'Do not interrupt me while I am drawing circles', so scientists and sciences cannot remove themselves from the history in which they draw their circles. So-called boundary questions, therefore, should, rather, promote traffic across these boundaries. If we ourselves do not mutually interrupt each other's 'drawing of circles', there might suddenly be a rude awakening.

We shall therefore try to transfer the historical enlightenment of history as we have known it for more than two hundred years, in terms of its presuppositions and its consequences, into a historical enlightenment of this enlightenment. We shall, in other words, ask ourselves in what way historical reason serves history and what effect it has on history.

On the other hand, however, we should have to attempt to clarify theological talk about the 'end of history', considered in terms of its presuppositions and consequences, within the context of that history which proclaims itself to be the 'end of history'; in other words, to ask both in what way theology serves history and also what is the result of theology on us in history today.

II Motives for historical reflection in history

Modern historical awareness is an awareness of crisis.[6] Modern history and the philosophy of history are, in their beginnings and in their intention, a philosophy of crisis and a science of crisis.

In the nineteenth century, all reflection on history including the investigation of events and their context by historians, sociologists and philosophers has the earth-shattering French Revolution behind it and the unforeseen consequences of the industrial revolution, which is bound up with the French Revolution, before it. In this double revolution, the familiar orders and institutions of society and patterns of thought were shattered. With it, the whole crisis in which the human world was involved became apparent. History, so to speak, had burst the banks of traditions which had confined it to familiar routes. The traditions were no longer equal to these new possibilities of history. They could now be preserved only with effort. They no longer offered man the salutary matter-of-factness of the obvious. In this way tradition became the object of reflection and of criticism. Men discovered the historicity even of those rules which history up to then had been able to control. Since then, 'history' has been experienced either as a permanent crisis or as a continuing, irresistible revolution in constant acceleration. The positive sciences which have developed in this atmosphere along with a new philosophy of history have been compelled to 'conceptualize their time' so that it is possible to perceive, control and finally master the course of historical events. The old cosmological orientation of the world has been replaced by one which is historical and philosophical. The mastery of the 'revolutions of nature' by the natural sciences has to be extended to master the revolutions of society through the science of history. So what 'history' really is in its as yet undiscovered possibilities for good and evil is experienced primarily from that revolution of which Hegel said: 'Thus the movement and the unrest goes onward. It is this collision, this knot, this problem that history faces and that it must solve in the time to come.'[7] But how ought this problem to be 'solved'? Before we turn to possible attempts at a solution, we must first ask how, and on which horizon of perception, history is experienced at this focal point of modern times.

(i) The first horizon in which the experience of history may be encountered is the *horizon of the threatened order*. Within this context, history is experienced as crisis, as the calling into question of all traditional political, social, and cultural orders. History can be turned into a temporary crisis by being imprisoned and brought under control in restored and renewed ordinances. In this sense, the new experience of history has been identified as 'crisis' by conservative as well as progressive thinkers.

For Saint-Simon, revolution meant 'crisis'. 'He means the revolution, but by pressing on towards its political foreground, he becomes aware of the reality of history and society in its totality. In other words, when Saint-Simon speaks of crisis, he means history – and he is the first person to mean it in a totally modern sense.'[8] Now if history is understood as crisis, its critical element, that which is at risk and has to be achieved is always already included: the ordering of chaos. If history is identified as crisis, this ordering is seen to be the task of the spirit both on it and in it. In political terms, this may be the restoration of the balance of power in Europe. In social terms, however, it can also mean the establishment of the sovereign jurisdiction of the positive sciences.

(ii) The other horizon in which history can be experienced is the *horizon of realized hopes*. When historical crises break out, because of the new possibilities which are suddenly within reach, the sense of what is possible also comes to life in man. Hopes which have been shattered along the way, visions which the old order has relegated to the kingdom of unreality, become actualities. Old dreams loom up and seem within the realms of possibility. For that reason, the history that dawned in the revolutions of modern times, has not only been seen as a crisis of order but also – as above all in German idealism, in so far as it is the intellectual answer to the French Revolution – as a 'glorious dawn' (Hegel), an unforgettable 'sign of history' for the plan and the final goal of nature with the human race (Kant), and as a concrete occasion for a messianic movement, which saw fulfilled in the new age the hopes of the West, including those of the Bible. In Hegel's theological *Jugendschriften* we find this sort of identification of revolution with the eschaton of hope:

The first disseminators of the Christian religion hoped for a revolution, to be brought about by these means, i.e. to be accomplished by a Divine Being, while men looked on passively. When this hope finally evaporated, men were content to await this universal revolution at the end of the world.[9]

Now, in the shadow of the French Revolution, Hegel, along with his young Tübingen friends, was convinced that

... it has been reserved in the main for our epoch to vindicate at least in theory the human ownership of the treasures formerly squandered on heaven; but [he goes on to ask] what age will have the strength to validate this right in practice and make itself its possessor?[10]

Friedrich Schlegel thought in the same way:

The revolutionary desire to realize the kingdom of God is the elastic point of progressive education and of the beginning of modern history. Anything that does not have some relationship to the kingdom of God is only a matter of secondary importance in it.[11]

If history is not understood as a crisis of order but rather as a new possibility within the horizon of actualized hopes – albeit with the addition that it is man who must realize this hope through the power of his spirit – then history is always qualified by the future and the future becomes the authentic category of historical thought, the 'spiritual principle of the time'. What dawns as new possibility is no longer measured against the existing order, which is breaking up, but against men's hopes, their essential concern.

In the nineteenth century, both modes of experiencing history were interwoven in many ways, and they greatly influenced historical consciousness and its work in history. However, the first experience of history as a crisis of order was the predominant one. 'Since Herder, historical reasoning has been reflection on threatened order.'[12]

(iii) If history is identified as a crisis of order, then order is the task of the spirit; if it is experienced as chaos, then cosmos is the task of the spirit; if it is experienced as discontinuity, then the establishment of continuity is the task of the spirit. It is, therefore, understandable that for the comprehension of, the designation of and the understanding of crisis, the old images of order must first be revised. The experience of history as crisis and terror makes it necessary for the spirit to investigate and to search in history and in the philosophy of history for the general in the specific, for the constant in the changeable. In the nineteenth century, the tendencies of historical understanding and the presentation of history were urgently directed towards the recognition of the homogeneous in the heterogeneous, towards the coherence in the fortuitous, towards the permanent substance behind the fleeting appearances, towards the meaningful integration of divergent historical powers. But if this attempt succeeds, it subordinates the puzzling events of history to a more general horizon of meaning, a background (usually seen in metaphysical terms) against which these events can be recognized, designated and, in their context, understood. For Ranke, 'the epochs succeed one another in such a way that there occurs in all of them what is not possible in any single one, so that the abundance of life which is instilled in mankind by the divinity is revealed through the centuries'.[13] As Carl Hinrichs has pointed out, the Platonic-type theology of history of Goethe's age and the restored balance of the European powers are the images of order which for Ranke represent the background of history. For Johann Gustav Droysen, the subject of the historical method is defined as the 'cosmos of the moral world', which develops teleologically in world history. Aim after aim is revealed and fulfilled and, on the basis of this, it is possible to infer the intention of intentions in which all motion comes to an end. What propels men restlessly onwards will become rest, consummation and the eternal present. For Wilhelm Dilthey, every single expression of life in the realm of the objective spirit represents a fundamental common reality. The main basis of the historical world is unfathomable life, 'this sphinx with the body of an animal and the face of a man'. The essence of history is present in the objectification of this unfathomable life.

Only through the idea of the objectification of life do we gain insight into the nature of the historical. Whatever characteristics the mind puts into its expression of life today, are, tomorrow, if they persist, history.[14]

Therefore, it is only one's own participation in this unfathomable life that makes historical understanding possible. 'We are first of all historical beings before we become advisers of history, and only because we are the former do we become the latter.'[15] These conceptions, which have only been hinted at here, show how time and time again in various ways, the substance, the whole, the foundation of history is suspected, desired or experienced and how, on the basis of a nucleus of history, which is established by one means or the other, the historical individualities, novelties and crises can be made understandable.

For the theoretical as well as the practical overcoming of history as crisis, still another conception is offered which is much more closely related to this revolution: scientific positivism. For Saint-Simon and Auguste Comte, the goal of the historical, political and sociological understanding of revolution is the conclusion of the revolution. If, however, for them revolution means crisis, and crisis in general means history, then the goal of their understanding is, generally speaking, the overcoming and the conclusion of history. 'We have the immense task of bringing to an end what Bacon, Descartes and Galileo began. Only then will the revolutionary upheavals be at an end.'[16] Their historical and sociological positivism is, therefore, a consequence of the scientific Enlightenment. The laws that govern crises in society can be recognized by 'social physics', and where these crises are recognized, they may also be controlled and avoided. This historical positivism of Bacon, Descartes and Galileo was certainly discarded by many people at the turn of the century on epistemological grounds when a distinction was made between the methods of the natural sciences and those of the humanities. Nevertheless, positivism has a universal scope which ought not to be overlooked. Saint-Simon, Comte and Hegel already recognized that the French Revolution was only the political and contingent expression of a much greater revolution, the industrial revolution. The latter cannot, however, be understood as a temporary shift of balance in Western society. Its effect is total and overpowering. There is no historical model for the conditions created by it which might serve for orientation. It not only outdates historical conditions but also leads humanity over a threshold of history beyond which everything hitherto called history seems to come to an end. Granted, it can be said that history is always very complex and does not allow itself to be explained by the scientific method. Still, the sovereign authority of the natural sciences has been able to produce a technical civilization in which these very conditions prevail. In that case, history does not become computable because it is computable, but rather because it can and must be made computable. The irrationality which both torments and delights could be eliminated from history if man began consciously to produce history. The meaning of the puzzles of history could then be recognized in that men realize such a meaning in practice. But in that case the positivism of scientific and technical civilization would bring an end to previous history and transform it into a history that could be recognized, planned and made. It could be that the complexity of history, which the positivistic historian no longer sees, no longer occurs and is no longer experienced. The renunciation of national history and slanted political history, the renunciation of the historical determination of man by his origin, tradition and religion become the conditions for the acceptance of this system. Functional determinations suppress the historical determination of man. History is – to use the terminology of automation – now only experienced in those 'badly-structured problems' which are made into 'well-structured problems' so that their optimal solutions are computable. That intermediate area of automata and cybernetics comes not only between man and nature but also between man and the future of history. This also brings with it the renunciation of history, the release from history and the repression of history. This system – in so far as it relinquishes historical leadership – again makes possible individual history, cultural history, religious history and national history, but it does so through as comprehensive a social and historical *quietus* as possible, in other words, in the area of the freedom that has been relieved of history. Everything again becomes possible on a new level, but on this new level nothing has any significance for the real forward movement of history. This, too, is an 'end of history' for which the positive sciences apparently provide the determinative instrument.

Scientific and technical civilization brings history to an end as a crisis, in the observable realm. Does it not, however, as an undertaking, produce in the end a crisis which can be much greater and which, therefore, remains intellectually uncomprehended and morally unconquered simply because man, caught within this system, can no longer see beyond it? Ought not the dominating character of the sciences to be disclosed so that people no longer work *in* science, forgetful of history and with the naïvety of children at play, but learn to work *with* it and to be responsible historically with it for this work? In order to do this, however, it is necessary to arrive at an understanding of history which is greater and more comprehensive than the 'far-reaching undertaking' which Bacon and Galileo began and which Saint-Simon and Comte tried to carry on. Truth must be thought of as history, so that in the history of approaching truth the historicity of human reason emerges. The latter must be realized in scientific endeavours for new, open possibilities so that it can be responsible for its scientific and technical acquisition of power to a hoped-for and sought-after future. The more history can be computed and made, the more we must look for an opening up of history on a level to which this history can be responsible. We must, as it were, look for the history of that history in which man is the subject.

III *Motives for theological reflection in history*

1. Faith in Christ and the 'End of History'

First of all, we might say, very generally, that for Israelite and Christian faith, history is experienced in the horizon of hopes for the fulfilment of God's promises. No questions are asked about the overcoming of history and the control of chaos through a divinely stabilized cosmos; the concern is, rather, for the fulfilment of the time of promise through the God of promise. By means of God's promise, men are led out of their stable metaphysical cosmic home and are exposed to history. If we speak in this context about eschatology, we mean the doctrine of hope which, on the basis of God's fulfilment of his promise, awaits the goal and end of everything which is now set into motion historically.

If history is revealed out of the past of God's promise for the future as a time of hope, then the question arises whether the corresponding horizon of hope is broad enough and strong enough to bear every new development in history, to make it understandable and to give it shape. The question is always whether hope has kept pace with historical experience, especially when this experience usually proves to be just the opposite of fulfilment. There is always more contained in the statement of hope for those who hope than can be realized in what is later experienced in history. In New Testament research, this is referred to as the problem of the 'delayed *parousia* of Christ'. It appears in other forms wherever history is sought and experienced in the mode of hope. How does hope overcome its disappointment in history? How does hope transcend the melancholy which history prepares for it through alleged fulfilments?

According to the New Testament witness, primitive Christianity hoped for 'the day of our Lord Jesus Christ', for his 'coming in glory', for his 'glorious appearance', for the making known of the freedom of the children of God in which not only the hope of those who hope will be fulfilled but also the longing of the whole creation which lives in the pain of transitoriness. What, however, did the first Christians experience? First, simply that this future of Christ kept them waiting and history calmly moved ahead. Even those who hoped were plunged into a transitoriness which has not yet been transcended. As Albert Schweitzer, the originator of this picture of primitive Christianity, said:

There is silence all around. The Baptist appears, and cries: 'Repent, for the Kingdom of Heaven is at hand.' Soon after that comes Jesus, and in the knowledge that He is the coming Son of Man lays hold of the wheel of the world to set it moving on that last revolution which is to bring all ordinary history to a close. It refuses to turn, and He throws Himself on it. Then it does turn; and crushes Him. Instead of bringing in the eschatological conditions, He has destroyed them. The wheel rolls onward, and the mangled body of the one immeasurably great man, who was strong enough to think of Himself as the spiritual ruler of mankind and to bend history to His purpose, is hanging upon it still.[17]

According to this powerful metaphor, history – understood as the wheel of transitoriness and the eternal return – swallows up all eschatology. All that remains of the hope against history aroused by Jesus and his followers is deep resignation. Since that time, eschatology has become impossible. History buries every hoped-for end of history. Its significance and fulcrum is found not in an ultimate goal toward which the wheel of history rotates, but rather within the wheel itself. Of course, this image is not historically accurate for Jesus, as he deliberately separated himself from John the Baptist, but it still calls attention to a problem in primitive Christianity. Certainly, particular groups expected the arrival of Christ and the saving end of the world in the coming future, 'not everyone will fall asleep'. As history went on and this generation also died, the question arose, 'Where is the promise of his coming? Ever since the fathers fell asleep, all things have continued as they were from the beginning of creation' (II Peter 3.4). In this way, expectations of an imminent end may have been postponed. On the other hand, however, early hymns and liturgies point out that this first experience of the nearness of the kingdom of God in Jesus' works and deeds and in his resurrection from the dead could change. The expectation of his real coming and the enthusiastic joy of already living in his presence became the cultic celebration of his epiphany and his eternal return and presence in spirit and sacrament. To the degree to which this representation in church and cult of his promised future established itself, earthly hopes for the end retreated to the border of the church's consciousness and were forced into heresies. The fulfilments which God was to prepare for believing hope in a real future were replaced by what the church was able to offer.

We come, then, to another solution to the conflict between hope and history, which is characterized by the catch-phrase *Eschatology swallows up history*. This solution presupposes the phenomenon of the sudden turning from the future to the present and from expectation to remembrance, and results from the following reflection: if all the glowing apocalyptic images of hope evidently reach out into emptiness and history goes on, then it could very well be that the authentic meaning of this hope is not to be found in their objective desires for the world in the future, but in the fact that they give naïve expression to something which, in fact, is already present. This is the sudden turn from what is hoped for to the hope itself which is accomplished by reflection. As a result, the question is no longer what these traditional images seek to communicate about the future, but rather what it is they express about human nature. There is a move from Christ's future – which has failed to arrive – as intended by such images to their lasting anthropological significance. Furthermore, there is a turn from the awaited 'revolution of the totality', as Hegel put it, to a revolution which has already occurred in a hidden way and which, therefore, now only has to be remembered and demonstrated. What is the result of this? The last judgment has failed to arrive, as historical experience teaches. It *must* fail to arrive, theological reflection teaches, because time was already fulfilled and because the revelation of God in Christ has already transcended the history whose end is sought. The end must fail to arrive because it is already there. If, however, the end of history is, in essence, already there, then every further question concerning the goal and the end of world history becomes meaningless. Where and how is this end already there? 'Today', it is said, 'where you hear his voice'. Because God is present, in his revelation there is only 'today' and never a 'then' or a 'once'. For 'God' is eternally present, and in the presence of his eternity, time, so to speak, stands still. There 'the arising is extinguished and the going down is lost', as Parmenides said. God's revelation, like God himself, has no extension into time. His truth stands in the 'now'. His eternity is present. Now wherever this divine 'now' occurs, history is at its end. What no longer is and what is yet to come no longer have power over the man who stands in God's eternal presence. He is free from the burden of history, from guilt; and free from the power of history, from death; and free from world history because he is free of the world. Faith practises this end of history. It no longer recognizes a past and a future. If this faith is faith in Jesus Christ, then Jesus Christ is not this end of history for it because it awaits the end of world history from him, but rather because Christ makes it possible for faith to exist in the eternal presence of God in which history finds its end. Here the solution of the puzzle is not an end of world history but rather freedom from the world; not an eschatology of the world's history, but eschatological existence. A present and anthropological eschatology swallows up history, or, more precisely, makes the question about history and its future end superfluous and meaningless. The true solution of this problem is found in the fact that Christ is the ever-present, particular eschatological event. The 'now' receives its eschatological character through the confrontation with Christ or the word which proclaims him, because in this confrontation with him, the world and its history comes to its end and the believer is freed from the world as a new creation.[18]

If, however, 'eternal presence' is to be the true solution of the problem of history and eschatology, and if Hegel's and Marx's ideas of universal history and final history are no more than secularized primitive Christian eschatology, as is often suggested, then the theological solution of the Christian problem just outlined can offer itself as a standard for parallel solutions to the nineteenth-century problem of the history of the world which has become meaningless. World history as such is without a meaning and an end. The meaning and the end of world history are present in that moment which man grasps as his very own present moment. By grasping the present moment, he understands the meaning of history.

2. Faith in Jesus Christ and the opening up of history

Enlightening though such a solution of the Christian problem of history may appear, we must investigate its cost. Faith has to pay the price in two places:

(i) If 'Christ' means the ever-present, particular eschatological event, then it is vague and unclear to what extent and why Jesus of Nazareth, crucified under Pontius Pilate, is this 'Christ'. The earthly, historical Jesus, the story of whose passion is told in the gospels, can now be considered only as a starting point, beginning, presupposition or even a cipher for a continually possible and always present eschatological event. Theological reflection, which sees the end of history in the eternal presence of word and faith, threatens the earthly Jesus and the historical remembrance of him with this 'end of history'. By praising the present event of word and faith as the presence of eternity and as the eschaton of history, it obscures the extent to which Christian faith is involved and Jesus is the Lord of this faith.

(ii) On the other hand, this presence of the eschaton in faith is only to be had at the price of the spiritualization and the individualization of that future which primitive Christianity expected from Jesus for the earth.

Now in its beginning and its nucleus, Christian faith is a resurrection faith and a hope for the resurrection. 'If you confess with your lips that Jesus is Lord and believe in your heart that God raised him from the dead, you will be saved', states the ancient confession in Romans 10.9. Here is a confession of who the Lord is and to whom the lordship of the world belongs. The crucified Christ is not only the Lord of the believers, but also the Lord of the dead and the living. Here, too, is a confession of who God is. It is 'God' alone who has raised the crucified one, who brings the dead to life and who calls those who have no existence into being. Christian faith, therefore, is faith in God in that it is a resurrection faith, and it is a resurrection faith in that it is faith in Christ. For it, the resurrection of the crucified one is not only the motive and the presupposition of faith but also the foundation for this faith. Christian faith is – as Kant says – the historical faith of the church. It cannot supersede the Christ-event and the Word, which reaches faith as proclamation out of history, by a moral, God-given faith in reason. The predicate of 'resurrection' further shows that an eschatological and universal expectation is bound up with this once-and-for-all event. The Easter event is not a miracle which is isolated in Jesus; rather, it can only be understood apocalyptically in so far as in it and through it the resurrection of the dead may be hoped for. The primitive Christian Easter faith teaches us that Jesus is always intelligible only in relationship to his future. Through the guidance of hope, we learn to understand him. Now if Christian hope finds its ground in the resurrection of Christ and its horizon in the overthrowing of sin and death by the lordship of God, then this hope is not swallowed up by history, nor does it swallow up history. The present is opened up by this past, which is characterized by the cross and the resurrection of Christ, for the future, as a time of hope and of patience. If this hope is a resurrection hope, then it is indebted to an event in which the transitory is past, and is directed towards a future in which the past is passing away. The impression of general transitoriness, which presents itself to the sorrowing glance backwards at what cannot be retained, has, in truth, little to do with history. The historical is much more the characterization of that transitoriness which arises in hope, and its breaking out towards another, new future. For the resurrection hope, it is whatever seems to make all life a passing thing that is transitory: where hope in the resurrection of Christ is kindled, death becomes transitory; where the absolution of justification allows one to hope for righteousness and freedom, guilt becomes transitory. History does not swallow up this hope.

This hope, however, does not swallow up history either. The resurrection hope which is based on the cross is satisfied with nothing less than the resurrection of the dead and the new creation of all things in the full lordship of God. As a result, here it becomes the motor, the spring, the happiness and the torture of history. The word of the promise provokes history incessantly, and hope keeps open the experience of reality as history. As identity is promised to man and comes into view, he observes his permanent non-identity in historical terms. As the full lordship of God and physical freedom is promised to men and brought into view, he begins to suffer from the God-forsakenness of the world and the inhumanity of man in it. He experiences a great difference between existence as it is and that existence which may be hoped for. In this difference he experiences in himself solidarity with all the eager longings of creation, which is subject to futility (Rom. 8.18ff.). With his freedom and his hope, with his suffering and his expectation, he becomes a hope for the whole creation. The 'end of history' is not yet present in such a way that time and history stand still and no longer exist, but rather in such a way that this 'end of history' allows time, makes the future possible and affects history. In the word that calls the crucified Christ into life, in the word which calls those who are guilty into righteousness, and in the 'spirit of hope' which permits suffering in the unredeemed state of the world, the 'end of history' comes into the present and does not allow the present to remain as it is. So the present is qualified by the eschatological future as history. The 'end of history', which so happens and is understood, makes history. This does not turn the present into the present of eternity or into the eternal present, but it does make it an advancing front line which is freed from the past and is propelled into the oncoming newness.

How does this resurrection hope effect history? It effects history in that man can hold fast to it only in obedience to mission. The 'spirit of hope' and the present 'power of the resurrection' have an explosive effect. The progressing mission to all nations and the liturgy in the physical everyday world perceive the new possibilities which have been opened up through the eschatological word and grasp them. A Christian consciousness of history, for that reason, is always, above all, a consciousness of mission. This consciousness does not ask about God's universal plan for the coming ages, but asks rather about Christ's universal mission to all men. Christian consciousness of history, for that reason, is primarily a new relationship to the future and only then a new relationship to the world and a new relationship of man to himself. The Christian mission infects all nations with hope and produces in them the breaking out towards the future. The practice of this hope in obedience, love and suffering works on the future of men and humanity so that they become what they have never been: 'disciples of Jesus' (according to the conclusion of Matthew), the 'new people of God' made up of Jews and Gentiles (according to Paul), the 'third race' (according to the early church).

Word and work of mission bring about the exodus of a new humanity from all peoples and nations, the *profectus ecclesiae e gentibus* (Irenaeus). This mission and the consciousness of history which is achieved from it are, without a doubt, revolutionary. The resurrection hope in this form produces 'unrest' in the world of the gods and in human society, as Celsus correctly pointed out. It allows nothing to remain as it was and is, but rather confronts everything with that transformation which it expects by reproaching it with its unredeemed and unfulfilled condition. This hope is not interested in stabilizing transitory things by supplying them with an eternal world foundation; its sole concern is, rather, the reconciling of all things with their real future. It therefore harries things, relationships and men because of the coming glorification of God in them, and it allows nothing either to be its own self-justification or to sink into nothingness. If this hope can only be kept in mission, then it only remains alive through patience. If it is based on the resurrection of the crucified one, then it shows itself in that patience which follows the patience of Jesus. This patience alone is able to survive the tension of the hope of history. Patience is the greatest art of those who hope. Hope accepts the 'cross of the present' in the 'power of the resurrection'. It takes upon itself the real unredeemed state of the present as it is, the torture and the pain of the negative, without resignation and without illusion. The political and social revolutions, which we have seen from the beginning of modern times, have always shown very little patience. They force man into reconciliation with their observable achievements. A hope, however, which is directed towards the transcendence of loneliness, towards the solution of real contradictions, towards the negation of the negative through the God of the resurrection, is able to establish reconciliation in patience. Only where Christian hope itself remembers the cross of Christ is it able to endure the crucifying pain of the 'delayed parousia' of its Lord. Where hope abandons the cross, it is inflated in an enthusiastic way and immediately collapses in helplessness.

IV   Historical reason and the opening up of history

Can anything parallel in meaning for the work of historical reason result from the observation and the opening up of history through Christian hope? Here the theologian can make no demands. He may, however, ask questions.

Every historian realizes that each single event remains silent and nebulous without a certain survey of the relationships. Only in comparison with and in the context of other events does it begin to light up and speak. Now the more comprehensively the comparison and the context are accepted, the more a single event or an individuality loses its character as event and becomes an appearance, becomes the case which demonstrates that which is typical and already known. Without the relationships, we can recognize nothing. In fixed relationships, however, the historical, the fortuitous, the once-and-for-all character is lost. For this reason, theories of historical relationships must always retain the flexibility of heuristic projects. They must be open over against that which has not yet been established in detail and over against that totality of history which has not yet been experienced. This raises not only the question of how and by what methods one arrives at a continually improving and more differentiated knowledge of history, but also the converse question; what significance can historical knowledge really have for history? With whom and with what can historical knowledge of past history reconcile? Is its task to reconcile transitory things with what is eternally immortal and to confront the mortal with the truth? Is it its task to rediscover the past history of men in the modification of their own spirit, to elevate history that has happened into history which can be perceived and recognized and, in this way, to make men more and more the subject of their history? Could it not also be the task of historical reason to reconcile historical phenomena with their own possible future? Every historical phenomenon has its very own future in which it reveals what it really is and its true concerns. It will only in the end reveal itself as 'what really happened' when history reaches its end. But which end will it reach? This is always at stake. 'To articulate what is past historically does not mean to recognize it "as it really was",' wrote Walter Benjamin in his *Geschichtsphilosophischen Thesen*. 'It means to seize a remembrance as it flashes in the moment of danger.' In preceding sentences he explained this danger in the following manner:

The Messiah comes not only as the Saviour; he also comes as the conqueror of the Antichrist. Only the recorder of history has the talent to kindle the sparks of hope from the past which is permeated with the idea that even the dead are not safe from the enemy when he is victorious.[19]

If we follow this line of thinking, then concern with past history cannot be only for the sake of its pure past, for the sake of the ascertainment of facts.

Concern with past history cannot, then, be exercised out of mere interest in the present, as has been said, to stylize the past into a pretty avenue lined with poplar trees which runs up to the glorious present, or to place oneself as a dwarf on the shoulders of gigantic ancestors. In that case, the work of historical reason would be necessary, from a historical point of view, and would take place for the sake of the open, unconcluded and for the most part still undiscovered future of the past. Future which has not come into being can lie in the past. Fulfilled past can be sought for in the future. For the historical is always found in the question-and-answer difference between what it becomes and its real concern. This unconcluded quality of what has come into being in what is authentically desired, hoped for and intended, appears to me to be the mainspring of history as well as of historical investigation.

We do not study Luther and the Reformation, the French Revolution and Napoleon only because they once were, or to give the present a new orientation to its past. Rather, we study them on the basis of that solidarity which, according to Benjamin, permeates 'even the dead . . .', as collective insecurity and collective hope. The historian does not have to make the last judgment on the past either in accusation or in justification. In that case, he himself would be its end. Nor can he merely record facts and reconstruct history. But in solidarity with the historical, he can reveal the rents and cracks of what is needed, the imperfections and unfinished quality of the past. He cannot redeem the past from its conflicts. He can, however, represent the solidarity of the unredeemed and, in this way, 'kindle the sparks of hope' on the cemeteries of history. His theme cannot only be the history of success and how and why history so succeeded; rather, it must be the history of failures and of the ongoing differences between the future that was sought after and the present that was achieved. He thus investigates the 'significance' of the event and in so doing considers what transpired in the event, progressing to that which *seeks* to have meaning, to proclaim, and to point the way. He also investigates what it needed and did not find in itself and its time. He investigates the future *of* the past and the future *for* the past and in his investigation also considers the significance of the past for the present and, conversely, the meaning of the present for the past. If hope discloses to him the meaning of the moving horizons of the future in history, then history brings him into a unique historical state of aggregation for him.[20] Past history comes alive when neither its temporal past nor death can be its end. The historian's historical images of the past, which he himself painted, acquire from the past a provisional character, for the 'movement and unrest' goes onward (Hegel).

The young Marx once said, 'One must make the stones of circumstances dance by singing their own melody to them.'[21] I would like to modify this and say: one can make the stones of historical circumstances dance when one tries to sing that melody which, on the basis of the transcendence of death and whatever is transitory, allows the future of reconciliation to resound over its cemeteries.

NOTES

This article was first published in: Reinhard Wittram, Hans-Georg Gadamer and Jürgen Moltmann, *Geschichte – Element der Zukunft. Vorträge an den Hochschultagen 1965 der Evangelischen Studentengemeinde*, 1965, 50–74.

1. K. Marx, *Die Frühschriften*, ed. S. Landshut, 1953, 346.
2. *Ibid.*, 525.
3. *Ibid.*, 235 [*Early Writings*, trans. T. B. Bottomore, 1963, 155].
4. In a somewhat simpler way, Alexi Tolstoy, the poet of the revolution, wrote, 'Do you remember? We have talked a great deal about what a tiring meaninglessness the cycle of history, the decline of great civilizations and ideas, which have turned into a pitiful parody, seemed to be . . . lies! The veil has been ripped away from our eyes. . . . A glaring light has illuminated the half-destroyed vaults of all the past centuries. . . . Everything is harmonious, everything is in accordance with the law . . . the goal has been found. . . . Every member of the Red Army recognizes it' (quoted from R. Wittram, *Das Interesse an der Geschichte*, 1958, 6f.).
5. R. Bultmann, *History and Eschatology*, 1957, 155.
6. G. Mann, 'Die Grundprobleme der Geschichtsphilosophie von Plato bis Hegel' in: L. Reinisch, *Der Sinn der Geschichte*, 1961, 13.
7. G. W. F. Hegel, *Sämtliche Werke*, XI, 563.
8. N. Sombart, in: A. Weber, *Einführung in die Soziologie*, 1955, 88.
9. G. W. F. Hegel, *Early Theological Writings*, trans. T. M. Knox, 1948, 158.
10. *Ibid.*, 159.
11. F. Schlegel, *Athenäumsfragmente*, No. 22.
12. H. Heimpel, 'Geschichte und Geschichtswissenschaft', *Vierteljahreshefte für Zeitgeschichte*[5], 1957, Part 1, 15.
13. Quoted from C. Hinrichs, *Ranke und die Geschichtstheologie der Goethezeit*, 1954, 162.
14. W. Dilthey, *Werke*, VII, 147.
15. *Ibid*, 278.
16. A. Comte, *Die Soziologie*, 1933, 15.
17. A. Schweitzer, *The Quest of the Historical Jesus*, [3]1954, 368f.
18. Cf. R. Bultmann, *Glauben und Verstehen* III, 1960, 105.
19. W. Benjamin, *Illuminationen: Ausgewählte Schriften*, 1961, 270.
20. For both this formulation and the reference that knowledge of an eschaton allows a powerful, solvent force to penetrate historical work, I am indebted to a letter from R. Wittram about my book, *Theology of Hope*.
21. Quoted by H. Popitz, *Der entfremdete Mensch*, 1953, 40.

7

HOPE AND PLANNING

I Future planned and hoped-for

Hope and planning are both related to the future, but they are
not identical with one another. Hope and planning represent
the future in different ways. Yet they are not separated from
one another, but live with each other and for each other.
Unless hope has been roused and is alive there can be no
stimulation for planning. Without specific goals towards which
hope is directed, there can be no decision about the possibilities
of planning; but without planning, there can be no realistic
hope. Both hope and planning have their foundation in suffering and in dissatisfaction with the present, though planning
only appears in business theory, while hope also involves the
perception and the acceptance of suffering. Over and above
this, both find, in new possibilities, ways leading towards
another future. Both are, then, based on the idea that the
reality of human life is that history in which the existing and the
possible can be fused with one another, in which the possible is
realized and the new can be made possible. Reality's horizon of
time is thus perceived by both, and both experience the changes
of reality in time. For both, the future has a special significance.
Man does not exist within a temporal framework, but is rather
directed out beyond it. This is, however, not always obvious.
There are cultures and religions without a sense of the future.
This sense of the future first had to be stimulated by Christianity
and by industrialization. Moreover, in both cases, man's freedom is realized in a changeable world. The field of hope and

planning is summarized historically, by means of the 'future'; ontologically, by means of 'possibility'; and anthropologically, by means of 'freedom'.

By *planning*, we understand an 'anticipatory disposition for the future' (Haseloff).[1] The greater the abundance of scientific and technical possibilities become in a society, and the more social conditions are affected by change, the more important it becomes to plan so as not to 'backslide in the future' (Paul Valery). Such anticipatory dispositions can make what is future and possible, through *deterministic systems*, into necessities. In the network of causes and effects, dispositions of this type are possible in limited areas and automatic complexes. They can also make what is future and possible, through *probabilistic systems*, into probabilities. Such dispositions are appropriate when they concern not only causes but also originators who do not have the delightful regularity of the stars in their courses. For many ways out are always possible for a history that has been disposed of, each of which can possess determinable degrees of probability. Finally, dispositions are still possible when not only causes and effects, or originators and their fortuitous interactions, but competitors, challengers and opponents are involved. Stemming from the *game theory of society* (J. von Neumann), actions and reactions may be meaningfully calculated by means of planned games and simulators. The goal which is envisaged can then be brought towards realization not only by computable laws and calculations of probability, but also agonally, by planned estimation of the possible counter-effects of others. Plans are therefore only at their lowest and most primitive level predictions and prophecies of what happens. In relation to greater and more complex realities, planning is always found in a dialectic relationship to history. A development which can be foreseen historically requires the making of plans to cope with it; anticipatory dispositions, on the other hand, compel history to develop towards specific goals. Simply by being made public, dispositions and prognoses themselves influence a disposed and prognosticized history. So in making plans, one must take into account the special influence of planning on history, for there can also be self-destroying prophecy, as is illustrated by the prophet Jonah, which often develops in negative predictions. This dialectical relationship between planning and history finally poses the question of the worth of goals and purposes. Which goals ought one to pursue when so many things are possible? What is urgent and what can one do without to begin with? 'The god of physics is there to give us what we wish, but not to tell us what we ought to wish for' (Santillana). In this way, planning finally leads us to the question of what it is that men actually wish, hope and search for. This question is always found in relationship to that which causes men to suffer, experience dissatisfaction and feel need. When the need is no longer there, suffering ceases – and so do wishes and hopes. At this point, both future and planning lose their meaning.

Hope, on the other hand, is more difficult to define. One can understand hope as a subjective feeling – hope and never despair. Hope can be called for when anticipatory dispositions become uncertain and mean by it the power to take risks. In that case, however, hope would refer to that remnant of destiny and chance which remains on the periphery of planning for the future. Hope would then come into consideration in our plans only in the context of 'unforeseen developments' and would be the human attitude in the face of the uncontrollable in the controllable, the unplannable in planning. Hope would relate to those incalculable and unplanned moments in history. Anticipatory dispositions of the future certainly presuppose that a specific future stands at my disposal and these anticipatory dispositions extend only as far as the future now appears to be disposable. The word 'hope', however, comes from the realm of inter-personal relationships. One does not like to make arrangements for another man or to have arrangements made for oneself. In personal relationships, hope presupposes the otherness of the other and his freedom and becomes a hoping trust in which one person promises himself to another for his future. Hope then refers much less to that future which is available out of my own powers than to that future which another man places at my disposal. In that case, hope is not the disposition of my future, but the expectation of the future of the other, based on his promise. So hope refers to the future of the other or to another future. That does not mean that I am able to know nothing about this future. This leads neither to fatalism nor to irrationalism, for such a future for another or such another future opens up real objective possibilities for me, a new sphere of life, new freedom in a wide-open field of action in which there are certainly plans. By way of comparison, it has been said that a man can hardly plan when and whom he marries. But the plans certainly begin to be made with the mutual promise of marriage.

When in the light of a *planned future* we speak of a *hoped-for future*, there is always the resonance of such an element of the otherness of the future over against the present, with regard both to the origin of this future and to the newness of this future over against that which is known in the present.[2] The question is how we might characterize this element of otherness more closely. If we mean by it the factors of destiny (*fatum*) and coincidence (*contingentia*) in the future of history, then these factors will be eliminated by planning as much as possible, for planning is the negation of destiny and fatalism, of coincidence and the irrational hazarding of pure decision in man's conscious and responsible arrangement of the future. The element of otherness of the future can, in essence, never mean destiny and coincidence, for both have nothing in common with 'future'. 'Future' must mean ontological possibility and anthropological freedom. The fascinating element of the otherness of the future is found much more in the 'new', which it brings as far as possible. The otherness of the future has significance for man not because the future is incalculable and uncontrollable, but rather because it generates something new. Coincidence and destiny are meaningless in comparison. This 'newness', which the otherness of the future determines, lies on the border between what is possible and what is impossible. The new is there when the impossible becomes possible, when the unthinkable is thought, when the undiscovered is found and discovered.

In this sense, the 'new' is, first, the making possible of the possible, the conditioning of the future which is coming toward us, and the opening up of freedom.[3]

What does planning have to do with such a *novum* of the future? If planning is an anticipatory disposition, then it is kept alive by the exploration of possibilities and represents forward-looking perception and development of what is different and unfamiliar. What does hope have to do with such a future *novum*? Everything, I think! Hope is always born from the emergence of the new. Hope sees the advent of the future and reaches out for it in open expectation. It forsakes the old and the inadequate both inwardly and outwardly. At the moment when the new awakes hope, suffering and dissatisfaction with the old are born. Hope has nothing at all to do, however, with 'destiny' and with 'coincidence'. Hope is the opposite of fatalism and decisionism. It is concerned with the removal of the irrational factors in history, for it likes to plan on behalf of that new which kindles it.

For the Greeks, hope was an evil from Pandora's box which was poured out to confuse the human spirit so that men were not over-presumptuous. For the Greeks, meaning and truth could be found only in the continual, the timeless, the always-being and the eternal present, but not in history and in the changeable.

For the Israelite and the Christian spirit, however, truth is found in the advent of that new thing which God has promised. Their relationship to truth is, therefore, one of hope. Changes in history and changes of history acquire meaning when the promised new thing must be expected in history.[4] The incalculable, which is called fate or chance, becomes secondary for Christian hope, for it is not directed towards a God of fate or chance, but rather towards the God of promise. For this reason, hope says, 'But seek first the kingdom of God (sc. for it is now at hand) and all these things shall be yours as well.' Therefore, it knows that to those who love God, all things, events and decisions will serve the good, namely, the goal of promise and of hope. Christian hope springs from the belief that the *novum* of salvation and of freedom for an unredeemed world has appeared in and through Christ. Therefore, hope directs itself toward the corresponding new creation of all things. It recognizes in the history of Christ an event in the mode of promise. What does that mean? A promise always has its time still ahead of it, and not behind it as a concluded fact. A promise directs the present which is effected by it towards the *novum* of fulfilment and, in so doing, turns the present into a front line for the breaking up of the old and the breaking in of the new. A promise is no Cassandra-like prophecy, but requires hope and a new mode of action. It does not prophesy history, but rather summons men to a historical life. For Christian faith, the fulfilment of the promise and the realization of the hoped-for *novum* is placed in God's hands. The hoped-for future is not only different because it is new but also because it is God's future. Still, this future does not, on the other hand, lie in the hand of blind fate or whimsical chance but rather in the power of this God who will create it. For Christian hope, the basis on which we can hope for such a future is found in the Christ-event. Hope recognizes the power and also the faithfulness of God in this story of the resurrection of the crucified one. Such an event cannot be forgotten! It is, therefore, more than the reason to hope for a once-and-for-all future of God. Faith also means that through the history of Christ and the promises of the gospel, God reveals his future to men and has, thereby, granted them freedom. Christian hope not only waits for its fulfilment as a fact but also searches for this fulfilment in the grasping of that which is historically possible. The prospect of this future coming from God already opens up here and now an open space of change and freedom which must be shaped with responsibility and confidence. Through Christ's resurrection and through hope aroused, the future of God exerts an influence in the present and makes the present historical.

For the prophets and the apostles, the catchword of hope is always the 'new'. The Old Testament speaks in this way of the New Exodus, the New Conquest, of the New Zion, the New Heaven and the New Earth. The New Testament speaks of the

New Covenant, the New Life, the New Commandments, etc. The simple fact that the basic scriptures of Christianity contain the antithesis between the 'Old' and the 'New' Testaments has already buried the tension between 'old' and 'new', and the 'new' is given pre-eminent meaning. That hope is kindled in this tension between 'old' and 'new' does not, however, balance out the flow of time toward the realm of the past; rather, with the judgment of 'old' and 'new', it cuts into it and in this way makes it 'historical' and gives it direction. The fulfilment of hope and the fulfilment of time is not just eternity as the unchangeable which at every moment is both near and far. This fulfilment evokes an interpretation of time for those realities from which one withdraws and which are close at hand.

Only when Christian hope recalls its own unique basis – the God of promise, the God of the exodus in the Old Testament and the God of the resurrection in the New Testament – can it become a critical and active partner of the present mentality of planning and the model of the world of tomorrow. For this, however, it must remove itself as much as possible from the stormy God of history, from the God of fate and of chance. Theologically, this means that we must again learn to differentiate between the promise of God and the providence of God. The promise of God is not based on the providence of God, but rather the providence of God serves the fulfilment of the promise of God.

The deterioration of Christian hope began in the history of theology and philosophy with the disintegration of the promise of the God who makes history into a general providence of God over history. With this levelling process, the translation of what had been revered as 'providence' into prognostic planning systems first became possible. The promise of God became merely the expression, the revelation, of the divine planning-mentality for history. The human spirit of planning could then be understood as the image of the divine, and that led to natural reversal which made 'providence' simply a hypostatized ideal of the still undeveloped human capacity for anticipatory disposition.

II   The enlightenment of time

1. Theological systems of hope in the enlightenment

It has been said that in today's planning systems, we are concerned with a conquest and an extension of time analogous to the conquest and extension of space. This parallel did not arise only today. It stems from the Enlightenment. The familiar movement of the explanation of space and its laws by mathematics and science from Galileo to Newton was matched by parallel movements of a historical and prognostic explanation of the periods of history and its laws. One movement sought divine wisdom in the creation, the 'book of nature', and found it in geometry. The other sought divine wisdom in history, and found in the books of the Bible the proclamation of the divine plan for history. The one first became popular in the higher échelons of society as *'physique amusante'*; the other, in pious, academic biblical circles as 'prophetic theology'. At the beginning of this interpretation of time stood the statement of Luther that history is the impenetrable mask of God. At its end is the conviction of the well-planned course of history towards the goals set before it. How did this change come about?

Even as early as the seventeenth century, the age of orthodoxy and absolutism, apocalyptic and chiliastic thought underwent a quite remarkable renaissance in Protestant theology.[5] It began in Holland and England and came into full bloom in Württemberg and Saxony. Through this sudden and universal renaissance of theological apocalyptic, a new historical sense developed in the middle of the age of an orthodoxy that was both without a sense of history and hostile to history. People began to question the Bible about its witness to past and future history and no longer sought it in heavenly doctrines (*doctrina coelestis*). Over and above the 'law' of the Old Testament and the 'gospel' of the New, a third kind of divine expression was discovered – prophecy. In the prophecy of the Old and the New Covenants, the revelation of the divine *providentia* was sought. Whereas previously the Revelation of John had been an incomprehensible book to the Reformers, it was now referred to as 'the princess among the scriptures'. As a result, the investigation of the *series temporum* became the main subject matter of 'prophetic theology' in the seventeenth and eighteenth centuries.

But what did 'prophecy' mean here? *'Prophetia est quasi rerum futurarum historia'*, wrote Johann Cocceius. All prophecy is *'antecipata historia'*, according to his pupil van den Honert. 'Prophetic exegesis has the purpose of teaching men an appropriate concept of the ways and the intentions of God', observed the Dutchman van Til. Gottfried Menken, who interpreted the French Revolution and Napoleon in apocalyptic terms – ideas which affected the 'holy alliance' – said, 'The Bible is the divine commentary on world history'. 'The history of Israel is the type of the training of humanity.' Long before him, we find the lyrical poet Adolf Lampe saying,

Where are the depths of God's wisdom more revealed than when one examines and compares with each other the various ways which God has led his church? How well the Lord has made everything here in his time! How is everything related to everything else? In what orderly fashion can one step follow the other when what is going ahead is always in the shadow of what is coming? Just as, through binoculars, one daily makes new discoveries in nature, what a miracle it is that also by means of increasing diligence in the investigation of the divine word, new discoveries are made and the promised growth in knowledge in the last days begins increasingly to be fulfilled.

Johann Albrecht Bengel and the Swabian fathers turned this into a 'system of hope', a 'beautiful, glorious coherent system which permeates all epochs of the world'. It is the 'divine plan of the kingdom', the progressing reality of which was thought to have been discovered. Since the promise and providence of God coincide, history itself becomes the progressing perfection of the kingdom, the *procursus regni Dei*. In Christian August Crusius, the pietistic philosopher from Leipzig,[6] this 'system of hope' turns into a *systema moralitatis*, which the history of man progressively masters. This completes all the necessary changes in theology, so that Lessing and Kant could replace and dissolve faith's system of hope by a system of a planned education of humanity or a plan and an ultimate intention of nature with humanity. The pious explanation of the providence of God in terms of an ultimate intension and plan was deistic through and through. 'God' faded so that he became the mere décor of a plan which could be understood, to which history corresponded and would correspond. If prophecy is nothing but anticipated history, then it is prognostic and predictive. The *novum* of God's promise becomes *fatum*. In place of the eschaton of the fulfilment, which must be searched for in hope on the basis of the promise that has been heard, emerges a *finale* of history which is to come to light in the course of time. A historical theology and a faith working in history become a theology of history and a faith in history. Basically, truth becomes apparent in the difference between hope aroused and experience undergone, in present suffering through the passion of hope. Here truth appears in the formula: *verum=factum*.

These first systems of hope produced by the Enlightenment accepted the pious rational interpretation of *fatum* and *contingentia* by introducing a so-called divine planning-mentality into past and future history. These systems of hope still accepted the planning of history by divine providence as *fatum*, but it was a penetrable *fatum*. It is no wonder that this Christian explanation of history very soon turns into a historical explanation of Christianity and an apocalyptic supersession of faith replaces an apocalyptic of faith.

2. The providence of God and the providence of man

When providence and the detectable plan of history become the mediating element between God and man, there emerges from this mediation a development in which the emphasis is placed on what is discovered by man. This change displayed by theology was met by the succession of Vico, Kant, Hegel and Marx.[7] Vico's *Scienza Nuova*, written in 1725, expresses the already mentioned principle of faith 'in history' – the true is that which is becoming, *verum et factum convertuntur*. His philosophy of history sets out to present the eternal, ideal history according to the principle that what has happened must necessarily so happen.

According to our first unquestionable principle, the historical world is most certainly made by us men and is, therefore, able to be rediscovered in the modifications of our own spirit. Nowhere can there be greater certainty than where he who creates things, also tells about them.

This insight offers the observer 'divine pleasure, for in God knowing and doing are the same thing'. This last statement elevates the historical acknowledgment of human history to a participation in the divine acknowledgment of divine history. At the same time, however, it erects a barrier. In God, knowing and doing are one. The *intellectus originarius* produces the world by thinking of it. It can also prophesy history, since it can make it. Man, however, can only recognize his history *after* he has made it. He rediscovers the history that has been made in the modifications of his own spirit. For Vico, God has the ability to look ahead; man, however, can only look back. Man can become a knowing participant in divine providence, but only in a retrospective way, for what is true is what has come into being, and providence coincides with the real circumstances of history. Even today, when we often ask why things had to happen as they did, we still unconsciously make this presupposition. This forecast of history, according to Vico, is finally possible because and in as far as historical processes repeat themselves cyclically in such a way that one is able to recognize again what is typical. These barriers of the human knowledge of history tumble when (1) the regularity of the accepted cyclical scheme of historical control is broken by the expectation of a final fulfilment of time and (2) the ideal image of a divine *intellectus originarius* is sacrificed for human intellect. In both cases, reason can no longer only reproduce future conditions according to the patterns of the past. Reason must be prospective and inventive. It then requires a new epistemological proof of its prognostic achievement.

Immanuel Kant considered precisely this problem when he asked, 'How is a history *a priori* possible?'[8] He answered, 'When the prophet himself makes and organizes the events which he announces beforehand.' He gave three examples of this, which he meant ironically. The Jewish prophets prophesied well because they themselves were the creators of their destiny. Our politicians say that we must take men 'as they are'. This 'as they are', however, must mean, what these politicians have made them by means of unjust force. Clergymen like to prophesy the disintegration of religion while, in the meantime, they themselves do just what is necessary to bring it about. In this way, men are prospectors of history in so far as they are subjects of history. Man is able to recognize and predict history in so far as he can become its subject. Yet for Kant, this human, designed and created world remains embedded in an allegedly great and comprehensive context of the intention and plan of nature for the development of the human species. 'One can consider the history of mankind, in general, as the realization of a hidden plan of nature to establish an internally – and for this purpose externally – perfect political constitution as the only condition in which nature can fully develop all its intentions in mankind.' 'One sees', says Kant in this connection, 'that even philosophy can have its chiliasm.' It all depends on whether experience can ascertain some proof of such a process of nature's intention for the human race, for 'the predictive history of mankind must still be attached to one experience or the other'. Kant found such an event to illustrate the moral tendency of mankind in the French Revolution; participation in it, even in spirit, found an echo which could be caused by nothing but a moral disposition in humanity.

In other words, according to Kant, history is *a priori* possible when and in so far as the prophet himself makes the events which he announces beforehand. But what he predicts and what he ought to begin and create in history is based, according to Kant, on a presupposed hope which knows itself to be one with the intention and the total plan of nature which is revealed in a revolutionary event, a 'sign of history', as Kant says, a *signum rememorativum, demonstrativum, prognostikon*, a phenomenon, 'which no longer forgets itself'. In this way, humanity is the subject of history and yet it is not, because human history only receives its meaning from a tendency of divine providence or from nature itself. History can be made, planned and predicted, but this planning and making is subordinate to a higher insight into the general tendency of nature.

The next step will now be the drawing together into a dialectic of this dualism between the tendency of nature and the history of man. There is always a reciprocal relationship between the supposed and postulated outline of meaning and the corresponding planning and making. What is presupposed as providence or the intention of nature always has an effect on the making of history by prospective investigation. These presuppositions can also be understood actively as ordinances of the spirit which brings forth history according to its own designs. Planning and acting are then not only equivalent in value but also value-producing. Only in this way does the knowledge of history emerge from *theoria*, so that it is no longer insight into fundamentals but, rather, the production of new things. Knowledge no longer looks into something that is there but rather produces something which is not yet there. It produces by prospecting. It does not bring to light facts or intentions, but rather sets in motion human action. Prognostication is then no longer an anticipation of fate but rather an anticipation of human practice. In this sense, the meaning of history for Karl Marx can be recognized theoretically to the degree to which men set about to realize it in practice. It is disclosed theoretically to the degree in which humanity makes, deliberately and consciously, that history which it has already made. The possibility of making history itself becomes the goal of making history. 'To the degree to which history can in fact be made, there also grows the awareness of the Enlightenment that it can learn to control history in an intelligent way.'[9] In this projection of the goal, however, there are pre-judgments and general concepts which cannot be proved purely pragmatically. The goal of being able to make history generally and as a community and the wholesale expression of human powers to be achieved in this has a 'sign of history' in itself. There is not only, as for Kant, the French Revolution, but also the industrial revolution. This is understood as a prognostic sign and as a real potentiality for the realization of the ideals of humanity held both by the Enlightenment and by German classicism. The inner progress of industrial growth, accepted without question, becomes the proof of the faith in progress which has been brought along with it.[10] These signs of history give information about a comprehensive horizon of makeable human history, namely, the longed-for union of mankind. What was only seen in ideal terms in Christianity, as a result of the mission 'to all nations', and in humanism as a result of universal understanding and tolerance, can now be realized through economic integration and universal interdependence. Through the industrial complex of communication, men are becoming for the first time what they have always thought themselves to be, but never were – men in one human race. For the first time, the history which up to now has only run its course as the history of nations, groups and classes, has been united into a history of the one world. The unification of the world and its destiny, which emerges in this way, is the presupposition for the common planning and the need for the making of one history.

Once these implications are made plain, then a series of critical questions arises:

(i) History becomes *a priori* possible when the predictor himself makes the events which he announces beforehand. For the whole Enlightenment up to and including Marx, the whole horizon of this plannable and makeable history was found in what Kant called 'philosophical chiliasm', according to which the unity and development and universal unfolding of mankind is to be realized and the kingdom of freedom and self-realization is to dawn through the deliberate possibility of making history. This chiliasm can easily be made historically relative: man has only recently become a historical subject of this kind and for the first time finds himself on the way towards being such a man. The categories of the unity of mankind and the one history now become the necessary task of mankind; they are not valid timelessly and universally but rather are valid only hypothetically and for an epoch.[11] One cannot subsequently throw over history the net of world-historical relationships which has only been formed today, and declare all history to be 'pre-history'. If we make a historical and critical study of the history of the development of the modern industrial world, then we can hardly understand it as the triumphant conclusion of all previous history, as if all previous history since the birth of man had only present conditions in mind. It is always the error of chiliasm to take a specific epoch of history for the 'end of history'. If, however, the modern world, as it is and as it can be, is not the end of history hitherto, but rather an epoch in history, then the modern world itself is not at its end; on the contrary it is faced with an open history. Through such a historical criticism, which reveals the origin and conditions of the modern system of man, who plans and makes history, the system stemming from this again becomes, so to speak, fluid. It loses its ultimate, apodeictic quality and its utopian reserve. In this way, the distinction which it conceals of itself is again revealed, namely, the distinction between the hopes with which it began and the conditions which it is creating, between the history which can be planned and made in hope, and the history of this history.

(ii) This can also be made plain from another side. In every breaking out into a new, unknown future, for which all historical examples are insufficient, more is contained for man than present experience can realize at that point. Israel experienced this distinction in its history, when it moved from Egypt into the land of Canaan, where milk and honey did not exactly 'flow'; it experienced it again in the return home from exile to its devastated homeland. This distinction permeated the whole western history of revolution. It will also be repeated in tomorrow's industrial planned society. 'The really disappointing thing is human existence itself, experienced or anticipated, as it emerges or will emerge from the industrial society.' As long as socialism is developing, it can retain the magic of a real transcendence. To the degree that it develops, it loses this magic. 'Can man', asks Raymond Aron,[12] 'live without all transcendence once the transcendence of the future follows the transcendence of God in being eliminated?' Will the subject which is moved by a transcendent hope have lost its capacity at the end of the process of its production?[13] In highly industrialized lands, the signs are increasing that the category of the 'future' is ending. The once progressive utopian thinking is dying out. In place of what were once necessary and substantial investments in an increasingly attractive future, there is a consumer relationship which is completely even with the future. The anticipation of disappointment gives birth to all those critical questions about great plans and models of a world of tomorrow. Does planning make man the free master of his history, or does it lead him into an organized adjustment to barren and unappealing developments? Does planning arouse a new consciousness of the future, or does it de-futurize the future? Shall we, as G. Anders put it so pregnantly, 'in the future no longer see the future as future'?[14] Does planning effect the overcoming of blind fate by seeing the responsibility of men or is man, through a totally planned life, the fatalist of his own timetable? Expected human existence is very clearly not what was promised in the first moments of enthusiasm. What, for example, did the programme for a shorter working week promise? An increase in leisure time, freedom and self-realization. Why did this not happen? Obviously the non-identity of man remains a torture and a piece of good fortune. *Horror vacui* asserts itself where men 'do not know what to do'. We must certainly be aware of this distinction for man if we are not to appropriate it and to produce those disappointments the consequences of which we cannot foresee.

III   Feed-back of planning in hope

If by 'feed-back' one understands a continual control of the impulse in the effect and of the effect in the impulse, then a fruitful relationship between hope and planning could, perhaps, be described as feed-back. The impulse of hope must be controlled in the effect of planning and, conversely, the effects of planning must be controlled in the intentions of hope. If specific hopes, as they come to life in the revolutionary signs of history and as they see new realms of possibility, are conveyed in planning, then such hopes exhaust themselves as soon as all these new possibilities are exhausted. If, however, the difference between hope and planning, hoped-for and planned future, is a mainspring of history, then in exhausting all the possibilities that have been opened up through anticipatory dispositions, we must continually observe the characteristic quality of hope and its different modes of action. Planning must be aware of its origin in hope and of the projection of hope. If it puts itself in place of hope, it loses the transcendent impetus of hope and finally also loses itself.

Through planning, this historical transition from the possible to the real and from the future to the present is consciously made and completed. In this way, planning is both reactive in the prevention of foreseeable evil and active in evaluative, particularized visions of a better world. In both cases, planning sets itself at the apex of history or, at least, at the apex of definite historical processes of production.

In the first place, hope has nothing to do with the historical transition from the possible into the real, but rather kindles itself on the *novum* in which the possible is first made possible and discovered. Hope invokes itself in an evolutionary contradiction to present reality, and not only in the name of the possible. Hope is not only, as Kierkegaard thought, the 'passion for the possible'. Hope reaches out further over against historical possibilities and can even be characterized as a 'passion for the impossible', the not yet possible. Yet this would be too formal a designation. So let us consider Christian hope in more concrete terms.

Christian hope has its origin in the event of the resurrection of the crucified Christ. For it, the cross of Christ reveals what is truly evil in the world, the torture of creation, the unredeemed condition of the world and its sinking into nothingness. For Christian faith, the saving future of God appears over this misery in the resurrection of *Jesus*. In his resurrection, hope is always kindled anew. In him, the future of righteousness and the passing of evil can be hoped for; in him the future of life and the passing of death can be hoped for; in him, the coming of freedom and the passing of humiliation can be hoped for; in him, the future of men's true humanity and the passing of inhumanity can be hoped for. Where this hope is applied to a human life, a great difference develops between what one believes and hopes for and what one sees and experiences. Man is involved in a contradiction between himself and his surroundings. He begins to suffer from it. If this hope is directed, as can happen in the Christian faith, not only towards the overcoming of this and that inconvenience but ultimately towards the overcoming of death, then Kierkegaard was correct when he called it a 'hope against hope'. This was what Paul also meant when he uses Abraham to illustrate that faith is founped on hope, where there was nothing to hope for (Rom. 4.18), and when he meant that hope in the visible and the probable is not yet hope. 'But if we hope for what we do not see, we wait for it with patience' (Rom. 8.24f.). Where such a hope comes to life, suffering from the unfulfilled and unfree aspects of life develops. It is not only a suffering from earthly anguish but, even more, a suffering from the anguish of the world,[15] the whole 'eagerly awaiting creation', which is expressed, revealed, and incorporated in the resurrection hope.

The new element which appeared in the story of Christ is not merely the prospect of a once-and-for-all end of history or of a life after death, but rather the historization of the world already here and now. It is through hope aroused and in suffering from the anguish of the world that such an open future comes to affect the present. Hope shows its power not in apocalyptic fantasies, but in the patience and in the contradictions of the world as it is.

Let us attempt to describe more precisely the ways in which this hope acts on the present.

(i) Suffering presupposes love. He who does not love does not suffer. One can avoid suffering by not attaching oneself to anything, by making oneself insensitive to happiness and pain. All things and conditions and life relationships then become replaceable and exchangeable. Only when one loves something or someone, does this thing or person become irreplaceable. At this point, one becomes open to injury, vulnerable, and the possibility of suffering develops. If we attempt to overcome suffering by the creation of a culture of non-attachment or of attachments which are loose and may at any time be dissolved, and create a consumer situation of the replaceability of all things, then pain can indeed be avoided, but the frustration of life, emptiness and boredom, ensues. Hope keeps love alive. Hope opens the freedom for love to express itself completely, to take on pain and suffering, for hope takes away from love the fear of losing itself where it attaches itself, considers something irreplaceably valuable and, in this way, becomes vulnerable. The dissolving of all attachments and the replaceability of all things is not equal to death and the pain of the past; this can only be done by that love which acquires its unending power of suffering and great stamina from the hope of overcoming death.

(ii) This hope places the life which is so loved within a purposeful horizon which goes beyond all the fulfilments which are possible and thinkable here, into the area of freedom from death. A man does not confront himself with the bare facts. He does not comfort himself by something which is invented and produced. In hope, he anticipates a future which reaches out beyond this and, therefore, permeates present history and the history that can be planned for the future. Here a permanent distinction arises between existence planned and achieved in terms that are possible here and now, and the main concern of this existence and what it really wants to be and intends to be. This difference, kept awake and made conscious, works like a permanent revolution, a permanent iconoclasm. It is the motor, the mainspring, the torture of history, for it points out the perennial incompleteness of that which has become and that which is becoming in the reality desired and sought for in hope. God's promises, which Christian faith understands on the basis of the history of Jesus Christ, are directed towards that kingdom in which God is God and in which men are true men. These promises are directed towards the true life, which will be free from transitoriness and death. They are directed towards righteousness and peace. What hope, in this way, hopes from God has an effect on the intentions of a corresponding activity. There are relationships and conditions which correspond to it better than others. This hope also produces evaluative, particular visions according to which some particular historical possibilities are to be taken hold of and others are to be left alone, without hope itself being incorporated in such particular visions.

(iii) The other side of this purposeful horizon of hope is the suffering and the dissatisfaction with the present in which man cannot become man as he hopes. It is the suffering from the earthly anguish and unfree human conditions which this love recognizes, that wishes happiness for the poor and freedom for the humiliated and is, therefore, ready to make investments. Here are not only the inconveniences which are seen by everyone, such as traffic congestion, the need for housing and hospitals, etc., which can be helped out by planning and investments. More urgent still is the anguish which will approach humanity in famines due to over-population. What is lacking to meet this anguish is a consciousness of the solidarity of mankind which does not close its eyes to the distress of others but rather accepts this distress as its own. This is just as valid for the unfree conditions of others. Is it not first of all important to make all men aware of such suffering? Is it not important to give the various economic, domestic, industrial and educational plans a certain orientation towards such a common recognition? One cannot pragmatically provide a planning corrective for this or that inconvenience which has appeared or will appear, but rather must include many individual purposes in one great undertaking.

We cannot abstain from hope for the future to enjoy our acquired happiness as long as most of the others have not yet acquired this future at all. The renunciation of consumption on the basis of self-preservation through asceticism for its own sake is not particularly sensible for its own sake, but it is valuable on the basis of necessary investments in the future of others.

Christian hope must be aroused to this task, if it does not want to become a private other-world by hope but rather the horizon of hope in love and in solidarity with all of creation involved in similar suffering.

We see the ways in which hope works, first, in the intentional horizon which it stretches out over a life. By means of this horizon, the driving superiority of the real future over the planned future can be seen. Secondly, we see the ways in which hope works in the capacity for suffering of that love which it arouses. If this is correct, then we can also say that this hope leads man to the origin of freedom, of what is future and possible.

Christian hope ought not, in a fatalistic way, to make the future tabu. Nor ought it to think that with the help of its faith in God, it could abandon the future. It ought, therefore, to see that men, in a world which is becoming unintelligible, should 'keep their heads up', recognize meaningful goals, and find the courage to invest human and material powers with this purpose.

NOTES

This article was first published in: Hermann Lübbe, Horst Karus, Fred Angerer, Wenzel Loff and Jürgen Moltmann, *Modelle der Gesellschaft von morgen* (Evangelisches Forum Heft 6), 1966, 67–87.

1. Cf. O. W. Haseloff, 'Strategie und Planung', *Griff nach der Zukunft*, ed., R. Jungk and H. J. Mundt, 1964, 122ff.

2. For what follows cf. J. Moltmann, *Theology of Hope*, 1967.

3. In a similar way, L. Kolakowski attempts to broaden the concept of utopia to the 'impossible'. The inadequate utopian consciousness always has goals which, at the moment, are impossible to achieve, but which give meaning to present transformations. He thinks that 'what is now impossible can only become possible at all when it is announced at a time in which it is still held to be impossible'. Cf. *Der Mensch ohne Alternative*, [2]1961, 147.

4. G. Picht, *Die Erfahrung der Geschichte*, 1958, 54. 'The Greek man lived in the epiphany of the eternal present. The man who experiences history in the future of truth lives within eschatological revelation.' 'It (i.e. time) does not represent what is already independent of it, but rather brings into the present what does not yet exist' (48).

5. Cf. the following references to the history of theology and of philosophy: J. Huizinga, 'Naturbild und Geschichtsbild im 18. Jahrhundert',

Parerga, 1945, 147ff.; G. Schrenk, *Gottesreich und Bund im älteren Protestantismus vornehmlich bei Johann Coccejus*, 1923; G. Möller, 'Föderalismus und Geschichtsbetrachtung im 17. und 18. Jahrhundert', *Zeitschrift für Kirchengeschichte* L, 1931, 393ff.; J. Moltmann, 'Jacob Brocard als Vorläufer der Reich-Gottes-Theologie und der symbolisch-prophetischen Schriftauslegung des Johann Coccejus', *ibid.* LXXI, 1960, 110ff.

6. F. Gerlich, *Der Kommunismus als Lehre vom tausendjährigen Reich*, 1920, has called attention to this pre-history of philosophical chiliasm in Germany.

7. For Vico, cf., K. Löwith, *Meaning in History*, 1949, 115ff. For the history of the problem cf., J. Habermas, 'Theorie und Praxis', *Politica* XI, 1963, 206ff.

8. I. Kant, *Der Streit der Fakultäten* (*PhB* 252), 1959, 78ff.; Akademie-Ausgabe VII, 79ff.

9. J. Habermas, *op. cit.*, 213.

10. H. Popitz, *Der entfremdete Mensch: Zeitkritik und Geschichtsphilosophie des jungen Marx*, 1953, 152, has referred to this.

11. Compare J. Habermas' critique of Marxism (*op. cit.*, 214).

12. Bergedorfer Gesprächskreis, *Zu Fragen der freien industriellen Gesellchaft*, Report No. 16, 1964, 8, 10.

13. So observes A. Metzger, 'Automation und Autonomie', *Opuscula* 17, 1968, 58.

14. *Griff nach der Zukunft*, 1964, 47.

15. I have borrowed A. Metzger's phrasing (*op. cit.*, 59) but understand it eschatologically in the sense of Rom. 8.18ff. rather than mystically.

8

THEOLOGY IN THE WORLD OF
MODERN SCIENCE[1]

I

The fate of the modern period is the scientific explanation of
the forces of nature, of the constitution of man, of social relationships and historical movements, and scientific technical civilization is its task. What kind of meaning can Christian theology
have in a world which has become man's world, and will become
even more so in the future? Where does the need arise for
theological reflection in a world in which men no longer live
with gods and demons, impenetrable powers in nature and fate,
but 'with the bomb' and revolution? In such a world, man is no
longer dependent on nature. Nature becomes dependent on
man, and man is more and more delivered over to himself and
to the actions of his fellows.

When the topic of theology and science, faith and reason, is
brought up, one immediately thinks of the long history of conflict between the declining 'religious' culture of the Middle
Ages and the rising, autonomous scientific culture of modern
times. One thinks of Galileo's trial and of modern slogans like
'knowledge is power' or 'faith and natural science are irrecon-
cilable'. One remembers that the meaning of theology in the
modern scientific world is really found in its increasing meaninglessness for that world. The time when one could argue who was
right, Copernicus or the Bible, where Joshua 10 states that 'sun
and moon stood still, until the nation took vengeance on their
enemies', is long past. Today the dilemma between theology
and natural science no longer lies in the conflict of contra-

dictory statements. On the contrary, the problem is the lack of conflict between statements which stand side by side but have no connection with each other and for the most part have nothing more to say to each other. Faith and secular reason are no longer engaged in the struggle for truth, but rather stand side by side in a meaningless coexistence.

How did this cool schism between the certainty of salvation and responsibility for the world, between faith and reason, theology and science, develop from this early conflict?

The work of Nicolaus Copernicus, *De revolutionibus orbium coelestium*, which, according to Kant, started the 'revolution in the manner of thinking', was published in 1543 by the Nuremberg Reformer, Andreas Osiander. In his preface, which was challenged by Copernicus, Osiander developed the significance of this new world-view by means of the rhetorical concept of the hypothesis: hypotheses are *fundamenta calculi*, not *articula fidei*. Faith does not bind science to a world-view that is necessary for faith, but rather frees the sciences for knowledge of the world within the open horizons of hypothetical outlines. Faith frees science from dogmas that are part of a particular world-view and constitutes its mobility in the progress from hypothesis to hypothesis.[2] But in that case, what is the aim of faith, if it is no longer the *magistra* that defines the foundations and purposes of scientific endeavour, but only guarantees the uncontested freedom of that endeavour?

Johannes Kepler had already recognized that God's purpose with the Bible could not have been the rectification of erroneous opinions of a certain era, thus sparing men scientific research. His sole intention was to reveal to men what was necessary for their eternal salvation.[3] This reduction of the contents of the Bible to the question of man's salvation – and at the same time the exclusion of its authority in all areas which do not relate to this personal, supernatural salvation – was then and is today felt to be a great liberation: it was the only possibility of affirming the Bible's validity. By this understanding, however, theology dissociated itself from the task of taking possession of the world through acquiring knowledge of the world. Its domain became a personal, supernatural doctrine of salvation. It could interpret salvation only for the inner self-certainty of tempted man. In this way, science and the shaping of the world lost their place in the framework of the hope for possible salvation and the fear of possible condemnation. The more this salvation is thought of as being unrelated to the world, the less important and significant the knowledge and the shaping of the world becomes. If the Christian expectation of salvation was dependent on a historical remembrance defined by the name Jesus Christ, then theology and the sciences also entered into the conflict between tradition and man's experience of himself. The place of the sovereignty of tradition through man's education by means of texts was taken by the liberation of man from tradition as a result of his education through his own experience and through experimentation.[4] When Galileo wanted to show Jupiter's moons to his opponents, they refused to look through the telescope. They believed – as Brecht put it – that 'Truth is not to be found in nature, but only in the comparison of texts'.[5]

A classic definition of this separation was given by Pascal. 'If we perceive this distinction clearly, we shall lament the blindness of those who only allow the validity of tradition in physics instead of reason and experiment; we shall be horrified at the error of those who in theology put the arguments of reason in place of the tradition of scripture and the Fathers.'[6] Only through the personal question of salvation does man find access to religion, for God is not manifest in all perceptible reality, as 'Deists and Jews say',[7] but is profoundly hidden. For René Descartes, too, the religious question is the question of God and the human soul.[8] It is possible to speak of certainty about God only within the context of radical doubt and self-certainty. Struggling for true divinity and the salvation of the whole in the knowledge of the reality of the world becomes meaningless when this world is reduced to the abstracted object-world of the *res extensae* and is made the mere object of the *res cogitans*. The gulf between subject and object, *res cogitans* and *res extensa*, humanities and the natural sciences, became the cause of the internal and external disorganization of the modern world. For, as Karl

Marx said, this materialism in respect of nature falls out of ongoing world history and becomes the 'enemy of man'.[9]

The concept of nature without the spirit which was given particular impetus by Cartesius inevitably resulted in a conception of the spirit without nature and a conception of them both without God.[10]

Modern theology agreed to this cleavage in the consciousness of the modern mind. It surrendered the awareness that the truth is always *one* and must therefore be the truth of the *whole*. It gave up the expectation of a total salvation or the salvation of the whole. Various spheres of truth were set up which did not conflict with one another: *esprit du coeur – esprit de géometrie* (Pascal), *vérités de fait – vérités de raison* (Leibniz), inessential truths of history – essential truths of religion (Lessing), practical reason – theoretical reason (Kant), mysticism and mathematics, existence and science, subjectivity and objectification, positivism and decisionism.

Schleiermacher praised this division in the modern mind.

If the reformation . . . does not have the goal of creating an eternal treaty between the living Christian faith and free and completely independent scientific research, so that faith does not hinder research and research does not exclude faith, then it does not sufficiently meet the needs of our time and we still need another reformation, regardless of how and from what sort of conflicts it may find its shape.[11]

Present-day theology has hardly got beyond this. From Bultmann, we hear:

From Christianity, there comes no protest against secular science, because the eschatological understanding of the world is not a method of explaining it, and because 'taking out of the world' can be implemented not by an explanation of the world but only in the decision of the moment.[12]

And Karl Barth states:

There is free scope for natural science beyond what theology describes as the work of the Creator. Theology can and must move freely where science which really is science and not secretly a pagan *Gnosis* or religion has its appointed limit.[13]

On this question, C. F. von Weizsäcker had already re-marked that 'any division between existence and nature that made existence the field of Christian faith and nature the field of exact science would assign to both faith and science too narrow a field, which was not really there in such a form'.[14] Such a division between objectivity and subjectivity cannot be carried out neatly in scientific terms, as its object is not nature in itself but nature exposed to human enquiry. To this extent man encounters himself again even here (W. Heisenberg). The price to be paid theologically is a self-mutilation, for it is hardly possible to offer a world without salvation a salvation without the world and a reality without God a God without reality. If God and salvation cannot be interpreted in respect of the totality that is torn open and rent asunder here, then they can-not be explained at all. A retreat into man's inwardness leads faith into a ghetto in which it perishes. Finally, in philosophical terms, one will be able to follow Hegel's insight into the dialec-tics of the enlightenment, namely that there is no possibility of escaping such a bifurcation by fighting on one side or the other to remove the opposition as inessential or irrelevant. On the contrary, subjectivity and objectivity, spontaneity and ration-ality are historically related and their mutual influence together makes up the totality of historical existence.[15]

II

If Christian theology is to overcome the two-track thinking of the modern mind in which it finds itself on a siding, it must insist on the following things in its conversation with the secular sciences:

(i) *Theology* does not dispute with the sciences only or primarily for the soul of the investigator on the one hand and for the non-objectifiability of the scientifically analysed and treated man on the other. Its purpose cannot be limited to the simple formula 'the doctor as a Christian' or 'the believing physicist'. For its own cause, the hope of the salvation and the fear of the condemnation of the world, it is interested not only in the existence of the scientific man but also in his understanding of the world and his scientific and practical concern with reality. In so doing it is not looking for a 'Christian science' and it is certainly not after a clericalization of the university. It does, however, stand for 'the world for God and God for the world',[16] since it *asks about the future – good or evil – of the whole*, which is gained or lost within the historical process of reconciliation between man and nature. The more world-events become part of a historical-social world, the more urgent becomes the question of the purpose, goal and end of this process. The greater man's power to make all things becomes, the clearer becomes his helplessness in knowing where he is going and why. Kant's question 'What may I hope for?' appears where the knowledge that is inherently unlimited comes up against its limits in fear of possible condemnation. It is therefore impossible to separate world history and saving event from one another, for it is impossible to hand over to condemnation the history that we create through the knowledge of nature and technology. Hope of salvation and fear of condemnation are the ultimate impulses behind human activity. The question 'What may I hope for?' is a reflection on the content of two other questions – 'What can I know?' and 'What should I do?' So it is not just the physicist and his possible sacrifice, but rather physics itself that has relevance as a theological question. The understanding of the world in knowledge and in action is not a matter of indifference or an arbitrary affair either in the Old Testament or in the New. If we go through their historically conditioned views, we find that precisely in the area of her relationship to the world, Israel grappled passionately with the religions of her environment, as did Christianity with Greek cosmology. In this struggle, Israel repudiated the theophanic glorification of the world as an image of the Godhead and learned to understand this world as God's creation, groundless in itself, and as an inherently open history of God's new unlimited possibilities. In this struggle Christianity, by virtue of the power of its hope in a new creation of God, transcended the Greek transfiguration of the cosmos as the prison of the soul.

Danger and salvation are found for both in historical time. This led to the reflection of temporal change and acceleration – to the recognition of history in terms of such a future and to the experience of time receiving its character from the future. It provided Greek thought with its turning point from the static to the dynamic, from substance to function, from a beatifying way of looking at things to an alteration of them in hope. Theology has discontinued a conflict of this kind with the scientific-technical civilization of the modern age.

For theology to acquire the necessary openness to the world for such a task it is essential that it should emerge from the status of being orthodox statements of truth *sui generis* and develop a *theologia experimentalis* which, together with the modern world, should subject itself to the *experimentum veritatis*. It must overcome its limitation to church, faith and inwardness in order to search, together with all others, for the truth of the whole and the salvation of a divided world.

(ii) Our concept of *theology* has its origin in high scholasticism, where it means the scientific presentation of the whole of the Christian tradition, the *sacra doctrina*.[17] Its character as a science and its position within the scientific system was determined by the Aristotelian framework: the first philosophy, metaphysics, reaches its high point in theology, the doctrine of God, which describes unity and totality within the structure of being as well as within the structure of knowledge. The God of Christian theology receives his name from the history and tradition of Bible and church. His universal divinity, however, is paraphrased with the help of the cosmological proof of God and Aristotelian metaphysics. This produced a harmony between biblical and philosophical theology. As a science of the highest being and of ultimate value, Christian theology became an ordering force in the scientific cosmos.

This unity of theology and science was dissolved at the dawn of the modern age. There is no reason to lament in romantic terms the 'loss of the mid-point', for the loss of this fixed mid-point has in fact led to the disclosure by science of an infinite number of ever-new horizons in the world. The God of the cosmological proof of God is not adequate for the new horizons of an open, investigable, changeable world. This God became obscure and was no good as a working hypothesis for the explanation of the world. Nietzsche interprets this process as follows: 'Who gave us the sponge to wipe away the whole horizon? What did we do when we loosened this earth from its sun?' But here the question remains and becomes more urgent than ever before:

Whither does it (the earth) now move? Whither do we move? Away from all suns? Do we not dash on unceasingly? Backwards, sideways, forwards, in all directions? Is there still an above and below? Do we not stray, as through infinite nothingness? Does not empty space breathe upon us?[18]

The obsolescence of the theological unity of reality expressed in Aristotelian terms certainly does not settle the question of the unity and truth, the salvation and meaning of the whole. Only now does it cease to be a traditional postulate and become an open question which keeps time and the progress of human history in suspense, continually provokes new answers and makes all answers obsolete and temporary. Truth and the salvation of the whole is understood in the form of the open question. As long as this question is open and still is recognized everywhere as a question, science remains science. Kant justifiably declared that 'a religion which, without hesitation, declares war on reason, will not, in the long run, be able to hold out against it'. Yet is became evident that even reason, in its enlightening victory over what it called faith, could not hold out alone, but developed highly unreasonable forms of naïve credibility.

The glorious victory which enlightening reason has won over that which, according to the low degree of its religious understanding, it regarded as opposed to faith is, when seen in this light, no other victory than that the positive, which reason set about fighting, did not remain religion, and reason, which was victorious, did not remain reason. The birth which hovers triumphantly over these corpses as the mutual child of peace, uniting them both, contains no more reason than true faith.[19]

Once the naïve positivism of science, this curious child of reason and faith, has begun to fall apart, starting points for a new mutual understanding and, over and above this, for a new community of theological and scientific thought have become recognizable in at least two areas. These areas are found, first, in the problem of the fundamentals of science and theology and, secondly, in the necessary construction of an ethos of the control of the world by science and technology.

III

1. The 'fundamental crisis' of the natural sciences

Positivism, as is well known, replaced the old mythical-theological interpretation of the world with the recognition of a relationship of all experienceable phenomena with each other according to natural law. In so doing, however, it remained just as naïve as the theological epoch which it wanted to replace. It assumed that reality was in itself what it revealed itself to be in the experiments of scientific research. It believed in a coincidence of science and reality, and it considered the objective truth of scientific knowledge to be the absolute truth of being. It was therefore unhistorical; it recognized neither the historicity of the phenomenon, the historicity of the observer nor the historicity of its communication in knowledge. It combined the recognizable and makeable world with the pathos of the conclusion of a mysteriously open history. Under its control, 'science' became the mystical word for a new magic of the world and the sole criterion of the awareness of truth.

Now Kant's critique of reason already showed 'that reason has insight only into that which it produces after a plan of its own, and that it must itself show the way with principles based upon fixed laws, constraining nature to give answers to questions of reason's own determining'.[20] This means that the objective truth of science only becomes possible when reason has given a preliminary definition of a horizon, a plan or a course of questioning in which the entity is brought to light as object under a particular aspect. Reason is forced to consider these conditions of the possibility of scientific objectivity. Kant understood by one such plan 'what reason itself projects onto nature'. The plan thus determines that questioning which nature must answer and eliminates other questioning as being irrelevant. The plan presents the horizon of meaning in which nature becomes understandable as it is put to the question, and meaningful judgments are reached. The objectivity of perception and judgment is thus always dependent on the perspective under which a piece of reality is observed. In an experiment, only that aspect is stressed in which nature is forced to answer the questions which are directed towards it. These questions must always be artificial in their elimination of abstract situations if the answer is to be given clearly and unambiguously. This becomes obvious in the preparation of any experiment, any series of tests and any questionnaire: the criterion for the accuracy of the results is the possibility of reproducing them, their uniformity in repetition.

In its Hebrew root, the verb 'to think' also means 'to separate', and scientific thinking consists in the elimination and exclusion of all those factors and aspects which are insignificant and inessential in a particular context.[21] Therefore the subject is prepared beforehand and the method is considered. This methodical abstraction from other contexts and questions constitutes the scientific infatuation with detail, without which science is not possible.

The so-called fundamental crisis in modern physics consists precisely in the fact that physics has run up against phenomena in which the illumination of the current horizon of meaning of classical physics can no longer be retained without question. The phenomena themselves compel reflection on the conditions and limitations of the traditional plan. In relation to atomic phenomena, for example, one is forced to consider the plan of classical physics as a 'plan which is only applicable under certain conditions'. One thus gains insight into the hypothetical character of that plan which was at first held to be universal. Precisely at its most problematical area, atomic physics, the hypothetical character of scientific knowledge becomes evident.

Scientific theories are no longer able to offer themselves as copies of the world existing in itself. They are models, i.e. observations within the limits established by experiment. The old and still wholly metaphysical suggestion of a world existing in itself is replaced by what has been called the 'field of constructive possibilities'.[22] It is a picture of particular relationships between man and nature rather than a picture of nature itself that can be produced.

The scientific method of differentiation, explanation and ordering becomes aware of the limits which are imposed by it; sees that the method can no longer be separated from its subject. The scientific picture of the world thus ceases to be a truly scientific one.[23]

The great 'world-pictures' of the past were in this way shown to be 'plans' with the help of which one could have definite and limited experiences. The success achieved in experiment justifies them. Their application to other phenomena, however, makes plain the difference between reality and mode of appearance in certain forms of questioning. Once one understands this, then that 'revolution in the manner of thinking' of which Kant once spoke occurs within the natural sciences themselves. This can be illustrated in a pointed way as follows:

Does not physics have the character of an art (*techne*) rather than that of a science of entities, namely, the character of an art of objectification? To this extent, exact natural science would not be a science of nature, but rather a science of an artificial man-made nature constructed after the idea of mathematics.[24]

With such an insight, natural science, as a result of its work on reality itself, emerges from the naïve, ontological protection of positivism and, in the knowledge of the hypothetical character of its plans, acquires a new understanding: (*a*) of the inter-relatedness between method and subject, (*b*) of the historicity of nature, and (*c*) of the historical character of the plan and production of scientific reason. Thoughts and questions appear which seem to be related to those of the humanities, for here the consciousness that plans and methods are only perspectives on the complex realities of human history is well developed.

Analogous changes are even more pronounced in the human sciences. The 'image of man', human life contained in a picture, has been replaced by insight into the character of pictures as models by which certain human phenomena are brought to light, their limited range, variability and only heuristic suitability. The anthropological attempts of the present are ' "aspect theories" of man, different in each case'.[25] Pavlov's Russian biographer has the discoverer of the conditioned reflex saying, 'There we have it, the truth. The "spiritual" has shown itself to be capable of manipulation. One can do what one wants with it.'[26] For scientific reasons as well as ethical reasons, the identification of the objective truth of a particular perspective with absolute truth has shown itself to be an error – an error over the conditions of the possibility of scientific objectivity. Objective truth remains objective truth, but it is objectively demonstrable that objective truth is not absolute truth, but rather a conditioned truth.[27] The world is not a machine simply because it permits machines to be made nor is man an aggregate of pre-determined social modes of behaviour because in certain respects he appears to be such and is predictable in regard to those commodities which he will purchase. Marxism, which to a large degree confronts one with such a scientific positivism of fixed laws in nature and society, is nothing but a grandiose lapse into a pre-critical era and, with its insights into the necessity of fixed determination, is itself a betrayal of the original dialectic of the historical process of communication between man and nature discovered by Marx. The materialistic scientific credibility of Marxism is an enemy of both history and of man, as Marx himself justly objected against the abstract materialism of the Enlightenment.

Whenever there is self-critical reflection in the way just described on the conditions of the possibility of scientific assertions, the possibility of asking about truth is again raised; it is possible to ask about the truth and the salvation of the whole and about the real and whole human being. Wherever the question of truth is asked and considered, man truly becomes man, for in the horizon of this question about the salvation and condemnation of the world, freedom, responsibility and education become necessary. 'The truth is the whole,' said Hegel,[28] and the whole is the good.

We thus return to the meaning of this open question for the scientific knowledge of the world and for world change. 'The whole of reality' obviously eludes our grasp. Scientific knowledge is forced into limitation, diminution, demarcation and abstraction in order to arrive at a certain and verified knowledge. But in what way does scientific reason become conscious of its limits and the aspectual character of its concerns? When partial aspects appear everywhere, the question arises – parts of what? For the self-critical reflection of reason cannot produce an agnostic relativism and ultimately a complete atomization of the consciousness of truth.

What kind of reality, then, discloses itself to the scientific compulsion for an answer, so that it may achieve a successful control of nature – yet in its totality nevertheless eludes scientific abstractions so that the process of knowledge never ends? Like Goethe, one can begin by saying that that dark totality of reality is at the basis of all phenomena and all individual insights.

In nature, which is alive, nothing occurs which does not have a connection with the whole. Even if the experiences seem to us to be isolated, even if we have to regard the attempts simply as isolated facts, this does not mean that they are in fact isolated.

If, however, one observes that scientific knowledge and the transformation of the world itself is also a part of reality, and not only stands over against it but also is an incredibly powerful element in the process of reality, then another thought arises, namely that this totality is not only hidden from knowledge but does not yet itself exist, that reality has not yet been rounded off as a whole but rather moves towards it in an open history. 'The whole', then, is not an eternal reality which provides the basis for each individual fact, but is rather always at stake in the process of history. It can be won, but it can also be frustrated.

For the whole, the true, the good, is that future towards which reality is recognized, shaped, changed and revised. In both fear and hope, we ask about the meaning and goal of this history in a world which becomes historical under our hands, and anticipate meaningful good in the face of possible evil.[29] If the whole announces itself out of the future of our historical world in the necessity of the question about it, then scientific knowledge falls into a twofold and contrary process of knowing. It is forced into limitation, diminution and abstraction in order to obtain certain knowledge; however, at the same time it is also forced to keep the individual steps of knowledge continually in touch with the reality of that totality which is still to come, that is, both to be aware of scientific abstraction and to transcend this abstraction in the coming totality.[30] Only where this questionability of the whole and of the future arises does man become aware of his limitation and temporality. Scientific knowledge is maintained by means of the unreachable question about truth and the future of the whole in historical process.

In the face of the open future, a new level of reflection develops in the process of historical differentiation and mediation, subjectivity and objectivity. Man stands not only *over against* 'nature' as the subject of knowledge and work but also *with it* in a history as the subject of knowledge and work. He has nature and grasps hold of it and, in this way, *is* at the same time himself that nature which develops itself further in him and his world. In that open future which is at hand for nature with him and for him with nature, man becomes aware not only of his power over nature but also of his solidarity with it. The subject-object relationship between subjectified man and objectified nature becomes obvious in his dialectical entanglement. It both has history and brings about history.

Through the same insight, reason acquires another facet. Obviously to understand reason as a finished power of man would be too rigid. Rather, it gains its historical structure within the open inter-relationship of plan, experiment and reflection in so far as it moves in an openness towards a truth which it does not already contain in itself but presupposes in outline planning, even if it has not already incorporated it. As long as the question of truth is open as the question of the salvation or condemnation of the future, man is aware of the finiteness and temporality of his plans. He finds no rest in his own plans and pictures, but with them moves out into the openness of history.

2. The theological dimension of science

It was an understandable misunderstanding when Christian theology occupied the place of metaphysical theologizing in the realm of the sciences and worshipped the God of biblical history as the Unmoved Mover of the universe or the Supreme Being. It was a similar misunderstanding when Christian theology abandoned its position in universal knowledge and withdrew to morals, inwardness and church doctrine.

In the meantime, not only science but also theology has been emancipated from all metaphysics. Science did this by finding horizons other than those illuminated by Greek cosmology; theology by remembering the God of Abraham, Isaac and Jacob (Pascal) and the God of the resurrection of Christ. If theology is thus renewed 'Christian' theology, it does not acquire its knowledge of truth from a particular understanding of being in 'what keeps the world together', but rather from the continual remembrance that, with the cross and resurrection of Christ, the 'end of history' has appeared. The horizon of meaning in which the divine element in the Christ event becomes understandable is not so much metaphysical as eschatological.[31] The *cross* of Christ is understood in its universal significance only in its connection with the last judgment, the crisis of all things at the end of time; his *resurrection* from the dead is understood only in the context of a transformation of the world, the future of which is the kingdom of God. Seen from this future of history, the appearance of Christ becomes meaningful. Conversely, through his appearance, the consciousness of a universal end of history has come into the world. Since then, this ultimate future of crisis and salvation is the 'soul' of time reflected as history. The question of the end of history is the question of the meaning that the historical-social world has for these expectations, by which this action is directed, an action which is always an anticipation in either fear or hope.[32]

Christianity, therefore, is neither 'metaphysics for the educated' nor 'Platonism for the masses' (Nietzsche), but is rather a universal hope for the future embracing the history of both man and the world. The Christ-event of the resurrection is 'historical' in as far as it creates history by opening up a new future. From this event of the past, which is still in no way a past event, the present is revealed for the future as the time of hope. Theological knowledge of the truth develops from the observation of this once and for all event and can only note the significance of this event by grasping the horizon of the future which is projected and announced by this event. Theological knowledge of truth may also be designated as historical; here it anticipates at the same time a universal future. The more one meditatively immerses oneself in the Christ event, the more strongly one is reminded of the open future of the world. Theological knowledge of the coming truth of the whole becomes aware of its own temporality in the Christ event. It does not therefore have a supernatural character, but has the character of a reminiscent knowledge of hope. Thus the characteristic of this temporality and openness also shapes man's knowledge of nature and himself. The fullness of all things, that totality of reality, is not concealed in a background of the world. The fullness of all things and all times for Christian hope is found in the fulfilment of that which is promised and, therefore, historically open here. The expression used by Paul 'that God may be all in all' (I Cor. 15.28) does not designate, as in Stoicism, the eternal present of being, but rather the future goal of all things, which are here grasped in history.

If Christian theology reflects on the historical Christ-event, the 'end of history', if it, therefore, sees the world and man within the struggle of crisis and salvation, then it can no longer be distinguished as supernatural – as opposed to natural – knowledge. Instead, it places natural knowledge in the open question of the ultimate future. God's revelation in Christ must be understood as a disclosure of the history of the world in which the future of salvation is at stake. This brings about not only a disclosure of man in the religious perspective of the heart, but also a disclosure of man in all those perspectives with which he seeks to make sure of himself, nature and society. Christian theology can no longer remain in a front line over against science; it joins it on that front which we call the present, where the future is either won or frustrated because the salvation of the world is hoped for and evil is feared. Theological considerations of this sort, therefore, do not belong in one particular faculty among other faculties, but rather within the horizon of knowledge for every science.

In our theological faculties we are essentially oriented in the direction of *pastoral theology*. Those professional goals for which one needs theology are reduced to the ministry and religious education in the schools. These purposes for which one 'needs' theology also determine the essence and structure of the discipline: from exegesis to the sermon, catechetics and pastoral care. Outside theological faculties a new lay theology is developing today which has scientific and practical, as well as theological significance. This lay theology is making itself felt in evangelical study groups, committees of the Evangelical Church of Germany (EKD), in the *Evangelische Akademien* and the national church assemblies. If the universities want to do justice to these changed conditions, then an institutionalizing of this theology as a department in non-theological faculties is necessary.

The horizons in which reality allows itself to be disclosed scientifically are the limited, finite and historically transitory horizons of our knowledge. The 'end of history' of which Christian theology speaks whenever it speaks of Christ is like an ultimate horizon which 'moves on' and continually invites a further advance.[33] Truth and salvation are not available as possessions, even for theology, but may be had only in the form of faith and hope. Theology knows of that ultimate meaning which the future of history can give only within the mode of anticipation. Hope, however, which is led by the anticipation of the future, exposes itself to the *experimentum veritatis*. If this is a hope which is not only directed towards the possible consequences of activity and its results, but also reaches out beyond all things visible and possible towards a meaning for everything that happens here, then it is a hope which receives certainty in the face of total uncertainty: 'Death, where is thy sting? Hell, where is thy victory?' (I Cor. 15.55).[34]

To the spirit which is active in modern science, theology will communicate its own peculiar unrest. 'For now we see in a mirror dimly, but then face to face. Now I know in part; then I shall understand fully, even as I have been fully understood' (I Cor. 13.12).

Modern science will, however, force Christian theology to take a new position, of which Teilhard de Chardin wrote:

Earlier there seemed to be only two geometrically possible positions for man – to love either heaven or earth. Here a third way can be found – to go directly through earth towards heaven. There is a community, true community – with God through the world.[35]

IV

On the other hand, theology and the sciences confront each other in a more fundamental way than ever before on the question of the *ethos* and responsibility of that technical acquisition of power which arises from scientific knowledge. The time is irrevocably past when the scientist could withdraw into his laboratory with a clear conscience, away from the demands of the time. The greater the sacrifice to scientific objectivity, in research and the more successful this work becomes, the more urgent the ethical and political human and historical responsibilities which have been excluded. Modern science is indissolubly bound up with the possibilities of modern technology. These possibilities, in return, are dependent on the investments which must be made in 'big science' and the national planning of society as a whole. Such investments are only meaningful when, in these projects, the future of a life fit for human existence is sought. Here we have an indication of the interdependence of politics, the social order and visions of the future which must be taken into consideration.

In the first place, scientific work must be abstracted from those questions which concern the whole. For a long time, the exactness of the method was also the embodiment of the scientist's ethical education. Its beauty was that it was an end in itself. Now, however, in the face of the unforeseen possibilities and the unavoidable consequences of the scientific acquisition of power, one must ask over and above this about the sense and meaning of the power in terms of the whole. Science acquired its power by means of abstraction from world history. Precisely in this way, a tremendous amount of control over the world fell to science – often without science knowing exactly how it had happened. The self-obliterating sacrifice to the cause thus led to a responsibility which demanded a new *ethos* beyond pure objectivity. 'Formerly one had perfect purposes but imperfect means. Today one has perfect means and great possibilities, but confused purposes' (Einstein). By what standards should the results of a value-free science be evaluated when the understanding of value is so arbitrary and therefore so confused? How ought optimal decisions to be reached when there is no clarity about the optimum? The transformation of the world by means of science and scientific technique becomes critical at that point where it is vital not only to know and be informed, but also to act decisively. Science has to diminish the question 'Why?' and 'For what?'. In this way, however, those questions are not discarded as unscientific, but rather emerge with unsuspected urgency. Natural science 'teaches us a method, but it does not teach us what we ought to do' (Dippel). 'The God of physics is there to give us what we wish, but not to tell us what we ought to wish for' (Santillana).[36] Originally man was dependent upon the impenetrable powers in nature and in history. Later he was able to understand these powers and explained their laws and relationships. History endured unconsciously then became history recognized. That was the first Enlightenment. Today we know that we can be free from these powers and can control them. But because of this, man himself has developed a new dependence on his own work. Processes have been released over which he no longer exercises control. His own products have got out of hand. He can no longer get rid of those spirits which he called up. The first Enlightenment wanted to understand and perceive what had previously been unconsciously endured. The new enlightenment must be an explanation of this enlightenment[37] in that man consciously shapes and brings under human control the power that hitherto he had conquered unconsciously and through self-forgetfulness. Today the old separation between theory and practice, between science and politics, is no longer feasible. Scientific theories acquire a practical meaning and everywhere practice is shaped scientifically. This interweaving has always been found in every natural science which has direct practical consequences. In medicine, the Hippocratic oath was and had to be an object of reflection because here man is not only an object of research but is also a life to be preserved and sustained. Today for the most part this reciprocal relationship is seen in all sciences – from atomic physics to bio-genetics. It was apparent in the intellectual conflicts between Einstein and Oppenheimer during their work on the atomic bomb.[38] It was formulated in the 'Göttingen Declaration' drawn up by eighteen German atomic physicists. Unfortunately the only reaction to it was the old division of competence – the political consequences of scientific work were not the scientist's responsibility. On the strength of this, the introduction of a professional oath for natural scientists has also been discussed.[39] Certainly such an oath could not prevent misuse today, for divided humanity is still a long way from an ethical solidarity in the responsibility for the scientific acquisition of power. But the need cannot be ignored. This responsibility can be practised only within a growing inner relationship of mutual trust, reciprocal control and a democratic control of the controller.

Every abstraction from world history without which we cannot learn scientifically must continually be transcended in man's responsibility for the whole. Only in the continual interplay of the release of technical reason from ethical and practical reason and its integration in this reason can each exert influence on the other. In itself, technical reason offers no criteria for the goodness of what can be done with the use of it. In itself, ethical reason has no means for its purposes. Only through continual discussion can one be reconciled with the other: scientific power on the one hand with the future goal of a hope for humanity on the other.

Hitherto Christian theology has yielded to the old division into 'areas of competence' and has neatly separated the kingdom of the preservation and formation of the world from its kingdom of salvation. When, however, it recognizes that the future of salvation for which it hopes is the future of the whole, which is more and more at stake here in human history, it must enter into that intermediate area between world preservation and world consummation[40] and reconcile that ultimate future of crisis and salvation with the historical goals of human activity so that in the light of the ultimate promises of God this world is both recognized and changed. The future of salvation, like that of condemnation, has never transcended history so that one could surrender oneself to it in fatalism or indifference, but rather in the process of history already acquires a shape so that one will only be able to find it by searching for it.

Max Weber closed his famous lecture on 'Science as a Vocation' with an allusion to the Bible.

For the many who today tarry for new prophets and saviours, the situation is the same as resounds in the beautiful Edomite watchman's song of the period of the exile that has been included among Isaiah's oracles: 'He calleth to me out of Seir, "Watchman, what of the night?" The watchman said, "The morning cometh, and also the night: if ye will enquire, enquire ye: return, come." '[41]

If theology answers for God in the world and for the world before God, then it does not see only night over the world, but has to arouse all the senses for the coming morning. It has to sharpen the sense for responsibility and the capability for anticipation in all disciplines. As Paul said, 'The night is far gone, the day is at hand' (Rom. 13.12). Only in company with the sciences can eschatological faith arrive at a historical self-consciousness.

NOTES

This article was first published in *EvTh* 26, 1966, 621–39.

1. This article is based on the following studies: H. Gollwitzer, 'Die Theologie im Hause der Wissenschaften', *EvTh* 18, 1958, 14ff.; E. Wolf, 'Theologie und Naturwissenschaft', *MPTh* 54, 1965, 321ff.; G. Howe, *Mensch und Physik*, 1963; G. Picht, 'Naturwissenschaft und Bildung', in: C. Münster, G. Picht, 'Naturwissenschaft und Bildung', *Weltbild und Erziehung* 3, n.d., 33ff.; id., 'Was heisst Aufklärung', *Frankfurter Hefte* 19, 1964, 503ff.; G. Gloege, 'Der Mensch zwischen Naturwissenschaft und Theologie', *Heilsgeschehen und Welt* I, 1965, 264ff.; C. J. Dippel and M.de Jong, *Geloof en Naturwetenschap* I, 1965 (these are studies which have been made since 1951 under the auspices of the Commission for Church and Theology of the Dutch Reformed Church).

2. Cf. W. Elert, *Morphologie des Luthertums* I, 1931, 363ff. and E. Hirsch, *Geschichte der neuern evangelischen Theologie* I, 1949, 115f. Against Hirsch, it must be noted that the concept of the 'hypothesis' derives from humanistic rhetoric and has only subsequently been interpreted in the sense of scientific hypothesis. H. Blumenberg has given a good account in his book, *Die kopernikanische Wende* (edition Suhrkamp 138, 1965, 92ff.) of the dispute between Copernicus and Osiander over the preface.

3. E. Hirsch, *op. cit.*, 205.

4. On this see G. Krüger, *Freiheit und Weltverwaltung*, 1958, esp. 71ff. and 213ff.

5. B. Brecht, *Leben des Galilei*, 1962, preface. Quoted from E. Wolf, *op. cit.*, 322.

6. Pascal, *Oeuvres* II, 133, quoted from J. Pieper, *Über den Begriff der Tradition*, 1958, 10.

7. Pascal, *Pensées* 603, trans. J. M. Cohen, Penguin Classics, 1961, 222: 'The God of the Christians is not simply a God who is the author of mathematical truths and of the order of the elements; that is the view of the heathens and of the Epicureans. . . . But the God of Abraham, the God of Isaac, the God of Jacob, the God of the Christians, is a God of love and consolation; He is a God who fills the soul and the heart of those whom He possesses; He is a God who gives them an inner consciousness of their misery and of His infinite mercy. . . . What meets our eyes denotes neither a total absence nor a manifest presence of the divine, but the presence of a God who conceals himself. Everything bears this stamp.'

8. Descartes, *Meditations*, Preface to the Reader, in: *Discourse on Method*, trans. J. Veitch (Everyman's Library), 1912, 71.

9. Karl Marx, *Die Frühschriften*, ed. S. Landshut, 1964, 330.

10. F. Baader, quoted from G. Howe, *op. cit.*, 120. Cf. also his insight

into the dialectical interpenetration of faith and knowledge, *Über den Zwiespalt des religiösen Glaubens und Wissens*, [2]1958, 49: 'That conflict, as one knows, is both historically and intrinsically related to the conflict between faith and action, for the action which has rid itself of faith is not real action, faith which has rid itself of action is not true faith, as knowledge which has rid itself of faith is not true knowledge and faith which has rid itself of knowledge is not real, true (i.e. effective) faith.

11. F. Schleiermacher, 'Sendschreiben an Dr Lücke', *Der christliche Glaube nach den Grundsätzen der Evangelischen Kirche im Zusammenhange dargestellt*, Part I, quoted after the edition in Bibliothek theologischen Klassiker, vol. 13, 1889, 36.

12. R. Bultmann, *Essays*, 1955, 88.

13. K. Barth, *Church Dogmatics* II/1, 1958, p.x. On the two see the study by G. Altner, *Schöpfungsglaube und Entwicklungsgedanke in der protestantischen Theologie zwischen E. Haeckel und Teilhard de Chardin*, 1965, 84ff.

14. C. F. von Weizsäcker, *Zum Weltbild der Physik*, [7]1958, 263.

15. J. Ritter, *Hegel und die französische Revolution*, 1957, 33; G. Rohrmoser, *Subjektivität und Verdinglischung. Theologie und Gesellschaft im Denken des jungen Hegel*, 1961.

16. H. U. von Balthasar, *Die Gottesfrage des heutigen Menschen*, 1956, 52.

17. Cf. G. Ebeling, 'Theologie', *RCG*[3] VI, cols. 754ff.

18. F. Nietzsche, *The Joyful Wisdom*, trans. T. Common (Complete Works X), 1910, 168.

19 G. W. F. Hegel, *Glauben und Wissen* (1802), (*PhB* 62b), 1962, 1.

20. Norman Kemp Smith (ed.), *Immanuel Kant's Critique of Pure Reason*, [2]1933, 20. Cf. G. Picht's interpretation, 'Naturwissenschaft und Bildung', *op. cit.*, 105ff., which I accept here.

21. Similarly W. Heisenberg, quoted by G. Howe, *op. cit.*, 74.

22. H. Weyl, quoted by G. Howe, *op. cit.*, 53.

23. W. Heisenberg, quoted by G. Howe, *op. cit.*, 74.

24. H. Hensel, *Studium generale* 15, 1962, 747.

25. See E. von Gebsattel, *Prolegomena einer medizinischen Anthropologie*, 1954, IV.

26. On this see H. Thomae, 'Psychologie', in: A. Flitner (ed.), *Wege zu einer pädagogischen Anthropologie*, Pädagogische Forschungen vol. 23, 1963, 92.

27. G. Picht, *op. cit.*, 115.

28. G. W. F. Hegel, *The Phenomenology of Mind*, trans. J. B. Baillie, 1910, 17.

29. L. Landgrebe, 'Das philosophische Problem des Endes der Geschichte', *Festschrift für H. Heimsoeth*, 1966.

30. H. Gollwitzer, *op. cit.*, 33.

31. J. Moltmann, *Theology of Hope*, 1967.

32. This has been demonstrated in a very illuminating way by L. Landgrebe, *op. cit.*, through Kant's writing *Das Ende aller Dinge* and Husserl's concept of time.

33. I take this expression over from H. G. Gadamer, *Wahrheit und Methode*, [2]1965, 288.

34. L. Landgrebe, *op. cit.*

35. See N. M. Wildiers, *Teilhard de Chardin*, Herder Bücherei 122, 1962, 9f. and S. Daecke, 'Bericht über die Teilhard de Chardin-Literatur', *MPTh* 55, 1966, 257–69, 312–28.

36. C. J. Dippel and G. de Santillana, quoted from E. Wolf, *op. cit.*, 331.

37. G. Picht, 'Was heisst Aufklärung?', *Frankfurter Hefte* 19, 1964, 506.

38. On this see the stylized 'scenic report' by H. Kipphardt, *In der Sache J. Robert Oppenheimer*, edition Suhrkamp 64, 1965.

39. E. Wolf, *op. cit.*, 332.

40. G. Howe, *op. cit.*, 117ff.

41. M. Weber, *Wissenschaft als Beruf*, [5]1967, p. 37, quoting Isa. 21.11f.; translated by H. H. Gerth and C. Wright Mills in *From Max Weber: Essays in Sociology*, 1947, 156.

INDEX OF NAMES

INDEX OF NAMES

This Index is confined to names mentioned in the text and does not include names referred to in the notes at the end of the chapters.